DR. CHARLES A. CRANE

Christianity & Mormonism

Copyright © 2002 Charles A. Crane

Printed and Bound in the
United States of America
All Rights Reserved

All Scripture quotations, unless otherwise indicated, are taken from the
NEW AMERICAN STANDARD BIBLE®. Copyright © 1960, 1962, 1968, 1971, 1972,
1973, 1975, 1977, 1995 by The Lockman Foundation. Used by permission.

www.covenantpublishing.com

P.O. Box 390 Webb City, Missouri 64870
Call toll free at 877.673.1015

Library of Congress Cataloging-in-Publication Data

Crane, Charles Arthur.
  Christianity and Mormonism : from bondage to freedom / Charles A. Crane
    p. cm.
Includes bibliographical references.
  ISBN 1-892435-43-8 (pbk.)
  1. Church of Jesus Christ of Latter-day Saints–Controversial
literature. 2. Mormon Church–Controversial literature. I. Title.
  BX8645 .C743 2002
  289.3–dc21
                                2002154171

Christianity & Mormonism

Abbreviations

BoA . . . . Book of Abraham

BoM . . . . *The Book of Mormon*

DC . . . . *The Doctrine and Covenants*

JD . . . . *The Journal of Discourses*

LDS . . . . The Church of Jesus Christ of Latter-day Saints

Pearl . . . . *The Pearl of Great Price*

Table of Contents

Preface   9

Introduction   13

CHAPTER ONE:
The Mormon Bondage to Suppressed Truth   23

CHAPTER TWO:
The Mormon Bondage to a False View of Scripture   43

CHAPTER THREE:
The Freedom in a Correct View of Scripture   65

CHAPTER FOUR:
The Mormon Bondage to Changing Revelation   79

CHAPTER FIVE:
The Mormon Bondage to False Prophets   117

CHAPTER SIX:
The Mormon Bondage to Fourteen False Doctrines, Part 1   131

CHAPTER SEVEN:
The Mormon Bondage to Fourteen False Doctrines, Part 2   147

CHAPTER EIGHT:
From Mormon Bondage to Christian Freedom   167

Conclusion   179

Preface

The Church of Jesus Christ of Latter-day Saints has been working hard to reshape its public image. Some have suggested that this had been in preparation for the winter Olympics in Salt Lake City. But in reality they have been trying to present themselves as a mainstream Christian religion for the past several years.

They have used magazine and newspaper advertisements, and television and radio commercials to present the idea that their church is little different than other Christian churches and denominations. Since so many Christians know very little about their church, this effort has had considerable impact.

Unfortunately many Christians and denominations have very little knowledge of the true teachings of the LDS[1] church. Because of their effort to be recognized as "not much different" than major Christian religions, other churches have taken time to study what they actually teach.

This has precipitated a strong response from several major Christian churches. The Presbyterian, Methodist, and now Roman Catholic Church have decreed that Mormons must be rebaptized before becoming members of their churches. Although many other churches have not issued public decrees, there are many other churches that insist that Mormons must make a total break from the LDS church if they wish to become recognized members.

The *Idaho Statesman* has reported,

Catholics: Mormons Must Be Rebaptized
The Roman Catholic Church declared Thursday that Mormon

---

[1] LDS will be used for The Church of Jesus Christ of Latter-day Saints. See Chapter 8 for their admirable traits as a class of people. Generally, unless quoted or used in a headline, church, prophet, president, and revelator will be lowercase when referring to the Mormon/LDS church.

converts must be rebaptized, a setback to the Mormon church's effort to characterize itself as a Christian denomination.

The Vatican's Congregation for the Doctrine of Faith declared that baptisms in the Church of Jesus Christ of Latter-day Saints are "not the baptism that Christ instituted."

The ruling was a departure from the Catholic church's usual practice of recognizing the baptisms of converts from most other churches. The Vatican held that Mormons' view of the nature of God was too different from Catholicism.

It was the second time, in as many years, that a major Christian church had ruled that Mormon converts must be rebaptized. Last year, the United Methodist Church, the nation's second largest Protestant denomination, took a similar stand.

Despite its distinctive doctrines, the eleven-million-member Latter-day Saints church has worked hard to cast itself as part of the American mainstream in this country and as a legitimate Christian church in developing countries where its missionaries are winning converts.[2]

First, this book will examine many of the reasons those who study the LDS church are surprised by how vastly different it is from Christianity. Their views of God, Christ, the Holy Spirit, the Bible, Revelation, the work of Christ, Heaven and Hell, as well as most other doctrines, are vastly different. Whereas most Protestant and even Roman Catholic Church doctrines are similar in regard to these doctrines, Mormon doctrine is not just somewhat different but *vastly* different. You will discover why major Christian churches cannot accept them as a "Christian" church.

We will address a second issue that has risen with the LDS church. It is their response to those who seek to inform the public of what their true teachings are. In times past they would willingly discuss what they believe with almost anyone. Today they seek to avoid those who are particularly knowledgeable of Mormon history.

While I was traveling in France with a Christian missionary we observed two LDS missionaries riding their bikes wearing black pants, white shirts, and black ties. We stopped to visit with them. During the introductions I was purposely introduced as "Chuck." After talking briefly one of them asked, "Are you Dr. Crane?" When I replied, "Yes," they said, "We have been forbidden to talk with you."

In addition, although not through official church channels, they have

---

[2] *The Idaho Statesman*, July 20, 2001.

used influential members to seek to silence any that would speak out. Would a "Christian religion" use all sorts of deceitful and often dishonest means to discredit those who seek to point them to the truth? The LDS attacks have not been addressed to the issues, but rather to destroy the reputations of those who have tried to teach them "mainstream" Christianity. These attacks have often been mean spirited.

This book is a call for The Church of Jesus Christ of Latter-day Saints to become what they claim to be—*Christian*. They will have to do a lot of changing if they want to become Christian. If they truly do have someone of "prophetic" impulses, motivated by the Christian spirit, they should not find it difficult to champion truth and begin casting out falsehood.

All Christians who approach LDS people should be loving, patient, and kind. They must prayerfully work with them recognizing that they are not enemies, but are victims of our mutual enemy. They have been brought into a bondage of error.

Over its history the LDS church has given up some of its more controversial doctrines such as polygamy and dropped its bar to blacks becoming Mormon priests. They should find little opposition to bringing their many errant doctrines back in line with established truth. This would qualify them as a *Christian* church rather than as a cult (I mean no offense but, in truth, the LDS system qualifies as a cult).

It is my dream of over fifty years that this change might begin, gain momentum and that, in my lifetime, the LDS church might move strongly towards the center of truth. This book suggests that the LDS need to go *From Bondage to Freedom*.

Dr. Charles A. Crane

"If you continue in My word, then you are truly disciples of Mine; and you will know the truth, and the truth will make you free" (John 8:31-32).

Introduction

Can the Latter-day Saints' religion be described as "bondage?" Or does political correctness require that we leave people alone, even if their church leaves them in spiritual servitude? Is there a time to examine another religion? What is the motivation, and is this motivation evil? Or could there be a deeper motivation of love? In my case it is love. For fifty years I have had many LDS friends. Living in the Western United States, it is nearly impossible not to know LDS people.

From all outward appearances they are some of the finest, cleanest, and most prosperous of any religious group in America. Most Mormon people have high standards and are astute politically. Their young men and women are clean-cut, groomed, and tastefully dressed. The average Mormon is, by American standards, a good person and citizen. The LDS church pictures itself as being as all-American and wholesome as mother, baseball, and apple pie. Some of this image is well deserved. For the most part they are good people. They do make good American citizens and have many characteristics that any community needs. Normally they do not smoke, drink alcohol, nor will they steal your wife. As neighbors they may be the first to help in time of crisis. Why disturb them in their routine of life? We'll call her Maxine Fields. Her recent letter probably expresses the view of many people.

> I would like to express a few concerns to you regarding your book, *Ashamed of Joseph, Mormon Foundations Crumble*. I have not read the entire book, but it is not the content that I am concerned with. It is the context. I have a very difficult time believing that a truly Christian person would write such a piece of literature. You see, a very dear person to me read your book, which spawned feelings of anger so deep he now would kill Joseph Smith himself. This disturbs me immensely. Feelings of anger, of

non-acceptance or disrespect of others' beliefs and right to choose are not of Christ, but of Satan. This person now experiences each of these feelings which he did not before reading your book.

Another concern I have is that of the time spent tearing down another religion instead of more serving activities a man of your position could participate in....

Should Christians remain quiet about false teaching? Especially when these teachings are drastically different from mainstream Christianity? This is a difficult question for most people because it is easier to remain quiet and not disturb people in their comfort zones. But is that what God expects of Christians? Christianity is based on truth. Error is bondage, particularly in describing Mormonism. In reality it often controls all of the LDS person's life, even what he or she thinks. Their "prophet" has already done the thinking.

If you are an LDS person I pray you will not lay this book aside with the thought that it is just another anti-Mormon book by some fanatic. In reality, the research upon which this book rests goes back a half-century. The motivation is that of the deepest love and respect for LDS people in general. The book comes out of the conviction that the vast good in the LDS church needs to be reclaimed and the church needs to continue restoration and the pursuit of truth. For all of us the pursuit of truth is a never-ending quest. It is time for them to have a leader strong enough to purge the errors inherent in their church and to point the church to mainstream Christianity.

As an LDS person, why should you object to a further restoration of truth? Can truth ever be damaged by investigation? Isn't restoring the church like keeping clean physically, a never-ending project, demanding the best of our efforts? If what I affirm can be proven to be true, how could this possibly harm you? If what I say is not the truth, please be the first to point out the errors!

IS MORMONISM BONDAGE?

Error in doctrine is no more appealing than dirty food, water, or air–ultimately it leads to harm and bondage. Truth leads to liberty and life. Jesus said, "Know the truth, and the truth will make you free" (John 8:32). Whether people followed Jim Jones, David Koresh, or the Rajneesh, they were duped. They wasted their lives and ended up in mental, spiritual, and physical bondage. Some ended up dead.

As lovers of the truth should we not be concerned about anyone

Introduction

being led into religious bondage? Where were those who should have warned them before they were brainwashed? Were friends and family silent too long? Was silence honorable? When we stand before the judgment seat of Christ what will our attitude be?

It is the truth that frees. Truth is like cleanliness, a constant pursuit. Dr. J. Edwin Orr spoke to a group of seminarians about the constant need for renewal in the Christian life and church. One student disagreed with him. Dr. Orr responded by using the illustration of bathing. He said, "This morning I arose, took a bath and shaved. I put on deodorant, combed my hair and brushed my teeth. After roaming around the Illinois prairie all day, amidst humidity and dust, I will probably need a bath again tomorrow morning." To remain clean requires a constant regimen of bathing, shaving, and grooming. He affirmed the same is true for the church, all churches including the LDS. To affirm that they have arrived at all of the truth can easily be proven false.

Real Christianity is never afraid of the search for truth and doctrinal purity. If what we believe cannot be scrutinized and survive, why would we want to believe it? Why should we get defensive when someone is pointing out a better way?

The church itself has passed the pragmatic test by being quite successful in business and in winning vast numbers of people to their movement worldwide. But is this success and wholesome image they portray proof they are of God?

To suggest that our LDS friends and neighbors are in some form of religious or spiritual bondage may at first appear to be un-American and even un-Christian. Why then would anyone want to suggest that Mormonism is bondage? It is because every falsehood they believe and teach leads people into bondage—unfortunately the church is filled with untruth. Although skillfully sold to unsuspecting people, investigation will reveal the web of deceit, twisted history, false and revised prophecies, and deeply damaging bondage. Being a Latter-day Saint is much harder than being a Christian! We are not suggesting that being a Christian is easy, but we are saved by grace, not by our own good works (Romans 3:24).

Surface appearance is vastly different from the reality found in the darker recesses of Mormon doctrine and practice. All doctrinal error is darkness and few religions have a higher level of outright error. The requirements bind them into a regimen of works, giving, serving, all the while shackled by the behavior of not questioning those who lead. After all this servitude they end up lost! What a shame when they have worked so hard to keep all the rules of their church.

How does the LDS church get away with this? The ignorance of both

CHRISTIANITY & MORMONISM

member and leader makes it possible. The whole church is "layman" led. The average Mormon, if he knew, would not believe what his own church teaches. Members accept the surface good and never take time to check more deeply into church doctrine. If it is suggested that they are *not* really Christian, they believe the accusation is absurd. This is because they are not knowledgeable of the Bible, *Book of Mormon*, their other scripture, theology, or the deeper teachings of their own church. Their ward leaders are basically laymen who also do not know theology or their church's deeper teachings.

Even among higher levels of leadership in the church, there is widespread ignorance of what their doctrines really are. This is because their church has few, if any, competent students of theology or the Bible. I have observed that, when a person becomes a competent theologian, he or she wants out and church leaders want them out. The saying is true: "When a Mormon becomes a competent theologian he will soon leave the church." Since this is true, isn't it time to reform the church?

If you are LDS and reading this, you may already be offended. Please hear me out, for your own freedom and salvation's sake you need to carefully check the facts. The Lord warned that if "a blind man guides a blind man, both will fall into a pit" (Matthew 15:14). Investigation is never harmful to truth. Those teaching the truth should not be alarmed by scrutiny. If you are afraid of investigating what you believe, it may be a subconscious admission that you fear what you believe will not stand the test.

Please accept my challenge to prove me wrong. In those areas in which I do not present convincing evidence, do not accept my conclusions. But if the evidence is clear, and I believe it is, turn to truth and freedom!

BAD APPROACHES TO WITNESSING TO MORMONS

Unfortunately, some of those who have sought to lead Mormons to the real Jesus have not always had the sweet spirit of Christ. Instead they have spoken with bitterness and rancor. It is understandable why someone who had invested many years of their lives in the Mormon system would be bitter when they learn how badly they have been fooled. This understandably can color the spirit of their testimony after they have left the church.

Nevertheless, bitter attacks or a critical spirit never help the cause of witnessing to Mormons. What works, and at the same time glorifies the Lord, is kindness, genuine concern, and truth from a heart of love.

If we cannot approach LDS people as their genuine friends, who are also in the search for truth, we may not help them much. If we do not

Introduction

take time to pray for and with them our words will fall on deaf ears.

Few people leave a cultist system without time, careful teaching, and with good reasons. They need to be given time to learn and grow. Check the information, study with them, and give them time to digest the information. Initially they may appear to be little affected. If they are motivated to think, they are on the way to truth and liberty.

IS MORMONISM A MAINSTREAM CHRISTIAN RELIGION?

Reading an advertisement in a magazine or seeing one on television gives the impression that the LDS church is not much different than the average mainstream Protestant church. They stress their belief in Jesus, God, salvation, and use theological words that sound much like what mainstream Christian churches use. They suggest they have all the truth and even more truth than other churches.

At the March 24-31, 2000, open house for the new Medford, Oregon, Temple there was a paid advertising insert in the Medford newspaper. Reading this makes the church sound just like the best from all other churches wrapped up into one.

They characterize themselves as "A People Devoted to Christ." They continue, "Church members believe that Jesus Christ is the Son of God, the Savior of the world, the promised Messiah, and the mediator between God and His children. Members of the Church love and worship Christ and try to honor Him by leading good and virtuous lives."

Attempted Name Change

Two recent *Idaho Statesman* articles appear to be a further effort to confuse the issue and remove terms that may make them appear different. One is entitled, "Mormon Church to Drop LDS Abbreviation."

> In a new move to identify their faith as Christian, leaders of the Church of Jesus Christ of Latter-day Saints will soon issue a formal statement dropping the term "LDS Church" and "LDS" as shorthand names.
>
> While the full name of the church–The Church of Jesus Christ of Latter-day Saints–will remain unchanged, leaders of the church will say that from now on the preferred shorthand or second reference should be simply "the church," or "the Church of Jesus Christ."
>
> The First Presidency and the quorum of the Twelve Apostles, the highest authorities in the eleven-million member church, will issue the statement within a week to 10 days, church spokesman

Dale Bills said in a telephone interview Friday from Salt Lake City.

For years, the church's detractors have charged that the Church of Jesus Christ of Latter-day Saints is not a Christian body because it claims to be the only true and 'restored' church of Jesus Christ. To counter such criticism, the church has taken a series of steps to re-emphasize its Christian roots. Several years ago it began to discourage the use of the name, "Mormon Church."[3]

The exact membership of the LDS church is probably unknown and may not come anywhere near the numbers reported by the church. Temple Mormons, those who may enter one of their Temples for heavenly marriages, or proxy baptisms, may be no higher than 10-20%. People who have ever been baptized into the church remain on the records unless they come to excommunication for some reason.

In 1995, it changed its logo to place the words "Jesus Christ" in larger letters than the rest of its full name.[4]

A few days later another article appeared in the *Statesman*:

> Mormons Want Church's Official Name Used. Salt Lake City—Mormon leaders are asking their followers and news organizations to stop using the informal name of their church.
>
> "The official, full name of the church should always be used by the church and its members," said a release issued Monday by The Church of Jesus Christ of Latter-day Saints. If that's too long, officials have sanctioned a new, more generic nickname: "the Church of Jesus Christ."
>
> It's not the first time the church has tried to move away from the name invented by 19th century critics to deride the new religion. Six years ago, the church—which some mainstream denominations insist is not truly Christian—redesigned its logo to emphasize the name of Jesus Christ in an attempt to play up its theological focus....[5]

Human nature moves us to shorten a nine-word name when it is used repeatedly. In a church with hundreds of teachings that are radically different from mainstream Christianity, it is understandable to offer some

---

[3]Ibid., February 2001.
[4]Ibid.
[3]Ibid., March 2001.

Introduction

designation delineating it from everything else. For the church to insist that they are *not* "Mormon" or "LDS" makes as much sense as it would for a Baptist or a Roman Catholic to insist on some other designation.

The major point being that The Church of Jesus Christ of Latter-day Saints may really want to move away from what they have always been, at least in the public eye. But has there been deep change within? Is the church identical to the rest of Christianity? This is the question we will investigate.

There are major differences between the church and most all of the rest of Christianity. The differences between the Roman Catholic Church and Protestantism are very minor in comparison to the differences between the LDS church and Christianity. On a scale using a percentage comparison, the Roman Catholic Church and Protestantism are 90% the same while the LDS church and Protestantism are only 20% the same. Even the vocabulary is predominantly different. Many commonly used words for Christians have a slightly, or sometimes drastically different meaning to an indoctrinated Mormon. God, Christ, the church, salvation, all are terms that have radically different meanings.

Differences in Terminology

Closer inspection shows that they have subtle or great differences of meaning from the Christian terms they so glibly use. Some examples:

1) "We believe in God the Father." Their meaning is that there is an exalted man who has become their God, one of millions of other gods.

2) "We believe in Jesus the Savior." They do not explain that they believe Jesus is a created being, son of a physical mother and father, not begotten of the virgin Mary.

3) "We believe in Heaven." The non-suspecting person does not know that they believe in *four* levels of heaven with people sent to different universes for eternity, a concept very different from that of Christian churches.

4) Their view of salvation, marriage, family, hell, conversion, the Holy Spirit, and most other common Christian teachings is often different.

For the above reasons the United Methodists claim that the LDS church is not really Christian. Another *Idaho Statesman* article records,

> United Methodists Claim LDS Not Really Christian. Cleveland–United Methodist Church delegates approved a new policy statement Wednesday declaring that the Church of Jesus Christ of Latter-day Saints, "by self-definition, does not fit within the bounds of the historic, apostolic tradition of the Christian faith."

CHRISTIANITY & MORMONISM

> As a result, Mormon members who become Methodists should be treated as converts from another faith and be re-baptized, the policy said.
>
> The United Methodist Church is the nation's third largest religious body, with 8.4 million members, while the Mormon church ranks seventh, with 5 million members.
>
> A nine-page paper, passed by the Methodist General Conference without floor discussion, said Mormonism has "some radically differing doctrine on such matters of belief as the nature and being of God; the nature, origin and purpose of Jesus Christ and nature and way of salvation."
>
> The Presbyterian Church (U.S.A.) and Southern Baptist Convention have issued similar assessments of Mormon doctrine....[6]

With three of the largest Protestant churches of America issuing similar statements in regard to the LDS church, it is no wonder the Mormon church is trying to spruce up their public image.

It is much like the story of two dogs. Two men were walking down the street and met with their dogs on leashes when one said to the other, "My dog can beat your dog in a fight. Your dog is the ugliest thing I ever saw." The challenge was accepted and the two dogs fought and in the very first attack the one dog bit the other in two pieces. The owner of the dead dog asked, "Just what kind of a dog is that anyway?" The other replied, "Before I cut off his tail and painted him yellow, he was called a crocodile."

What is the point? It doesn't make any difference how a crocodile is painted; it is still at heart a crocodile. Or put another way: If it quacks like a duck and walks like a duck, call it what you may, it is still a duck. More than re-naming the LDS church is needed for it to be really Christian.

Motivation for Identity Change

Presenting themselves as "mainstream Christianity" could come from several possible motivations:

First, they do not know the difference between their religion and Christianity. This option is quite unlikely, but may be true for many as there are so few leaders who really know either Christianity or their own religion.

Second, it may come from an effort to mislead people to get them hooked on their church without being candid about what they really believe. Their reason for hiding what they really believe may be because

---

[6]Ibid., fall of 2000.

Introduction

they realize it is radically different and people would be turned off if they told them the whole truth up front.

Or third, subconsciously they have begun to realize that some of their teachings are bizarre. They would like to distance themselves from these doctrines and become more Biblical and correct in their teachings. This is my hope. They are embarrassed (and should be) by their doctrines. They would like to move back to the real Jesus and truth. It is time for them to give up the untrue parts of their teachings. It would make them more believable and they could be what they claim to be. They would no longer have to run misleading advertising to disguise what they really believe. People would no longer have to use some term, like "LDS" or "Mormon," to indicate that they are significantly different.

Descriptive names, nicknames, applied to people are typically based on some fact about them. For example a person may be named "Shorty" or "Red" or "Irish" or some other designation, because the person may be short, red-haired, or of Irish descent. Such is the case with the LDS church. If they are not called LDS or Mormon then some other name will have to be used to indicate what they really are—different from Christianity.

Since the LDS church continues to claim that they are the only true church, then why would they want to be identified with all of these *false* Christian churches? It seems they would welcome being set apart as different. *The Doctrine and Covenants* says,

> And also those to whom these commandments were given, might have power to lay the foundation of this church, and to bring it forth out of obscurity and out of darkness the only true and living church upon the face of the whole earth, with which I the Lord am well pleased.... (DC 1:30).

Christianity and Mormonism: From Bondage to Freedom shows clearly the differences between the Mormon church and Christianity in general. A part of this book will deal with their many deceptions, how these lead to bondage, and will offer suggestions for how they can return to Biblical Christianity, and in truth be "The 'Restored' Church of Jesus Christ of Latter-day Saints." After 170 years the time is ripe for them to give up the long-standing errors, to launch a major study of what they teach in the light of truth, not according to what some of their church prophets have said God told them. They need a "Reformation" or "Restoration" movement within their church to restudy their teachings and make a major effort to return to the truth. It will be painful for Mormons but eternally profitable.

CHRISTIANITY & MORMONISM

A Lesson from the Worldwide Church of God

The Worldwide Church of God of H.W. and Garner Ted Armstrong had such a shakeup a few years ago, with their leaders admitting they had been wrong and for their members to merge back into mainstream Christianity. This came, in part, as a result of those who lovingly probed what they had been teaching and when it became known that church leaders had been found in open sin.

If the LDS church would take this course they would no longer have to defend what is indefensible. Someone could show the true signs of the prophet by pointing their church and its people back to Biblical truth. They could then use their vast resources and missionary pool to help mainstream Christianity turn our world back from the brink of disaster to the real truth, Jesus.

In contrast, their present method of dealing with those who have suggested they are teaching false doctrines is not to study the issues, but attack the messengers. They have trashed many peoples' reputations, including mine. One of the early Greek philosophers suggested, "If you cannot answer the message attack the messenger." This has been their method for the past 10-20 years. Frankly it has only had minimal success and made the church look dishonest. In Chapter 1 we will review Mormon methods of attacking others and investigate both Joseph Smith's and my credentials.

FROM BONDAGE TO FREEDOM

The Bars of Bondage
1. Why do Christians remain silent regarding false teaching? Specifically how can you turn bad witnessing approaches into good ones?
2. In what ways is it harder to be a Mormon than a Christian?
3. What are some differences in the use of Christian terms?
4. List at least two reasons for wanting to change LDS identity.

The Keys to Freedom
1. Begin a loose-leaf notebook for your personal or group study of Mormonism. Divide it into at least eight divisions corresponding to the chapters in this book.
2. Add a prayer section for listing the names of Mormon friends you contact. Keep notes of your encounters and answers to prayer.
3. Keep notes on Mormon advertising you will view on TV, hear over the radio, or see in print. What makes them appealing? How would you answer them?, etc. Discuss your notes with others and record your thoughts.

CHAPTER ONE
The Mormon Bondage to Suppressed Truth

"A good tree cannot produce bad fruit, nor can a bad tree produce good fruit" (Matthew 7:18).

THE LDS METHODS OF ATTACKING OTHERS

Why Destroy Peoples' Reputations?

A method that the LDS members have been using to defend their religion is almost as old as mankind. If you cannot answer those who point out your false doctrines, assassinate their characters. This, at best, is dishonest and some of their attacks have been, at worst, criminal.

I suspect that church headquarters does not officially authorize these attacks. Yet, it is easily within their hierarchical power to put a stop to it if they were not secretly pleased by these methods.

Recent attacks against others and me have been sleazy, dishonest, and villainous. Some individuals' lives, influence, and families have been irreparably damaged. I have personally felt the pain of being lied about, personally threatened with bodily injury, and having my reputation smeared. These attacks have been in print, on the Internet, over the telephone, and attempted in person.

Significant Change of Method

Over the past 30 years there has been a significant shift in how LDS people respond to those who point out errors in their teachings. In the 50s, 60s, and 70s, the LDS were willing to debate their teachings, privately and publicly.

CHRISTIANITY & MORMONISM

During the 70s, 80s, and 90s, researchers, using computer technology, directed good investigative methods on the church's history and doctrine. The church's efforts to defend themselves proved fruitless. When their true teachings were exposed to the light of truth and found wanting, they began to attack the credibility of those who pointed out their faults and inconsistent doctrines. Their stooping to mudslinging and character assassination is an admission that they can neither defend their doctrines nor answer their critics. The church, with their vast wealth, has even stooped to legal action against people of very modest resources to stop them from presenting the truth about the church. Their method is not to argue the issues, but silence anyone who dares question their teaching.

Having been a victim of their character assassination, it is tempting to be silent and thus not have to endure the pain and damage of widely published, untrue accusations from the well-financed Mormon propaganda machine. Imagine having such a huge and well-financed machine as your enemy. It is frightful, especially when truth is not a high priority for them.

They have tried to trash the reputations of Dee Jay Nelson and Jerald and Sandra Tanner. They tried to make Walter Martin, Wayne Cowdery, Howard Davis, and Donald Scales look like nincompoops. Their attacks on Ed Decker, Richard Fales, Charles Crane, and John L. Smith are examples of how deceptively they trash peoples' reputations with half-truths, faulty research, biased reporting, and outright lies. Although I do not know all of the above-named individuals personally, those I do know are misrepresented in the many accusations made against them. Some have had their lives destroyed by lies and deception. The church has made no visible effort to disprove these accusers.

Why would they not respond to the doctrinal and historical questions that their critics have raised? It is because the arguments the researchers have presented are valid and cannot be answered. It will be the goal of this book to present some of the most important of the Mormon inconsistencies, with a call for them to reform the church. When people turn from lies to truth, they will be turning from bondage to freedom in Christ.

Untrue Accusations about Their Critics

Several have experienced the deceptive and misleading writings of Robert and Rosemary Brown. Their publishing company, Brownsworth Publishing Company, is really a home-basement enterprise with one goal in mind: to discredit anyone who musters enough courage to speak against the LDS church.

The information in their books and floating around on the Internet presents a picture of me as having no respectable degree from any quality institution. Although I have four earned degrees, am the president of an accredited college, and in 1999 received the highest award presented by one of my Alma Maters, Lincoln Christian Seminary. (See details below.) Yet, they make it appear that I am poorly educated. I cheerfully gave them the facts, although they chose to publish false and misleading information based on their very poor investigative methods. I would welcome a fair investigation of the issues at stake. Why would they not discuss the issues? Because such investigations have proven their church to be in drastic error.

Attacks on Those Who Speak Out

The Browns have published the following books against the most well-known writers. Each volume in the series is entitled *They Lie in Wait to Deceive*. In reality the title applies more to the Brown's work than to those they write about.

They Lie in Wait to Deceive
Volume One: Dee Jay Nelson and Jerald and Sandra Tanner
Volume Two: Dr. Walter Martin, Wayne Cowdery, Howard Davis, and Donald Scales
Volume Three: Dr. Walter Martin again
Volume Four: Ed Decker, Richard Baer, Dr. Fales, Dr. Charles Crane, Dr. John L. Smith

In these books they have not tried to answer the arguments that have been brought against the LDS church or their doctrines, but their goal is rather to question the integrity or destroy the reputations of the people who have dared to speak out against the church. A public leader caught in sin tries to blackmail his opponents into silence. This has been the LDS effort to silence those who "have the goods on them." It is a similar method used in politics today.

The Nature of the Personal Attacks
in Books and on the Internet

Charges against Charles Crane
1) "Not educationally qualified to speak." (They have questioned other critics' and my education suggesting that we were from no credible institutions.)

Here is the truth of the matter. The following are earned degrees: Bachelor of Sacred Literature, Northwest College of the Bible, 1962; Master of Arts, Lincoln Christian Seminary, Magna Cum Laude, 1975; Master of Divinity, Lincoln Christian Seminary, Magna Cum Laude, 1977;

CHRISTIANITY & MORMONISM

CPEC, St. Luke's Hospital, Boise, Idaho, 1977; Doctor of Ministry, Luther-Rice Seminary, Summa Cum Laude, 1978.

2) "Not an expert in Mormon Archaeology"

They accused me of claiming to be an expert in Mormon archaeology. First, I have never made such an obviously untrue claim. The truth is that for thirty years I have repeatedly said that *no one* could be an "expert in Mormon Archaeology" since there is no such factual basis for *The Book of Mormon*. How can a person be an expert in the nonexistent, any more than he could be an expert in the Land of Oz or the Wonderland of Alice? It would make as much sense as being an expert in the geography of Santa's North Pole headquarters, or the land of the tooth fairy.

(Please forgive my forthrightness about this, but just where did the events in *The Book of Mormon* take place? North America, Central America, or South America? Possibly they may have taken place near the Great Lakes, as some of the names in *The Book of Mormon* are found there, modern and not ancient.)

They write other supposed authorities to prove that I am not what I *never* claimed to be. It is another example of the spurious methods and of the deception of the Mormon defenders. This deceptive trick is called the "straw man attack."

Charges against Other Writers
1) "Lack of education"

Why would they choose "lack of formal education" as a means to discredit those who speak out against them? This line of reasoning would discredit their own founder and prophets. What were the educational qualifications of Joseph Smith,[7] Brigham Young, or their other prophets? The answer: little or none. Joseph finished the eighth grade. What education do their missionaries, ward teachers, and bishops have for their church work? Little or no theological training. There is no formal theological education. Their missionaries hit the trail with a few weeks' training in how to give their "canned" testimony and other matters of behavior. Most are theological neophytes.

2) "Gross immorality" (Curious when considering the flagrant immorality of men like Joseph Smith, Brigham Young, and the widespread immorality and practice of polygamy in Utah still today.)

---

[7] I will use Joseph Smith, rather than Joseph Smith, Jr., as he is the best known of the several Joseph Smiths.

Men like Ed Decker and Dick Baer, if guilty as accused (which I seriously question) were only living like their leaders *while they were Mormons*. Their accusations only further discredit their own leaders. A more *valid* question would be, "What are they like now that they have become Christians?"

Some associated with the "Ex-Mormons for Jesus" movement have been attacked on the basis of moral depredations, extra-marital affairs, divorce, and pre-marital misbehavior. These accusations may well not be true. This also seems a curious approach, since many of the sins for which they accuse these ex-Mormons took place while they were *active members* of the LDS church. The sins were not after they left the Mormon church, but while they were yet members. (These accusations have not necessarily been proven, but, if like those against me, are probably distorted or outright lies.)

3) "Profiteering" (This accusation seems erroneous when considering that the LDS church has been a master at profiteering from religion and is a big business with enormous profits.)

4) "Deception" (The LDS do lie in wait to deceive. This accusation is hypocritical when considering the constant misrepresentation and changing of Mormon history, scripture, and doctrines.)

Could it be that Mormons find these faults so easily in others since they are so well acquainted with these sins in their own leaders? It is much like a skunk accusing a pig of stinking. Unfortunately their accusations have often been more lies than the truth. Their goal has not been to discover the truth about their own doctrines, but to discredit and vilify any that question them. Their response is more like what would be expected from a satanic religion whose head is the father of liars.

Getting Tough

The most recent method being used by the LDS church to suppress the truth about their teachings and practices is to sue those who would speak out against them. In 1999-2000 the church had gone to court against Utah Lighthouse Ministry to stop them from publishing material from one of the LDS handbooks. There has been little legal recourse available to people whose reputations have been slaughtered, since the courts view the whole discussion as a "religious matter." It is a Goliath versus David battle.

Is it necessary, with the church's huge financial and political power, to sue Mr. and Mrs. Jerald (Sandra) Tanner, whose purpose is to expose known errors the LDS church teaches? Since the mid-sixties, despite a low income, they have worked tirelessly to bring restoration and reform to the church in which they were reared. They do this out of genuine love for the people. Wouldn't it make more sense to discuss the inconsistencies and untruths of the LDS teachings? If in fact they support only truth why would they care if their teachings, writings, and practices are known?

If the LDS church really is a champion of truth, would they not be thankful that untrue things would be revealed so they could correct them? Evidently the LDS church does not wish to learn the truth, but rather wishes to threaten and intimidate anyone who has the courage to question their teaching and practice.

What has the church done? They have threatened, refused them access to historical records, intimidated, and now sued the Tanners. It is another indication how desperate the church has become to suppress the real truth about their history, what they believe, and what they have taught.

What is happening in essence is, "If you cannot refute the message, attack the messenger." It is an old and diversionary method to muddy the waters and divert attention from the prolific errors so rampant in church history and teaching. It is time for the LDS church to turn to mainstream Christianity and leave their fanciful teachings.

It is time for thinking people in the LDS church to stand up and hold their leaders accountable by the standard of truth. In our modern day it is no longer possible to maintain the cover-up. The church is going to have to face the music and begin the process of turning to mainstream Christianity and truth while there is yet time. This book is a call for restoration and renewal in the LDS church. It is time to free their members from bondage to freedom in Christ.

During the 2000 national political campaign some political candidates had their personal and private problems made public. When past sins have been made known, there are two courses of action. First, a person can stonewall and *deny* his sins. But usually after months of continuing investigation the facts come out. Second, the sooner failures are *admitted* the more credibility a person has.

Similarly, the church needs to admit its errors, openly and candidly. It is too late to do otherwise. The logical approach is for them to admit the faults. Point out that they have learned lessons and have returned to restoring truth. Thus the church could begin to lay their many problems to rest. It is suggested that candor on the part of the LDS church would be a breath of fresh air and would add credibility to the church's message of "restoration."

JOSEPH SMITH'S CREDENTIALS

Since Mormons have published so much about peoples' credentials, let's take a moment to look at the credentials of Joseph Smith, Jr. The criteria for assessment in this chapter are the same as those used against those who would seek to expose LDS doctrinal errors.

The record shows these facts about Joseph Smith's baptism and ordination, the very basis of his whole ministry:

a) Joseph Smith baptized Oliver Cowdery.
b) Oliver Cowdery then baptized Joseph Smith.
c) Joseph ordained Oliver and Oliver, Joseph. (Ordained each other?)
d) Supposedly the Holy Spirit fell on them both and they prophesied. Then Jesus, Moses, Elias, and Elijah appeared to them. (Strange that since Joseph Smith was a prophet that he did not know that Elias and Elijah were one and the same person.) *The Doctrine and Covenants* records the above event:

> Upon you my fellow servants, in the name of Messiah I confer the Priesthood of Aaron, which holds the keys of the ministering of angels, and of the gospel of repentance, and of baptism by immersion for the remission of sins; and this shall never be taken again from the earth, until the sons of Levi do offer again an offering unto the Lord in righteousness (DC 13; May 15, 1829).

e) Ten years later, in 1839, Oliver Cowdery had already renounced his Mormon membership, published a tract explaining why he left the Mormon church, and joined the Methodist church. There is conclusive evidence that he left the church within three years. Even the LDS church admitted so by publishing a poem about Cowdery's leaving:

A Mormon Poem

Amazed with wonder! I look 'round
To see most people of our day,
Reject the glorious gospel sound
Because the simple turn away;
But does it prove there is no time,
Because some watches will not go?

Or prove that Christ was not the Lord
Because that Peter cursed and swore,
Or Book of Mormon not his word
Because denied by Oliver?
Or prove that Joseph Smith is false,
Because Apostates say 'tis so?

CHRISTIANITY & MORMONISM

In my library is a rare, old, and fragile tract published in 1915 called, *Did Oliver Cowdery Renounce Mormonism and Join the Methodist Protestant Church at Tiffin, Ohio?* It was researched and written by R.B. Neal of Grayson, Kentucky.

If, to the LDS, credentials are so important and they want to accuse those who question their doctrines, they should examine Joseph Smith and Oliver Cowdery. Oliver admitted Mormonism was a hoax and left the church. Would he have done so if he had prophesied and had actually seen Jesus, Peter, James, John, Moses, Elias, and Elijah? You be the judge. Joseph Smith was baptized and ordained by a man who left the Mormon church to become a Methodist. *The foundation of the LDS church is sand.*

Who Was Oliver Cowdery?

Oliver Cowdery was one of the three witnesses to *The Book of Mormon*. (See the Preface in each *Book of Mormon*, which gives "The Testimony of" what is called, "Three Witnesses.") He was about twenty-two years old at that time. A fuller account of who he was and what he did is given in the Mormon Sunday school Catechism No. 1, printed in 1882, in a series of questions and answers intended to teach the newcomer and children.

Q. *When were Joseph and Oliver baptized?*
A. On the same day the Aaronic Priesthood was conferred on them.
Q. *Who was baptized first?*
A. Oliver Cowdery.
Q. *Who baptized him?*
A. Joseph Smith.
Q. *Who was next baptized?*
A. Joseph Smith.
Q. *Who baptized him?*
A. Oliver Cowdery.
Q. *What took place next?*
A. Joseph ordained Oliver to the Aaronic Priesthood.
Q. *What happened after this?*
A. The Holy Ghost fell upon Joseph and Oliver, and they prophesied.
Q. *By whom was the Holy Apostleship restored to earth?*
A. Christ's ancient Apostles, Peter, James and John.
Q. *Upon whom did they confer this power?*
A. Joseph Smith and Oliver Cowdery.
Q. *What glorious things were revealed on the next Sunday (April 3, 1836)?*

A. The heavens were opened to Joseph Smith and Oliver Cowdery, and the glories thereof were shown to them.
Q. *Who appeared to them on this occasion?*
A. Our Lord and Savior, Jesus Christ.
Q. *What did He say of Himself?*
A. 'I am the First and the Last. I am He who liveth. I am He who was slain. I am your Advocate with the Father.'
Q. *After this vision was closed, who next appeared?*
A. Moses, the great law-giver of ancient Israel.
Q. *What did he commit to them?*
A. The keys of the gathering of Israel.
Q. *Who appeared next?*
A. Elias.
Q. *Who appeared after Elias?*
A. The prophet, Elijah, who gave them the keys to turn the hearts of the fathers to the children and the children to the fathers.[8]

This gives the context for both who Oliver was and what role he played in the very foundation of the LDS church. He was the baptizer of Joseph Smith and both a participant in and recipient of reported glorious things. [How the two men can be considered reliable witnesses of these events when they confuse one man for two remains a mystery (Elias and Elijah). At the very source of Joseph Smith's credentials are two men who are seeing double!]

But it is more damaging that Oliver Cowdery later admits this was all a hoax and left the Mormon church to become a Methodist. In 1839, just three years after the above events, Oliver Cowdery published a booklet entitled, *Defense in a Rehearsal of My Grounds for Separating Myself from the Latter-day Saints*, By Oliver Cowdery, Second Elder of the Church of Christ.[9]

On the front of the booklet it says, "This Defense is not protected by a copyright, as I wish no man to be confined alone to my permission in printing what is meant for the eyes and knowledge of the nations of the earth."

Continuing, "God doth not walk in crooked paths; Neither doth he turn to the right hand, Nor the left; Neither doth he vary from that which he hath said."[10] Remember, their baptisms were less than three years earlier.

---

[8]R.B. Neal, *Did Oliver Cowdery Renounce Mormonism and Join the Methodist Protestant Church at Tiffin, Ohio?* (Grayson, KY: Gospel Dollar League, 1915), pp. 1-2. (This tract has been reprinted, and a copy can be purchased for $1.00 from Boise Bible College Press.)
[9]Ibid., p. 3.
[10]Ibid.; (Pressley's Job Office, Norton, Ohio, 1839).

The adopted daughter of Oliver Cowdery, Mrs. Adeline M. Bernard, says, "Mr. Cowdery adopted me as his own child." She wrote in a letter October 3, 1881, "I know that Mr. Cowdery joined the Methodist Protestant Church. He joined the church in 1841, and you can write to Judge W. Lang, of Tiffin, O., and he will search the church records and send you a transcript of his (Oliver Cowdery's) membership."[11]

Judge Lang said, "Cowdery entirely abandoned and broke away from all his connections with Mormonism."[12]

Again, "In the second year of his (Cowdery's) residence here (Tiffin, O.), he and his family attached themselves to the Methodist Protestant Church, where they held fellowship to the time they left for Elkhorn, Wis."[13]

G.J. Keen, a member of the Methodist church in question, says about Oliver's membership:

> "Mr. Cowdery opened a law office in Tiffin, and soon effected a partnership with Joel W. Wilson.
>
> "In a few years Mr. Cowdery expressed a desire to associate himself with a Methodist Protestant Church of this city.
>
> "Rev. John Souder and myself were appointed a committee to wait on Mr. Cowdery and confer with him respecting his connection with Mormonism and *The Book of Mormon*.
>
> "We accordingly waited on Mr. Cowdery at his residence in Tiffin and there learned his connection, from him, and his full and final renunciation thereof.
>
> "We then inquired of him if he had any objection to making a public recantation.
>
> "He replied that he had objections; that, in the first place, it could do no good: that he had known several to do so and they always regretted it. And, in the second place, it would have a tendency to draw public attention, invite criticism and bring him into contempt.
>
> "'But', said he, 'nevertheless, if the church require it I will submit to it, but I authorize and desire you and the church to publish and make known my recantation.'
>
> "We did not demand it, but submitted his name to the church, and he was unanimously admitted a member thereof.
>
> "At that time he arose and addressed the audience present,

---

[11] Ibid., p. 13.
[12] Ibid., p. 12.
[13] Ibid.

admitted his error and implored forgiveness, and said he was sorry and ashamed of his connection with Mormonism.

"He continued his membership while he resided in Tiffin, and became superintendent of the Sabbath school, and led an exemplary life while he resided with us.

"I have lived in this city upwards of fifty-three years, was auditor, of this county, was elected to that office in 1840.

"I am now in my eighty-third year, and well remember the facts above related.

[Signed] G.J. Keen

"Sworn before me and subscribed in my presence, this 14th day of April, A.D. 1885 Frank L. Emich.

"G.J. Keen, Esq., is one of our oldest citizens, is a respectable man and is very highly esteemed.

[Signed] O.T. Lock, Postmaster."[14]

As with other very damaging information like this, the Mormon church has tried to find conflicting testimony and to deny what actually happened. R.B. Neal presents incontrovertible evidence that Cowdery did become a Methodist and very shortly after his encounter with Moses, Jesus, Peter, James, John, Elias, and Elijah.

Does it sound plausible that he actually did see what he and Joseph Smith claimed? Would God, who knows the future, have chosen such a person to be the witness of the foundation events for the restoration of the gospel to the earth? Or does it seem more probable that Joseph and Oliver conspired to tell what amounts to a fish story?

Credentials? Joseph Smith's are pretty flimsy. Why then should they try to discredit people like Dr. Walter Martin, Dr. John Smith, Dr. Charles A. Crane, and others who have, in love, called them back to the truth? Isn't this a puzzling approach to a discussion of truth, to malign the good names of those pointing out inconsistencies and false teaching?

Wouldn't the time of Robert and Rosemary Brown and Russell Anderson (a man who put untrue things on the Internet about me) be better spent checking the credentials of their own church and "prophet" rather than trying to ruin the reputations of those who love them enough to show the errors of their religion? Are people their enemies because they tell them the truth? Several years were spent investigating my life, to see if they could dig up some dirt to discredit me. The same amount of time checking their own doctrines would have led them from bondage to liberty!

---

[14] Ibid., p. 13.

CHRISTIANITY & MORMONISM

CREDENTIALS OF CHARLES CRANE

What Is My Motivation to Speak Out?

So many have wondered and asked what my motivation is to speak out. Following is a brief review of my association with and the study of the LDS church. The researching of Mormonism has never been the main interest or emphasis my life. I have never considered myself a missionary to Mormon people. It is just one of my several interests in the religious realm. I do not recall having ever had a class on the Mormon religion in college or seminary. The emphasis of my life has been the study of theology and ministry. Many other areas of theology and religion are more fascinating to me than the study of Mormonism.

But from the time I was a child my life has been intertwined with LDS people. Out of necessity I have had to study their scripture and teachings. If they had not been so aggressive in proselytizing me, I might have lived among them without having to research their teachings.

It was because of their willingness to talk to everyone about their religion, especially me, that caused my study to find out if what they claimed was true. Having a good memory for facts and details has helped me to recall much of what I have read over the years.

Analysis and synthesis of vast amounts of information into a systematic scheme has been a long-time pursuit. The effort of this book is to boil down vast encyclopedias of material into its most significant essence. Following is my brief history of a lifetime of constant interaction with Mormon people.

I have never refused to study with any LDS person. Although most of my ministry (all but three years) has been in strong Mormon areas, only once has a member of a church I served been baptized into the LDS church. The story deserves telling.

I had been in the Middle East for nearly a month. Upon the day of my return one of my associates said, "Sister Christine (not her real name) is going to be baptized into the LDS church tonight." I went immediately with the staff member to visit her. She brushed us off and said, "My decision has been made." We left cordially.

At the prompting of her parents, and out of genuine concern, an elder and I went to visit her one evening the following week. She said, "I may not have done the right thing, but you and the church have not given me what I needed most."

I replied, "Since your recent divorce we have helped you with food and counseling, haven't we?" (She was a pretty but quite gullible young lady.)

She replied, "Yes, but I needed much more than that. I have been left feeling so worthless and lonely after the divorce, I have just needed someone to hold me. The missionaries and ward teacher have come and spent time with me. They have spent all night several nights, they have held me and made love to me. It has helped me feel more worthwhile."

You can imagine our response. "They have slept with you? Sex?"

To which she replied, "Yes."

We showed her from Scripture that it is sin for unmarried people (the missionaries) and married people (the ward teacher) to sleep with her. The very next Sunday she returned to church, responded to the invitation and asked forgiveness for being taken in by a false religious system. This is not to suggest that all missionaries and ward teachers are immoral, they aren't. But, if they have the keys of the gospel, why act in such a sinful way?

In all the years of my ministry she was the only member of a church I served that was ever baptized into the LDS church. Here is a summary of how I happened to have been involved so long in this study.

Homer Moxley

As a boy of 13, I was hunting on the back of our ranch in the foothills of Oregon's Cascade Mountains. I saw a caterpillar tractor pulling a large log. Thinking that someone was stealing our timber, I stood in the middle of the road so the cat had to stop.

The most handsome man I had ever seen got off, put out his hand and said, "My name is Homer Moxley. Your father gave me permission to yard some timber across the back of your ranch." We became friends that day and are still today. He is an old man, I'm not so young anymore myself. That was the beginning of my study of the Mormon church.

Homer was LDS and began to talk to me about their church. He gave me my first *Book of Mormon* and I kept my promise to read it. After reading it we discussed what it said. Although I was not the only reason he left the LDS church, he will tell you that I did help him develop questions about the validity of *The Book of Mormon*. I still have this *Book of Mormon* with all the marks and questions written in the margins that I made when I was thirteen years old. From that day onward I have had an interest in the LDS religion. Homer became a free-in-Christ Christian and has remained active all these years.

At Age Sixteen

I met a pretty and energetic girl at school, named Sally. We struck up a friendship and dated for a year or two. She was LDS and I studied with her and her family. They were interested that a prospective son-in-law be of their faith. I presented to them the questions that had come to my mind after reading *The Book of Mormon*.

Again, I was not the only influence in their lives, but I did have a small part in their leaving the LDS church. Sally and I did not date after I left for college. I was told that her father became a preacher and died in the pulpit while preaching the gospel.

While dating Sally I began work for a man who had been the LDS stake president. Like most Mormons he was a fine, honest, clean-living man. We became friends and remain close friends to this day. Because of his many admirable traits he had a good influence on my life, especially in encouraging me to attend college and to begin to invest.

We talked frequently and he has attended lectures that I have given about problems with the LDS religion. Because these presentations were fair and kind we have maintained our friendship, even though he has remained a Mormon. He and his family are not very active in their church today.

Dean Jacobs

Jacobs is not his real name. Dean and I worked together at Goodyear in Portland, Oregon. He was a zealous returned missionary. He was trying to win Mitch, the truck tire salesman, to Mormonism. Mitch asked me what I thought about what Dean was teaching. This led to discussions among the three of us and Mitch did not become a Mormon. Working with Dean, it was apparent that, although he held the LDS priesthood, he did not possess the Holy Spirit. A key indicator was dirty language and suggestive jokes. Jesus said, "A good tree cannot bring forth evil fruit, neither can a corrupt tree bring forth good fruit" (Matthew 7:18, KJV).

Larry Jonas

A fellow student at Bible College was affectionately called "Stretch." His name was Larry Jonas. He was a six-foot-five beanpole. He had studied the LDS religion and his Bachelor's thesis became a book published by Baker Book House called *Mormon Claims Examined*.

He and I became friends and the resident authorities on the LDS religion. We spent evenings responding to the call for help from area churches when the Mormon missionaries were teaching their members. This became an additional learning time for me.

Sutherlin, Oregon

After Bible college I was called to preach at a church in Sutherlin, Oregon. The LDS church was trying to begin a congregation there. The missionaries were working the area intensely. I was called out several times to study with the missionaries. In nearly every encounter people came to know the *real* Jesus.

My interest in Mormonism had grown to studying *The Doctrine and Covenants* and other LDS scripture. My confidence grew and I was willing to talk with anyone they could produce. There were several LDS families, or near converts who came to the real Jesus, rather than become LDS. Although there is a ward there now, its establishment was delayed several more years because a young preacher took an interest in studying the Mormon system.

Salt Lake City, Utah

In late 1965, I was called to minister to a Christian church in southeast Salt Lake City. This began an immersion in the study of Mormon teachings. For awhile so many LDS tried to win me to their church that I had trouble finding time to study for my teaching and sermons. They came to my church office day after day.

I made friends with Marvin Cowan, a fellow preacher, also interested in the study of the LDS church. He introduced me to Jerald and Sandra Tanner of Utah Lighthouse Ministries. During this period I was reading everything I could get my hands on, for and against Mormonism.

Although I have lost count of the exact number, about a third of the converts during the seven-plus-year ministry in Salt Lake City were converts from the LDS church, maybe as many as 200 during this period.

At first the LDS were anxious to talk with me. As time passed we baptized more and more of their members. During this period I had breakfast with Ezra Taft Benson, church president and prophet. We won more and more of them, and lost not one member to the LDS religion.

Finally their method began to change. When we began to study with one of their members they made no effort to confront us or keep their member from leaving the church. A large book would not hold the stories of all the studies, conversions, and experiences.

Since the evidence was so conclusive to disprove the LDS religion I grew more confident and agreed to talk privately or publicly with all that wished. The number that would talk diminished to none after a climactic study one winter evening.

A young couple was about to marry, the lady LDS, the man, as near as I can recall, Lutheran. Their eyes were filled with stars of love, but they wanted to settle the religion issue. I agreed with the couple to meet anyone they wanted to bring. The man they brought was, by his own admission, one of the church's top apologists and troubleshooters.

After talking two and one-half hours, the church authority was drenched with sweat, his shirt collar was totally soaked; under his arms the sweat had soaked through his shirt and down on his pants. He said as we concluded, "If I knew your religion as well as you know ours I could poke all sorts of holes in it just like you have ours."

I pleaded with him to keep what was good in his religion and cast aside anything that was false. He left in a state of mild shock. It was not that I was so bright, but that the evidence was so clear and conclusive. (A part of this book is a summary of the evidence gathered over a lifetime and what I had presented to him that night.)

Seminary

At thirty-four, a long-term goal of attending graduate school became possible. We moved to Illinois to attend Lincoln Christian Seminary. As partial fulfillment of the requirements for the Master of Arts degree I wrote a thesis called, *The Bible and Mormon Scriptures Compared*. This book was a condensation of the material I used in leading Mormons to know the real Jesus. It was published by College Press Publishing Company and sold out of print many times over the next 15 years.

Eugene, Oregon

After Seminary I ministered with a Christian church in Eugene. In 1984, the Christian campus minister set up a debate at the University of Oregon. An LDS professor was also a strong Mormon and head of the LDS missionary work in the State of Oregon.

We agreed that our only source for this debate was to be *The Book of Mormon*. I welcomed such limitation, because it was *The Book of Mormon* that had caused my earliest doubts about the LDS religion.

As the debate took place I began to feel sorry for the professor with a Ph.D. He was unaware of the many problems in *The Book of Mormon* and really not much more familiar with his book than many Christians are of the Bible. Before the debate was over the audience was laughing at him and I felt embarrassed for him. Although I do not have positive proof, I was told he later left the LDS church.

Are You a Mormon Fighter?

On one speaking occasion I was introduced as "Charles Crane the Mormon Fighter." Nothing could be farther from the truth. The study of the LDS church has been a special interest that I have pursued out of a genuine love for and respect of the LDS people. My motivation has almost always been love and concern for people who live in spiritual, financial, and social bondage. I say, "almost" because at times these discussions have degenerated into controversy, rather than searches for truth.

The Mormon Bondage to Suppressed Truth

(It has not always been a bed of roses. I have been threatened with physical harm. I have been run off of the road, and told on the telephone, "We are going to kill you.")

Even sadder than the rigorous demands made on the LDS members' lives is what their religion does to degrade and harm women and children. Their lives are truly in bondage and in danger eternally. It is a loving act to help them learn the truth.

Writings, Movies, and Cassettes[15]

In an effort to make available what I have learned, I began to write. The first booklet was entitled *Do You Know What the Mormon Church Teaches?* (Frankly it was pretty poor, but it was a beginning effort to state concisely the major issues between truth and Mormon doctrine.)

The second booklet was called *Mormon Missionaries in Flight*. The sub-theme was *Why a Mormon missionary does not want to talk to a knowledgeable Christian*. The emphasis was again a synthesis of the most basic problems the LDS church needed to solve in order to be founded on truth.

The next writings were scholarly papers presented at various conferences where I had been invited to speak. Below is a partial listing of these papers.

1. "The Bible and Mormon Scriptures"
2. "A Text Critical View of *The Book of Mormon*"
3. "Archaeology as Proof of *The Book of Mormon*"
4. "Why I Cannot Accept *The Book of Mormon* as Scripture"
5. "Deception in the Shadow of the Temple"
6. "The Restored Church?"
7. "The True God?"
8. "Revelation and Mormon Scripture"
9. "The Book of Abraham"
10. "Revelation and Contradiction"
11. "From Mormon Bondage to Christian Freedom"

Videos
1. *A Textual Comparison of The Book of Mormon and the Bible*
2. *Prophets for Profit*
3. *Confronting the Cults I* (Lessons 1-8)
4. *Confronting the Cults II* (Lessons 9-16)

---

[15]Unfortunately, many articles and speeches have not been preserved. This listing though, gives a picture of the steady lifetime activity in dealing with the Mormon religion.

CHRISTIANITY & MORMONISM

Movie: *The God Makers*

This movie was commissioned by Saints Alive in Jesus, a group of ex-Mormons who joined together to expose what they found wrong with their former religion. The film was the idea of Dick Baer and Ed Decker. Burbank Film Studio of Hollywood, California, made the movie. I was cited (unfortunately) as an expert in Mormon Archaeology. They included 5-7 minutes out of my two-hour interview. I have no apology for what I said, as it is fully the truth.

For the most part the movie is historically and doctrinally a fair representation of the Mormon position. It does show some of the deep hurt ex-Mormons feel towards the church that had kept them in bondage for so many years. (There are a couple of rather "cheap shots" taken at the LDS church. The church hates this movie so badly because it widely made known some of their dark secrets.) I have no regret for having had a part in this work.

Other Books

1. *The Bible and Mormon Scriptures Compared* (Joplin, MO: College Press, 1992).

2. (With Steven Crane) *Ashamed of Joseph: Mormon Foundations Crumble* (College Press, 1993).

3. *Is Mormonism Christian?: A Look at the Teachings of the Mormon Religion* (College Press, 1995). (A rewrite of Harry Ropp's The *Mormon Papers: Are the Mormon Scriptures Reliable?*, published by InterVarsity in 1977.)

A BRIEF LOOK AHEAD

The truth will make us free; deceit and lies bring bondage. The trip from Latter-day Saint bondage to Christian freedom begins with a search for and love of the truth. In each part of the following discussion we plead with the LDS church leaders to deal with the issues, show some spiritual courage, and turn from error to the truth. It will bring renewal to your life and could bring revitalization to the LDS church and make you what you claim to be—the *restored Church of Jesus Christ*.

With these introductory thoughts let us proceed by checking the works of Joseph Smith, founding prophet of the LDS church. If Joseph is not a genuine prophet of God, the church has a problem with its very foundation. What better place is there to begin than with the scripture the LDS church uses?

The Bible, other Mormon scripture, and Joseph's writings are some of the strongest evidences against the LDS church. The way they have changed and revised Scripture shows their callous disregard for truth. The Mormon Bible, *Book of Mormon, Doctrine and Covenants, Pearl of Great Price*, and *Journal of Discourses*, all have had major revisions and changes. We will apply very stringent tests to check the credibility of the Bible and then use the same tests on their other sacred books. By using the same tests on each we will be able to determine if Mormon writings are on the same level as the Bible and in fact Scripture.

Later we will compare some of their major doctrines with the Bible, as well as their other scriptures. Truth should be found consistent. If it is not, then we had better continue our search for truth. Many of their major doctrines are not Biblical nor does *The Book of Mormon* support them. The result is a system of bondage. Our LDS friends need to find the wonderful peace and liberty that are in Jesus.

Finally, since the LDS church apparently wants to portray itself as a mainstream Christian religion, we will suggest ways they can cull out false teachings and turn to Biblical Christianity.

This will take bold leadership on the part of the LDS church. It will take someone of courage like Martin Luther, Alexander Campbell, and other reformers and restorers if the church is to be really restored. Modern leaders will have to stand for major reform in their teachings, always with the goal of checking everything by the facts and discarding what is demonstrated to be false. If they can, in reality, be what they want the world to believe they are, then the church can become a champion of truth, rather than of false dogma.

When this becomes their focus they will no longer have to trash the reputations of those who are trying to help them return to truth and there will be no need to cover up, deceive, and attack those who want to love them back to the truth.

FROM BONDAGE TO FREEDOM

The Bars of Bondage
1. What has been the significant change in method for Mormons to confront their critics?
2. List at least three charges the LDS church has made against those who would point the way to truth.
3. Describe the basis for Joseph Smith's ordination to ministry.
4. Who was Oliver Cowdery and what role did he play in the beginning of Mormonism?
5. Summarize in six points the author's motivation to reach Mormons.

CHRISTIANITY & MORMONISM

> ***The Keys to Freedom***
> 1. Seek someone who has been personally attacked for witnessing to LDS members. Interview the person and offer to pray with him or her about continued efforts to evangelize the Mormon people.
> 2. Make a list of resources about Mormonism that you want to study. You may wish to add a section to your notebook for "resource swapping" with friends and/or small group members.
> 3. As you read this book and other resources, begin your own list of loving methods for witnessing to Mormons. Remember to update your changing prayer journal with personal contacts, actions, and answers.

CHAPTER TWO
The Mormon Bondage to a False View of Scripture

"But even if we, or an angel from heaven, should preach to you a gospel contrary to what we have preached to you, he is to be accursed!" (Galatians 1:8).

AUTHORS' STYLES OF WRITING

An author's style of writing is almost as distinctive as is his handwriting. One of the tasks of the higher textual critic is determining how many authors were involved in producing an ancient manuscript.

Styles in the Bible

The Bible has many different writers; their writing styles are as varied as those of Moses, Amos, Paul, and Peter. A cursory thumbing through shows the obviously different styles of the numerous writers. Over forty different writers and styles of writing have been verified in our Bible.

Such things as vocabulary, phrases, sentence structure, length or shortness of sentences, make up a writer's distinctive style. Ezekiel delivers his message in strange visions. Jeremiah speaks in figurative actions. David writes in poetic form. Hosea speaks in allegory. Isaiah speaks in most styles of writing common to literature. Paul writes in long and involved sentences with bursts of brilliant literary prose. They tell God's message, each in their own distinctive style.

Although the case can be made for common *authorship* by the Holy Spirit of the Bible, no case could be made for common *writing* of the Bible. In fact one of the evidences for the inspiration of the Bible is that

CHRISTIANITY & MORMONISM

so many different writers, writing over a period of 1,500-plus years, in at least three different languages, could tell a common story, historically, geographically, and factually accurate. A few people have argued a common writing, but the evidence clearly does not support this idea. The Bible is as multi-faceted as the rays of refracted sunlight.

Style in *The Book of Mormon*

By contrast, a text critical study of *The Book of Mormon* finds a similar style of writing from beginning to end. There are a number of distinctive fingerprints of the author throughout. (The only exception to this rule is in the places *The Book of Mormon* quotes the Bible. Here varied styles of writing suddenly burst upon the textual scene.)

There are some obvious indications that many different prophets who engraved them on gold plates did *not* write *The Book of Mormon*. Here is some of the evidence that points to a one-person authorship.

The first and most obvious is the continual use of the phrase "And it came to pass." This phrase is used many times in the King James Version. However, this represents a very poor translation of the Hebrew verb *hayah* with its many possible variations.

The KJV's indiscriminate translation of the many variations of the Hebrew verb *hayah* into "And it came to pass" or "It came to pass" amounts to a very poor, unimaginative translation of its nearly fifty possibilities and robs the translation of clearer meaning.

The Book of Mormon writer, to make his work sound Biblical, copies this distinctive style and phrasing. This plagiarism of the King James' style, and particularly in one of its poorest translations, shows *The Book of Mormon* not to be of God. A proper translation of the Hebrew would render very few of these "And it came to pass" instances.

The New Testament KJV translates *kai egeneto* "And it came to pass." This phenomenon is found in four New Testament books: the synoptic Gospels and Acts. Mark was likely written first. Matthew and Luke used Mark as a source for their Gospels and thus the common "And it came to pass" terminology. Luke wrote Acts and used this familiar style. Here again a careful translation renders few of these passages, "And it came to pass."

The Book of Mormon is caught plagiarizing the poor translation style of the King James Version to appear to be what it really isn't: Scripture. [For this reason I suggest the use of a more up-to-date and accurate translation than the King James Version. Translations such as the New American Standard Bible (Updated) or New King James represent more accurate renderings.]

Following is a list of the "And it came to pass" passages in *The Book* of Mormon. (This is my own incomplete count but shows the tendency.)

Book	Count	
1 Nephi	179	
2 Nephi	23	(Quotes extensively from Isaiah–but phrase never found in a direct Isaiah quote. Plagiarizing Isaiah explains why so few.)
Jacob	42	
Enos	5	
Jarom	4	
Omni	10	
Words of Mormon	2	
Mosiah	155	
Alma	351	
Helaman	110	
3 Nephi	124	
4 Nephi	19	
Mormon	15	
Ether	133	
Moroni	0	
Total	**1,172**	

Without a doubt this can be called a distinctive mannerism of a single author. As a textual critic, the tendency to use "And it came to pass" statements throughout, except for one book, and only when the Bible is directly quoted, is evidence for a single writer. Since *The Book of Mormon* claims to have been written by numerous authors, we can hardly accept it as an authentic record.

In the New Testament the five books that demonstrate this style indicate their dependency on a common source, or Mark's Gospel. This is not a problem for authenticity, since it is generally understood that Mark was the first of the synoptic Gospels. However, this becomes an insurmountable problem for those who would suggest that *The Book of Mormon* is authentic and written by many different prophets over many years. This idea could be greatly expanded, but is sufficiently strong evidence that one person authored *The Book of Mormon*, with the exception of those long quotes out of the King James Version.

Other textual criteria that indicate single authorship are

1) long, involved sentences
2) a similar vocabulary
3) outlandish distinctive names, many never found anywhere else

CHRISTIANITY & MORMONISM

4) similar plot with little variation from beginning to end
5) similar prophetic message: the coming Messiah, yet always in very similar words
6) most of the books quote from the King James Version of the Bible, hundreds of years before its translation from Hebrew and Greek sources
7) poor grammar and English usage throughout the original 1830 edition
Only one conclusion can be reached: *One author* wrote *The Book of Mormon!*

Extensive Quotes from the King James Version
As stated previously, *The Book of Mormon* quotes repeatedly from the King James Version of the Bible. Why are the quotations always from the KJV and never from other translations? The rule of textual criticism is that if a supposed ancient book quotes from a "modern" book, then the supposed "ancient" book is not in fact ancient.

There are two possibilities. Either the Bible quotes from *The Book of Mormon*, or *The Book of Mormon* quotes from the Bible. It seems unlikely there could be another explanation. Did the King James translators have a *Book of Mormon* by their sides? Was the King James translation inspired of God? If so, why were there poor and sometimes inaccurate renditions? Why would God not clear up some of these problems in *The Book of Mormon* if *The Book of Mormon* had been translated by "the gift and power of God?" *The Book of Mormon* is thus demonstrated to be a relatively modern book, written after AD 1611, with many parts directly copied from the KJV.

Poor Grammar
In many places the grammar is quite poor in *The Book of Mormon*. Here are a few examples. In 2 Nephi we find "… many of which sayings are written upon mine other plates; for a more history part are written upon mine other plates" (2 Nephi 4:14).

Or, "O Lord wilt thou not shut the gates of thy righteousness before me, that I may walk in the path of the low valley, that I may be strict in the plain road," (2 Nephi 4:32) and again, "and the stiffneckedness of men" (2 Nephi 32:7). This type of poor sentence structure and grammar can be found throughout the book.

The book claims to have been translated "by the gift and power of God …" Who made the mistakes, God? With the Bible, no claim is made that the *translators* were inspired of God. If so there would only be one totally accurate and infallible version. Yes, according to the example of *The Book of Mormon*, the Mormon god is a god of mistakes.

The Mormon Bondage to a False View of Scripture

Origins of Names in The Book of Mormon

Just where did the ideas for many of the names in *The Book of Mormon* come from? This subject deserves a lot more research, but here is a preliminary example of possible origins for some of the names in the book.

1. Nephi—comes from 2 Maccabees 1:36 (second century BC)
2. Lehi—a Hebrew word meaning "jawbone of an ass"
3. Mormon—a classical Greek word; one meaning is "monster"
4. Moroni—moron with an "i" added
5. Amaron
6. Amlicites
7. Helaman
8. Mosiah
9. Enos
10. Jerom
11. Omni

Such singularly different names and words are found throughout the book. Some have meaning. Some are the product of the author's own fertile imagination. Who knows their source for sure?

If Solomon Spaulding was the author, as affirmed below, he was an avid reader. He had a consuming interest in Indian folklore and archaeology. He had a master's degree.[16] He was a preacher and familiar with the King James Bible. This amply supplied him with the sources he needed to write the book. When his manuscript was found at Patterson's Print Shop it was only left to the devices of a scheming man and his friend to publish it as "Scripture" and to present it to an unsuspecting public, in a time of religious fervor. Can you imagine all the bondage this has brought to so many people? How many millions have been deceived, others discouraged, and many disgusted with all religion by the cumulative false and misleading claims?

THE BONDAGE AND DECEIT OF *THE BOOK OF MORMON*

What Is *The Book of Mormon*?

What about the Gold Plates?

The Book of Mormon is an epic novel about Jewish people who escaped from the siege of Jerusalem when the Babylonians captured Judah

---

[16]Wayne L. Cowdery, Howard A. Davis, and Donald R. Scales, *Who Really Wrote the Book of Mormon?* (Santa Anna, CA: Vision House Publishers, 1977).

about 600 BC. These 15-18 people escaped into the Judean wilderness and Sinaitic desert. God prepared a special boat for them in which they escaped to the Americas. There they split into two nations, the Nephites and Lamanites. This resulted in wars and the building of great civilizations.

Eventually the Lamanites, the bad guys, won out over the Nephites, the good guys, leaving the Lamanites or Native Americans, commonly referred to as Indians. The words of the prophets of these people were eventually written on gold plates and buried in the hill Cumorah. Joseph Smith found the gold plates and purportedly translated them into *The Book of Mormon*. The matter of the gold plates: their reality, who has them, where they went, and how much they weighed, have all been perplexing questions.

Brete Thomas is writing a book entitled *In the Name of Joseph Smith: Amen*. Following is a brief excerpt from his work regarding the gold plates' weight. Thomas says,

> Let's approach this scientifically and make the following conservative assumptions (in favor of a lower weight):
> 1. The plates were inscribed on both sides, thus cutting the number of plates in half.
> 2. The plates were inscribed in 10-point font (virtually impossible to do by hand with the tools available at the time *The Book of Mormon* was supposedly written,)
> 3. The plates were of 24-karat gold.
> 4. The ancient language used to inscribe the plates is as sophisticated as modern English. In other words, you can communicate the same information in the same amount of space, which is highly unlikely. Ancient, and therefore relatively unsophisticated, languages invariably consume more space than Modern English—a language with the largest vocabulary of any known. For example, while we can simply say "reservoir," ancient languages would need to say something like "very large, man-made holding place for drinking water." Let's ignore this point and assume this "ancient language" is as sophisticated as modern English.
> 5. The plate was at least 1/4 inch thick, (24-karat gold being quite soft, even at this thickness, would bend hopelessly.)
>
> So, if we imagine a plate of approximately 5" by 7," the size of a page from my friend's copy of The Book of Mormon, the plate would contain 8.75 cubic inches of gold (5x7x1/4.) One cubic inch contains 16.19 cubic centimeters (2.53 cubed). Therefore,

our plate would contain 141.66 cubic centimeters of gold.

The specific gravity of water is 1. Meaning, one cubic centimeter of water, weighs one gram. The specific gravity of 24-karat gold is 19.3. Thus, one cubic centimeter of 24-karat gold weighs 19.3 grams (an ounce is approximately 27 grams and there are 16 ounces in a pound.) Thus, our plates would weigh 141.66 x 19.3=2734.04 grams or 6.33 pounds. There are approximately 530 pages in my friend's copy of *The Book of Mormon*. However, at the bottom of each page are scriptural references added after the original "translation." Let's discount for this, very generously I might add, down to 450 pages of 'translated' material, Cut that in half, remember we're assuming inscriptions on both sides, and we have 225 plates. The total weight would be 1,424 pounds (225x6.33.) Historical accounts of the number and size of the actual plates are irrelevant, this is simply the calculation of the minimum surface area needed to contain The Book of Mormon, and the weight thereof, if such surface is 24-karat gold at minimum thickness....

While being outrageously conservative on every variable, we calculate a whopping 1,400 pounds that Joseph Smith claims he ran with for three miles. Let's add back some of my generous conservatism and see where we end up. The plates were inscribed on only one side so they could be stacked with less chance of eroding the inscriptions—doubling the weight. The plates were a more realistic 1/2 inch thick—again, doubling the weight. The inscriptions were in a more realistic size, say that of normal handwriting—conservatively tripling the weight (even with a modern ballpoint pen and paper, let alone a chisel and 24-karat gold, I challenge you to write legibly in 10-point font.) I must stick with the original 1,400 pounds, so 'scholars' won't even bother trying to punch holes in it, but you don't: let's see ... 1,400 x 2x2x3 is how much? 16,800 pounds of gold?

The notion *The Book of Mormon* was translated from an ancient language, carved on plates of gold, is absurdity beyond comprehension. I have avoided such language throughout this book, but, Joseph Smith [is] a liar.[17]

Previous estimations of the weight of *The Book of Mormon* have

---

[17]Brete Thomas, *In the Name of Joseph Smith: Amen*, (forthcoming) and recommended reading.

ranged from 700 pounds upward. Yet, when Joseph Smith found the plates, he fled from persons trying to steal them, jumped a fence, beat off an attacker, and ran a total of three miles! When reading Mormon stories it is wise to keep your mind engaged. Think, can this be a truthful story, or not? Truth liberates; falsehood brings bondage.

Why Quote the King James Version?

The Book of Mormon claims to have been written from 600 BC to AD 421 (note dates given at the bottom of each page). Yet about one third is a direct quotation from the King James Version of the Bible, AD 1611. This means that it was almost 1,200 years after *The Book of Mormon* was completed before the King James Version was translated. How did the Mormon prophet get a copy of the KJV 1,200 years before it was translated? Why didn't the prophet clean up some of the poor translations of the King James when he had the chance, if in fact he was a prophet?

Although the King James was a remarkably good translation for its time, it had been revised when Joseph Smith wrote. How did he make the choice between the original and revised version? Was it just more convenient for him to copy out of the one he had in his possession? If so, how could the book be ancient? This remains a valid question for those who would defend it as a valid record of the actual words of ancient prophets.

What is another scenario? Maybe the ancient prophets had a copy of the King James Version. If so, how did they get it 1,200 years before it was written? Why, if they were prophets, did they not clean up the works of the non-inspired King James translators? We find no such outlandish claims for the Bible. Rather, manuscript evidence supports the accuracy of, not only the documents, but of their logical origin.

Either way, the defenders of *The Book of Mormon* are caught on the horns of a dilemma, from which there is no escape, how could they quote from a book not yet written? How could Reformed Egyptian be translated into exact KJV English? But we have not yet considered the major problems.

Why So Many Mistakes in The Book of Mormon?

If *The Book of Mormon* was "translated by the gift and power of God" and was true, why did it have over 4,000 mistakes in the very first version, an average of seven errors on each side of each page? "The Testimony of Three Witnesses" was,

> BE IT KNOWN unto all nations, kindreds, tongues, and people, unto whom this work shall come: That we, through the grace of God

the Father, and our Lord Jesus Christ, have seen the plates which contain this record, which is a record of the people of Nephi, and also of the Lamanites, their brethren, and also of the people of Jared, who came from the tower of which hath been spoken. *And we also know that they have been translated by the gift and power of God, for his voice hath declared it unto, wherefore we know of a surety that the work is true.* And we also testify that we have seen the engravings which are upon the plates; and they have been shown unto us by the power of God, and not of man....[18]

An original (1830) copy of *The Book of Mormon* is available by photocopy from one owned and printed by Wilford C. Wood. The copy is called, *Joseph Smith Begins His Work*, Volume I. In the preface is a signed and notarized affidavit, subscribed and sworn by the Deseret News Publishing Company, the official printing house of the LDS church, that this is an authentic copy of the original *Book of Mormon*, reproduced from uncut sheets. Also there is a similar affidavit from Wilford C. Wood.

As a young man, "The Testimony of Three Witnesses" and "Eight Witnesses" seemed unnecessary if the book was in reality the Word of God, Scripture. An honest person is known by his works and does not need others to certify his honesty. If this is necessary, why are there not similar witnesses in the front of the Bible? Nonetheless, the witnesses proclaim that the angel told them that *The Book of Mormon* was "translated by the gift and power of God ... wherefore we know of a surety that the work is true...."[19]

Joseph Smith said about *The Book of Mormon*, "It is the most correct of any book on earth."[20] Is this the truth? The testimony of the translator and witnesses certainly sound like it should be.

When I purchased Wood's book, I was surprised to find many errors in the original *Book of Mormon* and the changes that have been made throughout the text from beginning to end as evidenced in present-day editions. There are no footnotes to explain the changes from the original.

The mistakes average seven on each side of each page, or over 4,000 mistakes. Although most are not of a serious nature, they show lack of skill in writing English. The question is, who made the mistakes? Did

---

[18]"The Testimony of Three Witnesses," Preface to *The Book of Mormon*. (One of the three witnesses was Oliver Cowdery whom we have already shown to have recanted his part in Mormonism.)

[19]Ibid.

[20]*History of the Church*, vol. 4, p. 461.

Joseph? If so, what about the content? How is it the most correct book on earth? If the gift and power of God translated it, is English too hard for God? Can't God spell? These and many other questions are embarrassing.

There are some outright mistakes in *The Book of Mormon*, words added and words deleted. The book makes mistakes of chronology and gives the wrong names to people. The book confuses Biblical places.

If the LDS church really wants to be a Christian church they should upgrade Joseph Smith's claim about the book being the "most correct book on earth." Maybe a more accurate statement would be, "We are trying to get it fixed up so it is correct." But these are still not the biggest problems.

Why So Many Earlier Books Like *The Book of Mormon*?

If *The Book of Mormon* is a singularly true record of history, why were there at least eight other books published over previous years with a similar theme? One book is a direct parallel: Ethan Smith's *View of the Hebrews*. Ethan Smith's book was written in 1823 and *The Book of Mormon,* in 1830. Even one Mormon scholar has admitted the similarity. Mervin B. Hogan wrote an article called, "A Parallel" with the subtitle "A Matter of Chance versus Coincidence."

> Unless an individual has experienced an unusual and an extensive historical education, he little realized that a speculative relationship of the American Indian to a Hebraic origin is a most time-worn thesis which must have sprung from the imaginations of some of the theologically inclined soon after 1492....
>
> Undoubtedly the listing of representative titles will substantiate the above statement as nothing else will. To that end the following titles, authors, and dates of publication are presented:
>
> 1. *Origen de los Indios del Naevo Mundo, e Indias occidentales. (Origin of the New World and Western Indians)* by Gregorio Garcia; Pedro Patricio Mey, Valencia, 1607. A second edition of the work was published by Francisco Martinez Abad, Madrid, 1729.
> 2. *The History of the American Indians; etc.,* by James Adair; Edward and Charles Dill, London, 1775.
> 3. *An Essay upon the Propagation of the Gospel,* by Charles Crawford; J. Gales, Philadelphia, 1799. A second edition of this treatise was published by James Humphreys, Philadelphia, 1801.
> 4. *A Star in the West; or, A Humble Attempt to Discover the Long-Lost Ten Tribes of Israel, etc.,* by Elias Boudinot; D. Fenton,

S. Hutchinson, and J. Dunham, Trenton, 1816.

5. *View of the Hebrews; etc.*, by Ethan Smith; Smith and Shute, Poultnery, (Vt.), 1823. A second edition of this volume, the most interesting by far in its relationship to the present subject, was issued by the same publishers in 1825. There were two printings of the second edition.

6. *The Wonders of Nature and Providence, Displayed*, by Josiah Priest; E. and E. Hosford, Albany, 1825.

7. *A View of the American Indians, etc.*, by Israel Worsley; R. Hunter, London, 1828.

8. *Antiquities of Mexico: etc.*, by Lord Kingsborough (in seven volumes); Augustine Aglio, London, 1830. Eighteen years later Vols. VIII and IX were published by Henry G. Bohn, London, 1848.[21]

The Tanners show 27 parallels between Ethan Smith's work, *View of the Hebrews*, and *The Book of Mormon*. This gives more than a strong suggestion that whoever wrote *The Book of Mormon* plagiarized Ethan Smith, whose work predated *The Book of Mormon* at least five years. It can be certain that Ethan Smith did not copy *The Book of Mormon*, since it was still in the ground, or Joseph Smith's hands.

What explanation could be given for the major thesis of *The Book of Mormon* having been a long-standing theory that had been around since 1492 or shortly thereafter? Evidence like this just keeps hanging around and is awaiting a credible answer, not just some spin reply. This theory has been thoroughly discredited in our time. But stronger evidence is ahead.

Did Solomon Spaulding Author *The Book of Mormon*?

If it is a revelation from God, why is it so similar to Solomon Spaulding's book, *Manuscript Found*? Spaulding probably used some of the previous books listed above to gain his basic premise that the American Indians were of Jewish descent.[22]

The LDS church took another of Spaulding's books (he wrote several) and proved it was not the same as *The Book of Mormon*. The evidence is substantially strong for the Spaulding authorship, since his wife and eight of his close friends heard Solomon read his book and later testified that it was the same as *The Book of Mormon*.

Spaulding's book was stolen from the print shop that was a hangout

---

[21]Mervin B. Hogan quoted in Jerald and Sandra Tanner, *Mormonism–Shadow or Reality?* (Salt Lake City: Modern Microfilm Co., 1964), pp. 410-411.

[19]Ibid., pp. 411ff.

CHRISTIANITY & MORMONISM

for Sidney Rigdon, a friend and companion of Joseph Smith. Strange that when the print shop lost some of the pages from *The Book of Mormon*, Joseph Smith ran home and came back with the pages known as those of "the unknown scribe," the handwriting was none other than that of Solomon Spaulding.

The "smoking gun" points to Solomon Spaulding having written *The Book of Mormon*. Joseph probably edited and enlarged it. Spaulding had plagiarized other books in print at that time. Although there remains some controversy and uncertainty about the Spaulding authorship, it does add another question to the many others. It is another smoking gun in Joseph Smith's hand, pointing to him as the perpetrator of a hoax. We will find an arsenal of smoking guns.

The Most Damaging Evidence against *The Book of Mormon*

Nephi's Sword Factory and Temple

The most damaging evidence against *The Book of Mormon* is reading it thoughtfully. As a young boy of thirteen, reading *The Book of Mormon*, there was one story that stood out as being totally unbelievable. It is the story of Nephi's Sword Factory and Temple (2 Nephi 5:13-17). Probably this one story has had the strongest impact on people with whom I have reasoned about the LDS church.

A little background is necessary to understand how lacking in facts *The Book of Mormon* really is. Let's review the basic premise of *The Book of Mormon* as this will help us understand the problem to be discussed. The events begin in Jerusalem 600 BC with the Babylonians marching upon the city. According to *The Book of Mormon* a few Jews escaped into the desert, went to the sea, entered a boat prepared by God, and came to America. The exact number is not given in the book, but the number had to be somewhat less than twenty. I called the LDS church offices in Salt Lake City and asked this question and was told the reputed number was fifteen. From carefully reading the story it appears that there could have been as many as eighteen.

These people were 1) Lehi; 2) His wife Sariah; 3) Laman; 4) Lemuel; 5) Sam; 6) Nephi; 7-8) two daughters of Ishael; 9) Ishael; 10-15) two sons of Ishael—their families; 16-17) Jacob and Joseph 590 BC. The church office estimated their number to be about fifteen souls plus two boys born in the wilderness. Then, 18) Zoram somewhere enters the story (2 Nephi 5:6).

When the groups separate, Nephi takes with him 1) Nephi; 2) Zoram; 3) Sam; 4-5) Jacob and Joseph, now 20 years old; and 6-8) the women. This makes their number three men, two boys, and three women (give or

The Mormon Bondage to a False View of Scripture

take a man or woman).

By the time of 2 Nephi 5:13, from twelve to no more than thirty years have passed. (See the footnote at the bottom of the page in *The Book of Mormon*.) The wicked Lamanites had separated from the righteous Nephites. Considering the original group was probably half men and half women and each of the eight or nine women had a child every year without fail, their total number would have been no more than 180 and that number divided in two since they had separated. This number could be reduced downward if part of the original 15-18 were children, which is almost certain.

There still would have only been four or five men in each camp, with a flock of children to feed and house in the wilderness. Mortality would most certainly have taken the lives of some of the children, so the maximum total in each camp would have been no more than fifty or sixty and most of them children. Here again these numbers may be inflated as much as 100% from the actual numbers.

Let's now read the text of 2 Nephi 5:

> And it came to pass that we began to prosper exceedingly, and to multiply in the land. And I, Nephi, did take the sword of Laban, and after the manner of it did make many swords, lest by any means the people who were now called Lamanites should come upon us and destroy us; for I knew their hatred towards me and my children and those who were called my people (2 Nephi 5:13-14).

As a young man this puzzled me. Having been raised back on the edge of the wilderness and I had done my share of exploring for gold and silver. While we barely scraped out an existence, Nephi's story seemed highly unlikely. How could so few people do so many things? Why were there so many precious things in such a limited area? Did they have a sword factory, mines, and build great temples?

This prompted some research what it would have taken to make swords. What I found was that to make "many swords" would take iron ore, coal, limestone, fluxing, smelting, forming, and grinding. When did they have time to discover an iron mine? Where, nearby, did they find the coal, and limestone? Did they in reality have a smelter? Grinder? Fluxing? And why did four men need "many swords"? Maybe they made the children fight also. But how many boys were there? Ten or fifteen maybe. It reminds me of the old saying often repeated to me as a child, "One boy is a whole boy, two boys are half a boy and three boys is no boy at all." This whole story smells of being a fairy tale. Did they have a sword factory, with iron, coal, and limestone mines? Keep your mind engaged a few minutes longer. The story gets much harder to believe.

Let us read on:

> And I did teach my people to build buildings, and to work in all manner of wood, and of iron, and of copper, and of brass and of steel, and of gold, and of silver, and of precious ores, *which were in great abundance*. And I, Nephi, did build a temple; and I did construct it after the manner of the temple of Solomon save it were *not built of so many precious things, for they were not to be found upon the land,* wherefore, it could not be built like unto Solomon's temple. But the manner of the construction was like unto the temple of Solomon; and the workmanship thereof was exceeding fine (2 Nephi 5:15-16).

Not only did they have an iron ore mine, coal mine, limestone pit, but they had a gold mine, silver mine, brass mine(?), and they worked in all manner of wood. Nephi has mentioned all of the precious things used to build Solomon's Temple, saying they were in great abundance. But in the very next verse he says they could not be found in the land. Which is it—there wasn't any, or they were in great abundance?

Did the Nephites have a steel mill? Not only does this passage refer to steel, but also 1 Nephi 16:18 speaks of spring steel. "And it came to pass that as I, Nephi, went forth to slay food, behold, I did break my bow, which was made of fine steel...." In order for a person to have spring steel several things are needed. It takes a craftsman with iron ore, coal, limestone, and a blast furnace. After finishing the blast furnace process, he would need semi-finishing mills, and finishing mills. Is it really likely that four or five men had a spring steel factory? Especially since steel was not invented for many years afterward, over twenty-three hundred years to be exact. When a purported ancient book tells of anachronistic, modern inventions it is proof that its claim of antiquity is bogus.

The *World Book Encyclopedia* says some steel may have been made in very small quantities, as early as slightly before the birth of Christ. It wasn't until 1722 that a French physicist learned how to make steel in large quantities, enough steel to have a sword factory to make many swords. Steel was not made in America until 1832. Modern research gives us good reason to question the statements of spring steel in 1 Nephi 16:18 and a steel mill in 2 Nephi 5. Can you believe this account? Only if your eyes are blinded by a condition of bondage.

The probability that this account is true history is nil. It is a fabricated and untrue fairy tale. Did four or five men and a few boys build a temple like Solomon's, while doing all this sword making, mining, farming, working in all manner of wood, building their houses and hunting? Not a chance! Solomon's Temple took 170,000 men seven years and cost an estimated ten billion dollars to build. Till this day it has not been reduplicated for wealth nor splendor. While taking a Temple tour the guide stressed how wonderful *The Book of Mormon* is. He kept saying there are such fantastic stories that "you just can't believe them." We agreed. We could not believe them.

Could four or five men, some women, and a few boys do these things? Hardly, maintain an iron mine, coal mine, sandstone pit, steel, brass foundries, while building a huge temple?

The King of a Few
Why would fewer than fifty people need a king? The Nephites did. "And it came to pass that they would that I should be their king. But I, Nephi, was desirous that they should have no king; nevertheless, I did for them according to that which was in my power" (2 Nephi 5:18). Why would so few people even need a king? A king over three to four other men? Does this story have the ring of plausibility to it? Or is it a copy of the Israelites wanting a king when they entered the promised land and then being given King Saul?

Dark Skin a Mark of Sin
That the pigmentation of a person's skin has anything to do with sinfulness or godliness is right out of Southern America and people trying to justify slavery. A study of the nations of the world and great people will show that all nationalities and skin colors have their saints and their sinners. But *The Book of Mormon* is caught in the most flagrant racism. Suggesting that dark skin has some link to ungodliness is absurd and ungodly. This idea has no basis in history, human nature, or observable testing. Some of the most godly and creative people in the world have had dark skin. Yet, 2 Nephi 5:21-22 says,

> And he had caused the cursing to come upon them, yea, even a sore cursing, because of their iniquity. For behold, they had hardened their hearts against him, that they had become like unto a flint; wherefore, as they were white, and exceeding fair and delightsome, that they might not be enticing unto my people the Lord God did cause a skin of blackness to come upon them. And thus saith the Lord God: I will cause that they shall be loathsome unto thy people, save they shall repent of their iniquities.

CHRISTIANITY & MORMONISM

For one hundred and fifty years the Mormon church would not permit a black person to hold the priesthood. They understood the clear implications of these verses. The Book of Abraham, another of Joseph Smith's scriptures says, "Now, Pharaoh being of that lineage by which he could not have the right of Priesthood...." (BoA 1:27).

This teaching flies in the face of clear Bible teaching, "There is neither Jew nor Greek, there is neither slave nor free man, there is neither male nor female; for you are all one in Christ Jesus" (Galatians 3:28). Skin color has nothing to do with godliness.

Are little black babies "loathsome"? For a time the church taught that if black people became good Mormons in time their skin would turn white. Brigham Young said that if any person, with even an ounce of black blood, was given the priesthood, the priesthood would be lost to the church.

As a young man, this chapter in 2 Nephi was a stark warning that the LDS church was built upon the sand. A few men, living in the wilderness, doing all of these things. Who could believe that four or five men and women needed a king? Who could believe a message of skin color having anything to do with godliness? Yes, there are stories in *The Book of Mormon*, "that you just can't believe."

Cowboy Snakes

While reading *The Book of Mormon* one should ask the question, is this story plausible? We are not suggesting that God does not work miracles. This is not to discount actual miracles, as through the centuries God has brought about many notable miracles. Each miracle is just that, a miracle, not a ridiculous narrative.

Ask yourself the question while reading the following account, did this really happen, or is it the result of a fertile imagination and poor logic? The people had become sinful and "... that exceeding great wickedness upon the face of the land...." (Ether 9:26).

> But the people believed not the words of the prophets, but they cast them out; and some of them they cast into pits and left them to perish. And it came to pass that they did all these things according to the commandment of the king, Heth. And it came to pass that there began to be a great dearth upon the land, and the inhabitants began to be destroyed exceeding fast because of the dearth for there was not rain upon the face of the earth. And there came forth poisonous serpents also upon the face of the land, and did poison many people. And it came to pass that their flocks began to flee before the poisonous serpents, towards the

land southward, which was called by the Nephites Zarahemla. And it came to pass that there were many of them which did perish by the way; nevertheless, there were some which fled into the land southward. And it came to pass that the Lord did cause the serpents that they should pursue them no more, but that they should hedge up the way that the people could not pass, that whoso should attempt to pass might fall by the poisonous serpents. And it came to pass that the people did follow the course of the beasts, and did devour the carcasses of them which fell by the way, until they had devoured them all.... (Ether 9:29-34).

This has been characterized as the story of "Cowboy Snakes." Use your imagination as to what is actually described. The people were very wicked. God sends snakes, to do what? To round up all of the people's cattle and drive them to the land southward, Zarahemla. Exactly where this was is not clear, some have supposed it may have been as far as Mexico or even farther south.

Picture the little snakes slithering along on their bellies, singing in snake language, "Get along little doggies." Over hill and dale, through swamp and stream, up hill and down, they pursue and bite the cattle. The dead cattle are left strewn along the way, bloating in the sun and rain. Does it seem plausible that the snakes set up guards to keep the cattle and people apart?

The people follow the snakes, and cattle, eating all the poisoned carcasses until they are all cleaned up. Really now, eating poisoned cattle? If there had been such a drought, what had the cattle been eating? Why healthy cattle and starving people? Does this story have the ring of plausibility to it? Doesn't it seem more reasonable to believe this is a fairy tale?

Other Incredible Stories

Reading *The Book of Mormon* with the mind engaged can be good entertainment. The story of the man who had the top of his head cut off and fought on for days. Or the story of the man who had his head cut off. The text says, "... he breathed his last and died." After his head was cut off?

Actually there are parts of *The Book of Mormon* that reach a pretty high literary standard and very high level of credibility. When those places are found, check it out; sure enough the writer is again quoting the Bible. When the Bible is quoted, how is it that the Mormon prophet translates from Reformed Egyptian (600 BC) the same chapter and verse divisions that the King James used 1,200 years later? Or, did the writer of *The Book of Mormon* just copy it out of the King James Version? Use your own good judgment.

Why mention things not yet invented? *The Book of Mormon* mentions electricity in 1 Nephi 17:53. The compass is used according to 1 Nephi 18:12 in 590 BC. Why were modern inventions mentioned, not predicted, if this is an ancient book? In truth, it is not an ancient book at all!

MORMON THEOLOGY AND *THE BOOK OF MORMON*

An early surprise for me, as a reader of *The Book of Mormon*, was to discover that its basic theology is not much different from that of the Bible! If in fact Solomon Spaulding wrote it, you would expect that a Congregational preacher would have espoused traditional doctrinal beliefs.

Today's LDS church does not really live by *The Book of Mormon*; if they did, they would be much closer to Christianity. Many of the book's teachings are ignored or viewed as unimportant. This is hard to understand since the Mormon people claim such allegiance to it as a direct revelation from God, equal to, or even superior to the Bible. Here are several illustrations of this point.

Baptism for the Dead

One of the cardinal doctrines of the LDS church is "baptism for the dead." You will not study with them very long before the subject will come up. Much of their temple work centers on getting the unbaptized dead, baptized. Their work with genealogy is to learn who has not been baptized. They see the graveyard as a great place of evangelization. Yet it is strange that *The Book of Mormon* teaches that once a person has died without being saved, he is sealed to Satan forever. Notice what Alma the prophet has to say on the subject.

> For behold, this life is the time for men to prepare to meet God; yea, behold the day of this life is the day for men to perform their labors. And now, as I said unto you before, as ye have had so many witnesses, therefore, I beseech of you that ye do not procrastinate the day of your repentance until the end; for after this day of life, which is given us to prepare for eternity, behold, if we do not improve our time while in this life, which is given us to prepare for eternity, behold, if we do not improve our time while in this life, then cometh the night of darkness wherein there can be no labor performed. Ye cannot say, when ye are brought to that awful crisis, that I will repent, that I will return to my God. Nay, ye cannot say this; for that same spirit which doth possess your bodies at the time that ye go out of this life, that same spirit

will have power to possess your body in that eternal world. For behold, if you have procrastinated the day of your repentance even until death, behold, ye have become subjected to the spirit of the devil, and he doth seal you his; therefore, the Spirit of the Lord hath withdrawn from you, and hath no place in you, and the devil hath all power over you; and this is the final state of the wicked (Alma 34:32-35).

Such plain language is hard to misunderstand. Mormon leaders excuse this passage by saying that God makes mistakes and has to constantly upgrade His doctrine to remove such errors! How can we know what is truth and what is not, if God is so untrustworthy?

God Has a Body of Parts and Passions

Another doctrine of the LDS church is that God is a "God of body, parts, and passion." Mormon theology pictures God as an exalted man who has gone ahead of us in what is called "eternal progression." Their teaching goes so far as to suggest that Jesus was physically begotten by God, through sexual relations with Mary. At the present, observe that *The Book of Mormon* teaches the same doctrine about God that the Bible does. That is, that God is Spirit.

> And the king said: Is God that Great Spirit that brought our fathers out of the land of Jerusalem? And Aaron said unto him: Yea, he is that Great Spirit, and he created all things both in heaven and in earth. Believest thou this? And he said: Yes, I believe that the Great Spirit created all things, and I desire that ye should tell me concerning all these things, and I will believe thy words (Alma 22:9-11).

When we consider the Mormon doctrine of eternal progression, that "God is growing and becoming wiser and stronger," *The Book of Mormon* does not agree with Mormon doctrine:

> For do we not read that God is the same yesterday, today, and forever, and in him there is no variableness either shadow of changing? And now if ye have imagined up unto yourselves a god who doth vary, and in whom there is shadow of changing, then have ye imagined up unto yourselves a god who is not a God of miracles. But behold, I will show unto you a God of miracles, even the God of Abraham, and the God of Isaac, and the

God of Jacob; and it is the same God who created the heavens and the earth and all things that in them are (Mormon 9:9-11).

Moroni seems to agree. "For I know that God is not a partial God, neither a changeable being; but he is unchangeable from all eternity to all eternity" (Moroni 8:18).

Man Can Become God

Another doctrine that is currently taught by the LDS church, which is not taught in *The Book of Mormon*, is that "man can be exalted to being a God." *The Book of Mormon* repeatedly states that there is only one true God.

> Now Zeezrom saith again unto him: Is the Son of God the very Eternal Father? And Amulek said unto him: Yes, he is the very Eternal Father of heaven and of earth, and all things which in them are; he is the beginning and the end, the first and the last (Alma 11:38-39).

Neither the Mormon church nor the Bible affirms that Jesus and the Father are the same Being. They are three with the Holy Spirit, yet one. Beyond this fact, we find here a statement that God the Father is the beginning and end of all things. This does not sound like it teaches that there are other Gods, or that man may become God.

These doctrinal issues about God, Christ, eternal progression, and baptism for the dead will be considered more fully in Chapters 6 and 7.

Contradictions Between *The Book of Mormon* and *The Doctrine and Covenants*

One simple rule, dictated by common sense, is that truth does not contradict itself. If God cannot lie, and He cannot, then you would expect His revelations to be consistent throughout. Something cannot be bad and good at the same time. Yet, examination shows that *The Book of Mormon* and *The Doctrine and Covenants* definitely contradict each other. Concerning the matter of polygamy, *The Book of Mormon* records,

> And now it came to pass that the people of Nephi, under the reign of the second king, began to grow hard in their hearts, and indulge themselves somewhat in wicked practices, such as like unto David of old desiring many wives and concubines, and also Solomon, his son (Jacob 1:15).

> Behold, David and Solomon truly had many wives and concubines, which thing was abominable before me, saith the Lord.... Wherefore, I the Lord God will not suffer that this people shall do like unto them of old. Wherefore, my brethren, hear me, and hearken to the word of the Lord: For there shall not any man among you have save it be one wife, and concubines he shall have none (Jacob 2:24, 26-27).

Yet when we turn to *The Doctrine and Covenants* we find an entirely different view of the matter, for it says,

> David also received many wives and concubines, and also Solomon and Moses my servants, as also many others of my servants, form the beginning of creation until this time; and in nothing did they sin save in those things which they received not of me. David's wives and concubines were given unto him of me, by the hand of Nathan, my servant, and others of the prophets who had the keys of this power, and in none of these things did he sin against me.... (DC 132:38-39).

How can a man be both condemned and justified for the same act? This is a sure, open contradiction. Apparently one or both records are not of God.

SUMMARY

Therefore, since *The Book of Mormon* has had to be changed so many times to correct it, yet claims to be translated by a prophet with God's help, it is difficult to accept it as Scripture. Because the book contains so many textual problems, unbelievable stories, modern words, quotations from modern books, poor logic, theology contrary to the Bible and current church teachings, as well as many other problems, we must reject it as Scripture.

What, then, is *The Book of Mormon*? It is an epic novel, poorly written, that has some high quality sections, that is, those that quote directly from the King James Version of the Bible. When a person accepts it and its representative church, he or she will end up in all sorts of physical and spiritual bondage.

It is time for the LDS church to give up the farce and admit that Joseph Smith's gold plates were a hoax, that semiliterate and civilized people were hoodwinked into believing it. They need to admit to the world that, although they have sold and given away millions of copies of it; it never has been on a par with the Bible, nor worthy of being classed as Scripture.

CHRISTIANITY & MORMONISM

Instead of the LDS vilifying those who love them enough to show them the truth, it is time to get to work and show a true prophetic voice. It is time for them to do a thorough, theological house cleaning.

FROM BONDAGE TO FREEDOM

The Bars of Bondage

1. Explain what author's style means in comparing the Bible with *The Book of Mormon*.
2. Discuss your own theory for the origin of *The Book of Mormon*. Include an explanation for the supposed gold plates.
3. Which of the most damaging evidences against *The Book of Mormon* do you find the most interesting? Why?
4. How does *The Book of Mormon* teach the same theology as mainstream Christianity? Cite some examples.
5. How does *The Book of Mormon* contradict *The Doctrine and Covenants*?

The Keys to Freedom

1. Prepare a written response to Mormon missionaries so that you will be ready to do more than slam your front door in their faces. Limit it to two pages. If possible include key Bible quotations from the King James Version, as that would be "common ground" with Mormons.
2. After you have studied the most basic evidences for the Christian faith and points against Mormonism, invite a Mormon friend to study the Bible with you or your group.
3. Visit an LDS congregation with a well-grounded Christian friend or two. Be polite and courteous but explain that you are a disciple of Jesus and you want to learn how to share Christ's truth in love.

CHAPTER THREE
The Freedom in a Correct View of Scripture

The Bible Says
"Forever, O LORD, Your word is settled in heaven"(Psalms 119:89).

Joseph Smith Said
"I believe the Bible as it read when it came from the pen of the original writers. Ignorant translators, careless transcribers, or designing and corrupt priests have committed many errors."[23]
Who is to be believed, David or Joseph?

Other LDS Writers Say
LDS prophets have so often criticized the Bible. Other Mormon leaders have made similar accusations against the Bible's accuracy. A son of Joseph Fielding Smith, recent prophet of the Latter-day Saints church, made the following statement about the Bible.

> Scholars do not deny that the original text of the Bible has been corrupted. Truths have been removed to preserve traditions. Faulty translations and omissions of phrases and clauses have resulted in confusion.[24]

---

[23]B.H. Roberts, ed., *History of the Church of Jesus Christ of Latter-day Saints*, vols. 1-6: Period I. History of Joseph Smith, The Prophet, by Joseph Smith; vol. 7: Period II. From the Manuscript History of Brigham Young and Other Original Documents; 7 vols,. m 2nd ed. (Salt Lake City, Utah: Deseret News Press, 1963) 6:57.

[24]Religious Truths Defined, p. 337, quoted in Tanner, *Mormonism–Shadow or Reality?* (1964), p. 64.

The early "Apostate Fathers" did not think it was wrong to tamper with the inspired scripture. If any scripture seemed to endanger their viewpoint, it was altered, transplanted, or completely removed from the biblical text. All this was done that they might keep their traditions. Such mutilation was considered justifiable to preserve the "purity" of their doctrines.[25]

The Book of Mormon *Says*
Even The Book of Mormon claims that the Bible has been tampered with and changed. "... for behold, they have taken away from the gospel of the Lamb many parts which are plain and most precious; and also many covenants of the Lord have they taken away. And all this have they done that they might pervert the right ways of the Lord, that they might blind the eyes and harden the hearts of the children of men" (1 Nephi 13:26b-27).

What Do We Say?
Are these statements true? Can we verify them? Consider the evidence. The LDS leaders should want to know the truth as much as anyone, because the teacher will be held to a higher standard of judgment (James 3:1). We will examine the facts so that we can know beyond any shadow of doubt the answer to this question. The evidence is plentiful to show the accuracy of both Old and New Testament Scripture.

Can you imagine what kind of bondage of error a person is left with, if when he picks up the Bible to read, he cannot depend upon it as the true Word of God? Is John 3:16 really the truth, or has it been revised? Did Jesus really rise from the dead, or did some "designing priest" add it?

PROOF OF OLD TESTAMENT ACCURACY

Let's begin with the Old Testament. The best proof that can be brought forth is of fairly recent origin, the Dead Sea Scrolls. Most of the Dead Sea Scrolls were found in several caves at a place called Qumran, which is at the northwestern end of the Dead Sea. Many of these documents now rest in the museum in Jerusalem called the Dome of the Scroll of the Book. This building is located near the Knesset building. Its roof is shaped like a scroll jar lid. Inside this small, climate-controlled building are displayed, for viewing, some of the Dead Sea manuscripts. Today, most of the displayed books are copies and the originals are kept in especially

---

[25]Ibid., *Religious Truths Defined*, p. 175/Tanner p. 64.

The Freedom in a Correct View of Scripture

secure storage. Every Old Testament book is found among the Dead Sea Scrolls with the exception of the book of Esther.

I have personally visited with the man who purchased the first scrolls from the Beduins. He confirmed the basic facts commonly related as to the finding and nature of the many scrolls. The jars in which the scrolls were sealed are from 12 to 18 inches tall, made of fired clay. The scrolls were wrapped in linen and sealed in the jars.

They were hastily hidden, as the Essenes at Qumran valued them as priceless copies of the Word of God. Fearing that the Romans were about to invade and destroy their community they hid them, thus preserving them for posterity. The arid dryness of the area preserved them perfectly. It was as if God was providing an additional testimony to the accuracy of His Word in the latter times. They were hidden about AD 60-70. Of the over 600 Dead Sea Scrolls, 330 were of Old Testament books.[26] Conservative scholars have dated these manuscripts from 325 BC to about 100 BC. Some of the Biblical manuscripts have been dated as early as 225 BC. These manuscripts were found between 1946 and 1960.

The question is, Have these documents proven our Old Testament Scriptures to be accurate or changed? The answer is that they have proven that the Old Testament has *not* been changed.

The oldest manuscript that we had before this time, of any Hebrew Old Testament book, has been dated AD 916. It was the Leningrad Codex and is in the Leningrad Royal Library in Russia. One other partial manuscript of the first five books of the Bible may date around AD 840. These are Hebrew manuscripts. Therefore, when the Dead Sea Scrolls were found they were supremely important in establishing the accuracy of our Old Testament text in that they were one thousand years earlier. They can settle the discussion as to whether "designing and corrupt priests, during the Dark Ages removed many plain and precious truths."

When the American scholar Dr. John C. Trever first found and read the Isaiah Scroll and compared it with the much later Hebrew manuscripts, he was disappointed that they were the same. He said they shed no new light. They only established that the Hebrew text had come down over one thousand years with remarkable accuracy. For all practical reasons the later ones were as accurate as the earlier, establishing the fidelity of our Hebrew text. Dr. Trever says, "Thus, as has been repeatedly stated, the ancient Isaiah Scroll is a witness to the antiquity and faithful preservation of the traditional Masoretic text from at least as early as the

---

[26] The first manuscripts were found when a shepherd boy, hunting his sheep, threw a rock into a cave and heard a jar break. His curiosity led to the discovery of the first scrolls.

first century BC."[27] Dr. Trever later explains in his book how the Daniel Scroll confirmed the accuracy of the manuscripts we already had.

> With the sixth layer removed, the remainder of the largest fragment was revealed. Now parts of Daniel 3:22-31 (3:22–4:1 in English) had appeared on two fragments. Having impressed me at first as revealing a script somewhat similar to the Manual of Discipline (IQS), I tentatively thought of the fragments as belonging to the middle of the first century BC. Although the text contributed nothing new, its significance among Biblical manuscript was immediately apparent.[28]

Having personally seen some of these Hebrew documents, they are remarkably clear and readable. Many past statements, such as the one we quoted from Joseph Smith at the beginning of the chapter, are outdated and inaccurate in the light of recent manuscript discoveries. A knowledgeable Bible scholar today would not make the untrue statement: "Many plain and precious truths have been removed from the Old Testament Scriptures."

In addition to the Dead Sea Scrolls we could point to the Septuagint (Greek) translation of the Old Testament. This provides additional evidence of what the Old Testament Scriptures were in the several centuries before Christ.

Additionally, the Samaritan Pentateuch gives us an ancient test of the first five books of the Old Testament from a separate history, the text of the ten northern tribes after the divided kingdom. We could add the evidence of ancient commentaries, the Halakah and the Haggadah. To suggest that there is any serious question to the accuracy of our Old Testament Scriptures is unenlightened.

The LDS church needs to correct these false and misleading statements made by their prophets and leaders. The bondage of falsehood rests on the LDS people. It is time the church cleans up the glaring examples of untruths spoken by their prophets and scriptures.

Rules for Copying Scripture

What could account for the remarkable preservation of the Scriptures? The scribes, so often mentioned in the New Testament, were

---

[27]John C. Trever, *The Untold Story of Qumran* (Westwood, NJ: Fleming H. Revell Company, 1952), p. 117.
[28]Ibid., p. 129.

a guild of men whose primary duty was the copying and preservation of Scripture. When we learn the rules that guided them in their work it is not surprising that the Scriptures have been preserved. The Talmud gave the following rules to govern the preparation of a manuscript to be used in the synagogue.

> 1. The parchment must be made from the skin of clean animals; must be prepared by a Jew only, and the skins must be fastened together by strings taken from clean animals. 2. Each column must have no less than 48 nor more than 60 lines. The entire copy must be first lined, and if three words were written in it without the line, the copy was worthless. 3. The ink must be of no other color than black, and it must be prepared according to a special recipe. 4. No word nor letter could be written from memory; the scribe must have an authentic copy before him, and he must read and pronounce aloud each word before writing it. 5. He must reverently wipe his pen each time before writing the word for 'God,' and he must wash his whole body before writing the word 'Jehovah,' lest the holy name be contaminated. 6. Strict rules were given concerning the forms of the letters, spaces between letters, words, and sections, the use of the pen, the color of the parchment, etc. 7. The revision of a roll must be made within 30 days after the work was finished; otherwise it was worthless. One mistake on a sheet condemned the sheet; if three mistakes were found on any page, the entire manuscript was condemned. 8. Every word and every letter was counted, and if a letter was omitted, an extra letter inserted, or if one letter touched another, the manuscript was condemned and destroyed at once. And so on. Some of these rules may appear extreme and absurd, yet they show how sacred the Holy Word of the *Old Testament* was to its custodians, the Jews *(Romans 3:2)* and they give us strong encouragement to believe that we have the real *Old Testament*, the same one which our Lord had and which was originally given by the inspiration by God.[29]

With such rules it is reasonable to expect that there would be few places where there were mistakes or differences of real significance. The Dead Sea Scrolls have given us undeniable proof of the accuracy of our Old Testament. The evidence is so remarkable that it appears that God has

---

[29]H.S. Miller, *General Biblical Introduction* (New York: Houghton, The Word-Bearer Press, 1959), pp. 184-185.

taken special pains to show us, in the last days, that His Word, the Bible, is accurate. Christians ought to be grateful for this added testimony to the fidelity of the Old Testament in our time. There are far too numerous other proofs for them to be mentioned in a book of this nature.

PROOF OF NEW TESTAMENT ACCURACY

An examination of the New Testament discloses even more remarkable evidence to support its accuracy than with the Old Testament. In fact, there are over 5,300 Greek manuscripts of New Testament books. (This may be a very conservative estimate of the total number.) It was my delight to visit St. Catherine's Monastery, at the traditional site of Mount Sinai, in June of 2000. In that library the librarian showed us over 3,200 ancient Greek manuscripts of the New Testament. The librarian said it was the second largest collection of ancient Biblical manuscripts second only to the Vatican Library in Rome.

The oldest New Testament manuscript, of a significant portion of Scripture, is a partial and fragmentary copy, called the Chester Beatty Papyri.

> The Chester Beatty Papyri is the greatest discovery of the new Biblical manuscripts, at least since the Freer collection, and possibly since the Codex Sinaiticus, was made... All the manuscripts are on papyrus, in codex form, and of an early date, from the 2nd to the 5th century; in fact, the really Biblical manuscripts are, with one exception, dated in the 2nd and 3rd century.[30]

It is possible that portions of this manuscript may date back into the year AD 150 or even earlier, some suppose as early as AD 125. If their date is as late as AD 250, it is still wonderful proof of what the New Testament was like at that time. The manuscript fragments contain nine epistles, almost complete, and in the following order: Romans, Hebrews, First and Second Corinthians, Ephesians, Galatians, Philippians, Colossians, and First Thessalonians.

These manuscripts give us proof that, at a very early date, these documents were bound together in a common book. They also prove that our later editions of the Bible were extremely accurate.

A second proof that the New Testament Scriptures have not been changed and revised is the Bodmer II Text of the Gospel of John. This manuscript is kept in the Vatican Library in Rome. It is dated, by able scholars,

---

[30] Ibid., p. 200.

The Freedom in a Correct View of Scripture

in the year AD 200. Since the Gospel of John was written about AD 95, this document takes us back within 105 years of the time that John wrote it.

I have personally seen this document, purchased a photocopy and translated it into English. It proves that the Gospel of John has not been tampered with, changed, or revised.

There are additional proofs of the accuracy of our New Testament Scriptures. The numbers vary, but there are well over 5,300 Greek manuscripts. As already mentioned St. Catherine's Monastery, near the traditional site of Mount Sinai, has 3,200 ancient Greek manuscripts of the New Testament, either partial or complete.

The four, often considered most valuable, New Testament Greek manuscripts are the Sinaitic (Codex Sinaiticus) which was written in AD 340; the Vatican (Codex Vaticanus) which is dated AD 325; the Alexandrian (Codex Alexandrinus) dated about AD 450; and the Codex Ephraemi dated about AD 450.

These four Greek documents are clear and readable, and in substantial agreement as to the New Testament text. They also contain the Old Testament in Greek. I have personally seen all four of these ancient manuscripts. The Vaticanus is in the Vatican library in Rome and the other three in the British Museum in London.

It is true that in later manuscript copies we have textual problems. It has been estimated that there may be as many as 350,000 or more textual problems or variations. At first glance this seems astoundingly high, but after a moment's thought it is amazing that there aren't more. Since there are over 5,300 Greek manuscripts, if there were only one difference between each of them there would be 5,300 textual problems. Thus, there are really less than one hundred significant textual problem passages. In fact, the really significant textual problems narrow down to less than twenty. Substantial agreement is found between the older copies, while variations appear in the later. Careful examination shows that the twenty or less textual problems do not involve any important doctrinal issues. While one passage might be questioned, another non-questioned passage says a similar thing.

Summarizing Charles Leach's comments: Add to the 5,300 Greek manuscripts 10,000 Latin Vulgate and at least 9,300 other early versions and we have more than 24,000 manuscript copies of portions of the New Testament. The Iliad by Homer is second to the New Testament in number of copies with 643 manuscripts that still survive. The first complete preserved text of Homer dates in the 13th Century.[31]

---

[31] Charles Leach, *Our Bible, How We Got It*, p. 145, quoted in Josh McDowell, *Evidence that Demands a Verdict* (San Bernardino, CA: Here's Life Publishers, Inc., 1979), p. 39.

> The interval then between the dates of original composition and the earliest extant evidence becomes so small as to be in fact negligible, and the last foundation for any doubt that the scriptures have come down to us substantially as they were written has now been removed. Both the authenticity and the general integrity of the books of the New Testament may be regarded as finally established.[32]

Scholar after scholar echoes Kenyon's words. The Bible, Old and New Testament, has come down to us with remarkable accuracy so as to leave no doctrine in question. Those who say otherwise have not done their homework. Many of the textual problems center on marginal notes, fragmentary ends of books, unclear copy work, writing outside the line. Modern scholarship has established our New Testament Scriptures beyond question.

Joseph Smith did not have sufficient education to have made such a charge as he did about the Bible. The fact that he did accuse the Bible of gross inaccuracies, while scholarship has shown his accusation to be false, places him in a very uncertain place as a supposed prophet of God.

For the LDS church to question the accuracy of Scripture and suggest that many "plain and precious truths have been removed" is just plain nonsense and leaves those who follow the church's line of reasoning in bondage to falsehood.

Some might suggest that the problem lies not with the original text, but with the translations of the original text. As one who has spent months in translation of the Hebrew and Greek texts and comparing them with modern translations, the modern translations are, for the most part, remarkably good. Although some English translations are better than others, few doctrinal problems are found in these translations. (Some insist on holding to the King James Version, not realizing its present form has been revised a number of times.) An honest seeker-after-truth can rely on most of the modern translations.

The LDS church is truly stuck with their traditional teaching about the inaccuracy of the Bible and Bible translations. It must be very embarrassing to them to explain why Joseph Smith made over 4,000 changes to the Bible in what he called his "Inspired Version."[33] His changes are ill informed and prove that he was not a prophet (Revelation 22:18-19).

---

[32]Sir Frederic G. Kenyon, *The Bible and Archaeology*, p. 288, quoted in Josh McDowell, *Evidence*, p. 40; see also pp. 39-78 for more textual information.

[33]Joseph Smith, *The Holy Scripture, Inspired Version* (Independence, MO: Herald Publishing House, 1970.

THE INSPIRATION OF THE BIBLE

Inspiration of the Old Testament

Most Bible writers claim inspiration for themselves. There is a certainty about their messages that gives them a ring of authenticity. For example, God said to Moses, "Then the Lord said to Moses, 'Write this in a book as a memorial and recite it to Joshua, that I will utterly blot out the memory of Amalek from under heaven.'" (Exodus 17:14). When the Ten Commandments were given it was said: "Now the LORD said to Moses, 'Come up to Me on the mountain and remain there, and I will give you the stone tablets with the law and the commandment which I have written for their instruction.'" (Exodus 24:12). There is a certainty about the writings of Moses; we can have little doubt that he spoke from God. We could give other instances in his writings. For example, examine Exodus 34:27, Numbers 17:2-3, and Deuteronomy 31:9.

This type of statement is repeatedly made throughout the entire Old Testament Scriptures. Whether it be Joshua, David, Solomon, Isaiah, Jeremiah, or any of the rest of the prophets, each emphatically claims inspiration for himself. There are never words of doubt about what they write. They write with a certainty seldom found in secular literature.

These men evidently wrote under a promise similar to that made to Moses. When Moses sought to be excused from the work he was to do, God said to him that He would guide and direct him.

> Then Moses said to the Lord, "Please, Lord, I have never been eloquent, neither recently nor in time past, nor since You have spoken to Your servant; for I am slow of speech and slow of tongue." The Lord said to him, "Who has made man's mouth? Or who makes him mute or deaf, or seeing or blind? Is it not I, the Lord? Now then go, and I, even I, will be with your mouth, and teach you what you are to say" (Exodus 4:10-12).

> Of David it records in 2 Samuel,

> Now these are the last words of David.
> David the son of Jesse declares,
> The man who was raised on high declares,
> The anointed of the God of Jacob,
> And the sweet psalmist of Israel,
> "The Spirit of the LORD spoke by me,
> And His word was on my tongue" (2 Samuel 23:1-2).

Each of the writers was positive about his message and his source of material. This is not so in *The Book of Mormon*. There is much uncertainty as we will see later in this chapter.

Inspiration of the New Testament

The New Testament Scriptures further undergird this teaching of the inspiration of God. Not only the apostles but also Jesus Himself affirm the inspiration of the Old Testament.

To quote Jesus: "Heaven and earth will pass away, but My words will not pass away" (Mark 13:31). And, "Now He said to them, 'These are My words which I spoke to you while I was still with you, that all things which are written about Me in the Law of Moses and the Prophets and the Psalms must be fulfilled.'" (Luke 24:44). This is a firm statement of the inspiration of the Old Testament and its writers, as they could have only known about Jesus through the avenue of inspiration. On another occasion Jesus said, "the Scripture cannot be broken" (John 10:35). To insist that Scripture can indeed be broken, or fallible, is to reject the divinity of Jesus.

The apostles are equally clear as to the infallibility of the Scriptures, both Old and New Testaments. We might begin with a passage from the book of Hebrews. This passage is quoted from the New American Standard Bible because the terminology of the King James is a bit obscure. "God, after He spoke long ago to the fathers in the prophets in many portions and in many ways, in these last days has spoken to us in His Son, whom He appointed heir of all things, through whom also He made the world" (Hebrews 1:1-2). This is an endorsement of the Old and New Testaments at once. God spoke through the prophets. God spoke through His Son. It would be hard to miss the meaning of this clear passage which asserts the inspiration of the Old and New Testaments.

Paul, writing to Timothy, makes it abundantly clear about the matter of the inspiration of the Scriptures. "All Scripture is inspired by God and profitable for teaching, for reproof, for correction, for training in righteousness; so that the man of God may be adequate, equipped for every good work" (2 Timothy 3:16-17).

Peter leaves no doubt about the matter of the inspiration of the Scriptures when he says,

> As to this salvation, the prophets who prophesied of the grace that would come to you made careful searches and inquiries, seeking to know what person or time the Spirit of Christ within them was indicating as He predicted the sufferings of Christ and the glories to follow. It was revealed to them that they were not

serving themselves, but you, in these things which now have been announced to you through those who preached the gospel to you by the Holy Spirit sent from heaven—things into which angels long to look (1 Peter 1:10-12).

Are we to suppose that God, who made the universe, created mankind, made man able to communicate with one another, is incapable of communicating with mankind in an accurate, intelligent way? So the Old and New Testament writers repeatedly, clearly claim that God had used them to communicate with mankind.

A God of such power as to make the universe, keep it running, and order this creation in such an intelligent manner, is capable of giving a revelation that is consistent, does not need changes, and is free of errors. Certainly for man to write such a book would be impossible. But we would expect just such a book from God. Anything less would be a disappointment.

God used men, giving them the power to receive and communicate divine truth. God used their own personalities, but guarded them from error, enabling them to speak His words in their own style.

Peter sums up the matter well when he says,

So we have the prophetic word made more sure, to which you do well to pay attention as to a lamp shining in a dark place, until the day dawns and the morning star arises in your hearts. But know this first of all, that no prophecy of Scripture is a matter of one's own interpretation, for no prophecy was ever made by an act of human will, but men moved by the Holy Spirit spoke from God (2 Peter 1:19-21).

We can safely say that the Bible writers spoke by the power of God. This explains why the Bible is accurate, when it speaks about medicine, when it speaks about science, when it speaks about history, human nature, spiritual truth, or any other subject. Otherwise it would be filled with the false information of the times in which it was written. But it is not.

This explains why Bible writers could predict such events as the coming of Christ with such remarkable accuracy. This explains how David was able to write the twenty-second Psalm that tells about Jesus' crucifixion. This tells us why Daniel knew about the four great world empires that he wrote about in the second chapter. This explains how Daniel knew that Jesus would come at the time he predicted he would in Daniel 9:24-27. We understand how Isaiah could write the fifty-third chapter of Isaiah, which tells so much about Jesus. When we begin to comprehend inspiration, we know how John could write Revelation, that great book of history, written in advance of history. All of this is because "... men moved by the Holy Spirit spoke from God" (2 Peter 1:21).

Sometimes these men didn't even understand what they had written. Many examples of this could be given such as Peter's sermon in Acts, where he says this salvation was to "all who are far off" (Acts 2:39). Then later, in the tenth chapter of Acts, God had to work a miracle or two to get Peter to accept what he had already preached.

The Old Testament prophets desired to know more about what they spoke but were not allowed to do so (2 Peter 1:10-12). They were curious, but God only gave them a partial view of what was to come.

So not only did Jesus claim inspiration for the Bible writers and they themselves claim that they were inspired, but also the works that they produced prove beyond any doubt that they were in truth inspired of God.

The Challenge of Inspiration to the LDS

The challenge for the current LDS prophet and leaders is to be in fact what they claim, Christian, and renounce this long-standing false doctrine: "that the Bible has had many plain and precious truths removed so as to leave hardly any passage the same as written." They should once and for all reject Joseph Smith's "Inspired Version" of the Bible with its unenlightened changes. They should rewrite the eight "Articles of Faith" that question the Bible translations. It would show good faith, a desire to be truthful, and a willingness to move from a long-standing position that has long since proved to be false. It would give credibility to their claim of being a truly Christian religion.

If they truly want their people to be led out of false teaching to the truth, they must renounce their criticism of the Bible by their prophets and by *The Book of Mormon*. There is great freedom when a person accepts the truth and salvation by faith in Jesus Christ and obeys Him. The LDS teaching of salvation by works, foreign to the Bible, is a terrible bondage. A great deal more will be said about this bondage in subsequent chapters.

SUMMARY

What has a comparison of the Bible with *The Book of Mormon* and *Doctrine and Covenants* shown? It demonstrates that the Bible is remarkably accurate. Although the Bible is an ancient book and the others are modern books, we find that the Bible has been preserved with such integrity that not one significant doctrine can be called into question. Yes, there are a few textual problems, due to its age and the thousands of Hebrew and Greek copies

The Freedom in a Correct View of Scripture

we have. Yet the problems are not problems of revision and alteration. The types of textual problems are commonly expected for such an ancient book.

The remarkable evidence available to us through ancient manuscripts—the Dead Sea Scrolls, the Bodmer II Text of the Gospel of John, the Vatican, Sinaitic, and Alexandrian Manuscripts—all give us undeniable proof that our Bible is accurate. There is no doubt that the LDS church criticism of the Bible by their prophets and leaders is ill informed.

After a close examination of a much later book, *The Book of Mormon*, we find that it was filled with mistakes, errors of chronology, grammar, and indications of the original copier's ignorance. Yet it claims to have been translated into English by the gift and power of God. Is it reasonable to blame God for these mistakes, or should we lay that at the feet of Joseph Smith, perpetrator of a fraud?

How can we hope to explain all the indications that *The Book of Mormon* was written at a much later date than it claims? How can it claim to have been written from 600 BC to AD 421 and yet quote so often directly from the future King James translation of the Bible? How can they explain the references to modern scientific discoveries? Why is it filled with theological problems?

The Book of Mormon has failed every test: the test of accuracy, the test of antiquity, the test of honesty. In every way it has been proven that it cannot be Scripture from God, except approximately one-third that is a direct quotation from the King James Bible.

FROM BONDAGE TO FREEDOM

The Bars of Bondage
1. Describe the Mormon attitude toward the Bible.
2. What is the significance of the Dead Sea Scrolls to the Old Testament?
3. Summarize the rules for copying Old Testament Scriptures.
4. What manuscript evidence is there for the New Testament?
5. How is the Bible inspired and why is that a problem for Mormon scriptures?

The Keys to Freedom
1. Keep a running list of questions prompted by this book. Be sure to leave room for their answers as you continue to study Mormonism.
2. Plan as a group to visit one of the museums that has early Bible manuscripts or a history of how we received our English Bible. If you do not have access to a museum, rent a videotape or DVD with the same information. Discuss how you can share this information with Mormons.

CHAPTER FOUR
The Mormon Bondage to Changing Revelation

"Every good thing given and every perfect gift is from above, coming down from the Father of lights, with whom there is no variation or shifting shadow" (James 1:17).

THE BONDAGE OF THE DOCTRINE AND COVENANTS

The second largest of the standard works of the LDS church, after *The Book of Mormon,* is called *The Doctrine and Covenants.* It is a series of revelations, supposedly given to Joseph Smith, with minor additions by later successors in the presidency of the LDS church.

The first revelation, according to his testimony, was given to Joseph Smith in September of 1823 and he received the last in June of 1844. There is one section given by Brigham Young, and short notes by presidents Wilford Woodruff and Lorenzo Snow.

For the most part *The Doctrine and Covenants* is the work of Joseph Smith. *The Doctrine and Covenants* introduces many of the different doctrinal ideas that were taught by the Mormon church. It is *The Doctrine and Covenants* that makes the Mormon church so different from most other Christian bodies in America. The serious theological problems come from this book. *The Doctrine and Covenants* is much more difficult for Latter-day Saints to defend than *The Book of Mormon.* While *The Book of Mormon* is a book about the size of the Old Testament, The *Doctrine and Covenants* is about the size of the New Testament.

Joseph Smith must be recognized as having produced quite a large volume of materials during his rather short life. It is a mistake to discount Joseph

CHRISTIANITY & MORMONISM

Smith as a person of ordinary talents. He was not; he was strong of body and mind. In many ways he shows the marks of genius, albeit misguided.

A Comparison of *The Book of Commandments* with *The Doctrine and Covenants*

Let's now examine the Mormon propensity for changing their revelations. An original edition of *The Doctrine and Covenants* is available through the means of photo reprint. It is printed by the Mormon church in Salt Lake City, Utah, and is called, *Joseph Smith Begins His Work*, Volume II. It is a companion volume to the photo reprint of *The Book of Mormon, Joseph Smith Begins His Work*, Volume I. Wilford C. Wood also published this volume through the agency of the Deseret News Publishing Company indicating that his is undoubtedly an authentic copy of the original *Book of Commandments*, now called *The Doctrine and Covenants*. The Mormon church leaders readily accept it. In the front is notarized documentation of its authenticity, both from Wilford C. Wood and the Deseret News Publishing Company.

The original *Doctrine and Covenants* (*Book of Commandments*) was published in 1833. The very first section of *The Doctrine and Covenants* tells us that these revelations are from God.

> What I the Lord have spoken, I have spoken, and I excuse not myself, and though the heavens and the earth pass away, my word shall not pass away, but shall all be fulfilled, whether by mine own voice or by the voice of my servants. It is the same. For behold, and lo, the Lord is God, and the Spirit beareth record, and the record is true, and the truth abideth forever and ever. Amen (DC 1:38-39).

After this affirmation it is shocking to learn that *The Doctrine and Covenants* has been greatly edited and changed. In fact, there are at least 2,786 changes. These are not changes of minor significance, but of major importance. By what justification could someone, Joseph Smith or anyone else, take out whole paragraphs, put in whole paragraphs, reverse the meaning, contradict what was originally said, when in no uncertain language Section One says these words would never pass away? If the original revelations were true, and the truth abides forever, why then would they have to be rewritten, revised, reversed, and changed?

If in truth these were revelations from God, like the Bible, why would any man want to correct what God had given? For a person to take in hand to change these commands, without telling the reader why or when he had done so, seems unthinkable, especially in the light of Section One which clearly affirms that these commands are God's words and that they will never pass away.

The next few pages of this book are photocopies of the original *Book of Commandments* with the changes marked to show how the present *Doctrine and Covenants* reads.[34] Remember that these are supposed revelations from God, recorded by His "prophet." Remember too, as you look at these pages, that Section One says these words would never pass away, that they were all true and would stand forever.

This is very damaging evidence. It is inconceivable that this book is the work of the God of the universe. We have already learned that the Bible has not gone through such mutilation. In fact, the men given charge of the Bible protected it most carefully lest they would lose a single letter and thus the very words of God.

Allow me to explain the code for the changes. The printed portion of the photocopies is the original *Book of Commandments*, now called *The Doctrine and Covenants*. The margin is marked to show how the present *Doctrine and Covenants* reads. Letters are used to indicate what type of change is made. T.C. means "textual change." W.A. means "words added." W.D. means "words deleted." In the margin are large printed letters: A,B,C, and so forth. These indicate "doctrinal changes." A brief explanation for some of these changes and their significance is in order as well. Some of the changes that involve the fewest words are the most serious.

The first change, marked "A," *Book of Commandments*, page 10, is a serious change. If you read carefully you will notice that originally Joseph Smith is told that he will have no other work from God than the translation of the gold plates into the English *Book of Mormon*. He is to pretend to have no other work from God. Then a few years later he decided that this wasn't enough, God supposedly changed His mind. It was changed so that he could have further revelations from God. We are forced to one of two conclusions: Either God changed His mind, didn't think ahead sufficiently, made a mistake, or Joseph Smith wrote the revelation. When he found out how well the people received his first work, *The Book of Mormon*, he decided that he had limited himself too much by saying he would get no further revelation, so he revised it in order to "receive" more. Either way we must realize that this cannot be a revelation from the God of the universe.

Under change "C," *Book of Commandments*, page 11, we see that the original teaches that the church was to be built up like the church of old, the New Testament church. When later, Joseph Smith wanted to change

---

[34]These pages are used by permission of Jerald and Sandra Tanner and are photocopies from their book, *The Case Against Mormonism*, vol. 1 (Salt Lake City: Utah Lighthouse Ministry, 1967), pp. 139-162.

CHRISTIANITY & MORMONISM

some things in the church from the original design, they had to change *The Doctrine and Covenants*. So they removed 154 words by the stroke of a pen. What was claimed to be a revelation from Almighty God had now been removed. Are we to believe that it really was a revelation from God?

Under change "D" is a document supposedly translated from some parchments written by the Apostle John, later found and translated by Joseph Smith. Jerald and Sandra Tanner report,

> This revelation is supposed to contain a translation of a parchment written by the Apostle John. Joseph Smith was supposed to have translated it by means of the Urim and Thummim. When this revelation was published in the *Book of Commandments* in 1833, it contained 143 words, but when it was reprinted in the *Doctrine and Covenants* in 1835, it contained 252 words. Thus 109 words had been added.[35]

Several explanations could be given for such changes. All of them boil down to the fact that the "revelations" have been very carelessly handled, changed, and revised at the will of those who received them. We can only conclude that those who claimed to be from God were not trustworthy people. To think that one would, without explanation, add to the letter of another is unthinkable unless the person doing the adding was not honest. This is good evidence that Joseph Smith was not a prophet of God.

Change "H," on page 35, is of significance since it provides for changing the church and its doctrine. Originally they were told to build upon the things which were already written. "For in them are all things written concerning my church, my gospel, and my rock" (BoC 15:3). When Joseph Smith wanted to change things later he had to change this. So, by adding three words, he made a way for changing the church of the Lord. It was made to read, "For in them are all things written concerning the foundation of my church, my gospel, and my rock" (DC 18:4). He gave himself license to change the church as he wished, and he did.

Change "J," on page 38, represents only one word, but it is a serious doctrinal change. Originally Joseph Smith supported his family "from" the church. Later when he wanted to do away with people getting salaries from the church, thus making a way for the church to grow great financially, the word was changed from "from" to "in." This changes the whole meaning and thus introduces a whole new doctrine. This is further proof that this is not a revelation from God.

---

[35]Jerald and Sandra Tanner, *Mormonism–Shadow or Reality?*, Enlarged ed. (Salt Lake City: Modern Microfilm, 1972), p. 27.

The Mormon Bondage to Changing Revelation

Change "L," on page 92, is a serious change of teaching. Originally the teaching was "and behold, thou shalt consecrate all thy properties, that which thou hast unto me, with a covenant and a deed which cannot be broken...." (BoC 28:26). Later, when the doctrine proved too hard, it was changed to "...and consecrate of thy properties...." (DC 42:30). This is a large change of doctrine. Who made the mistake, God or Joseph? Isn't this further evidence that Joseph Smith was not from God?

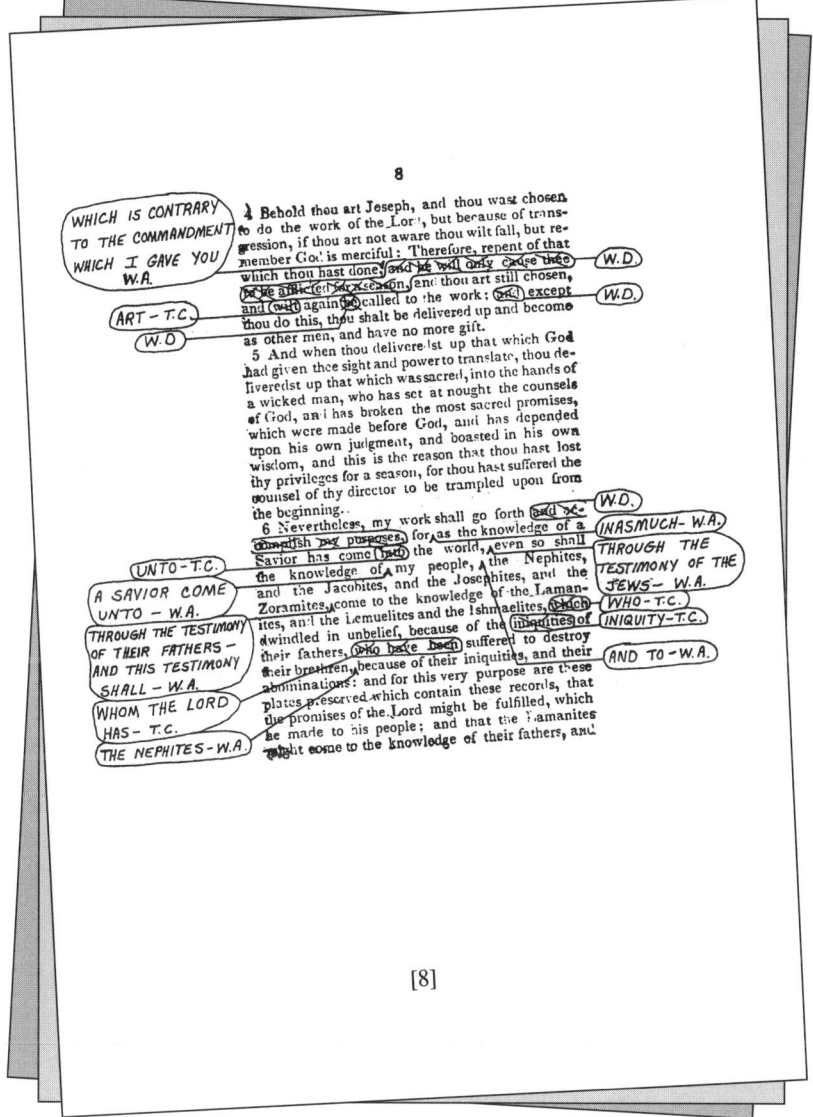

CHRISTIANITY & MORMONISM

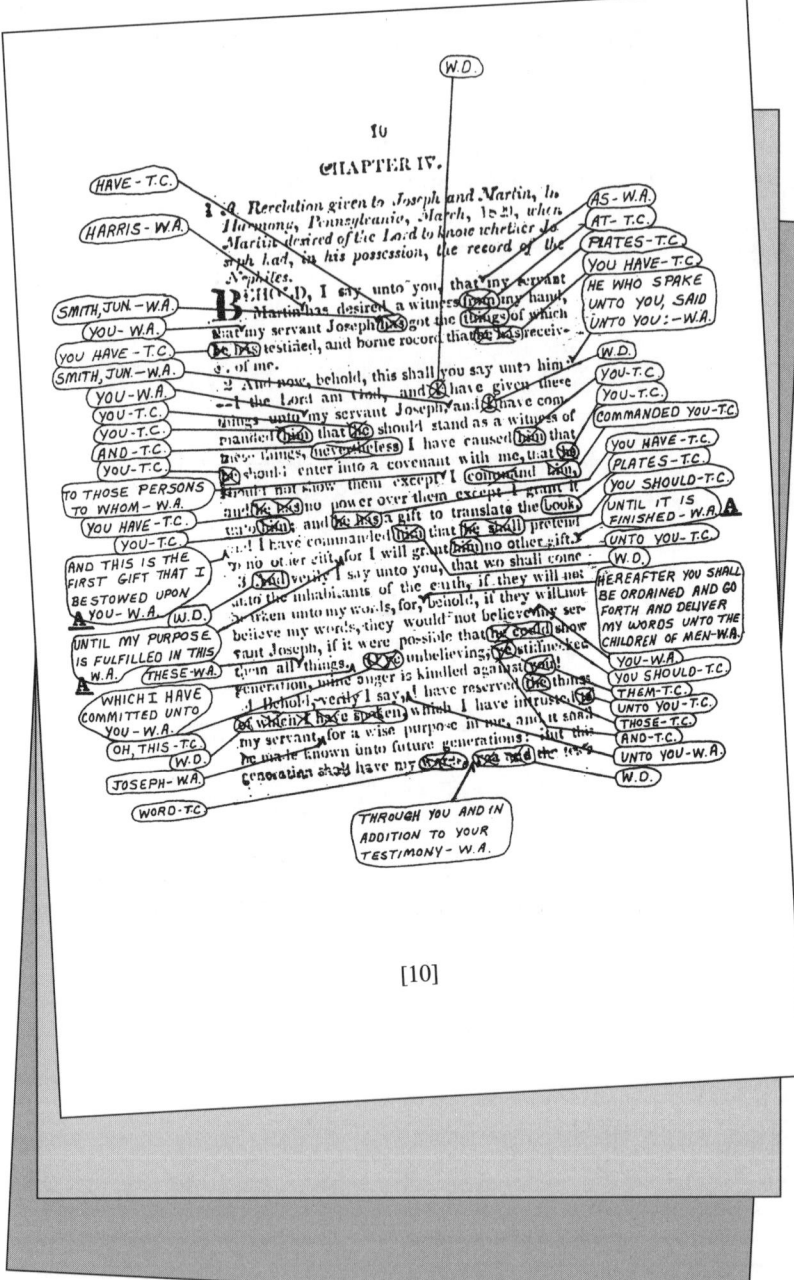

The Mormon Bondage to Changing Revelation

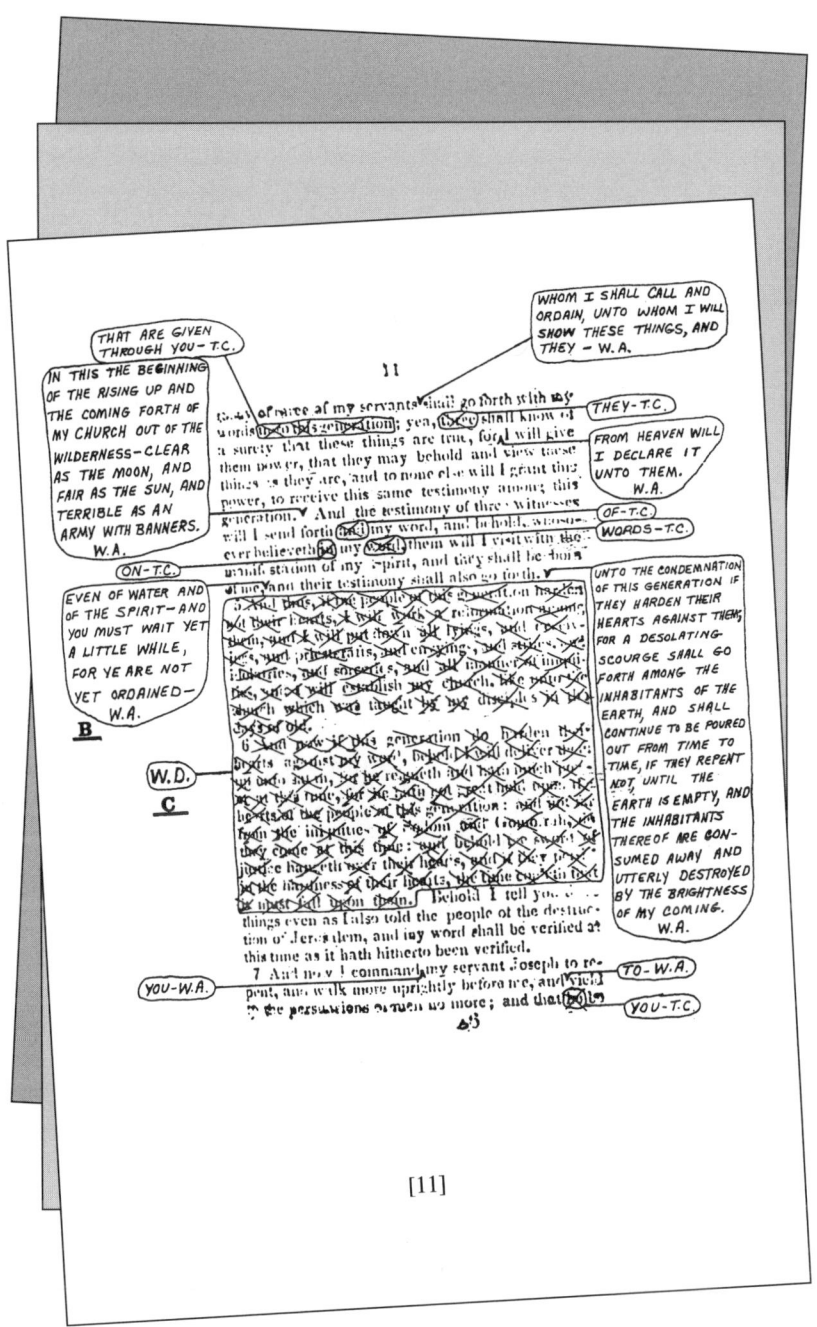

CHRISTIANITY & MORMONISM

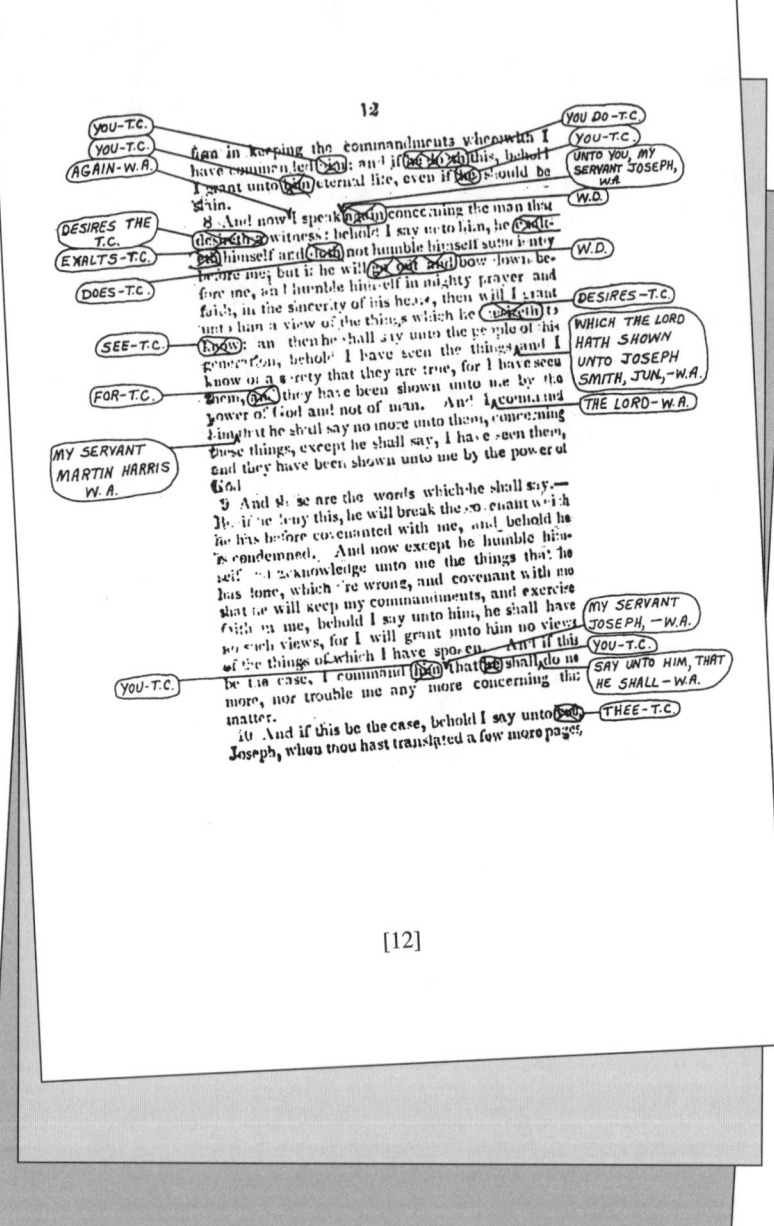

The Mormon Bondage to Changing Revelation

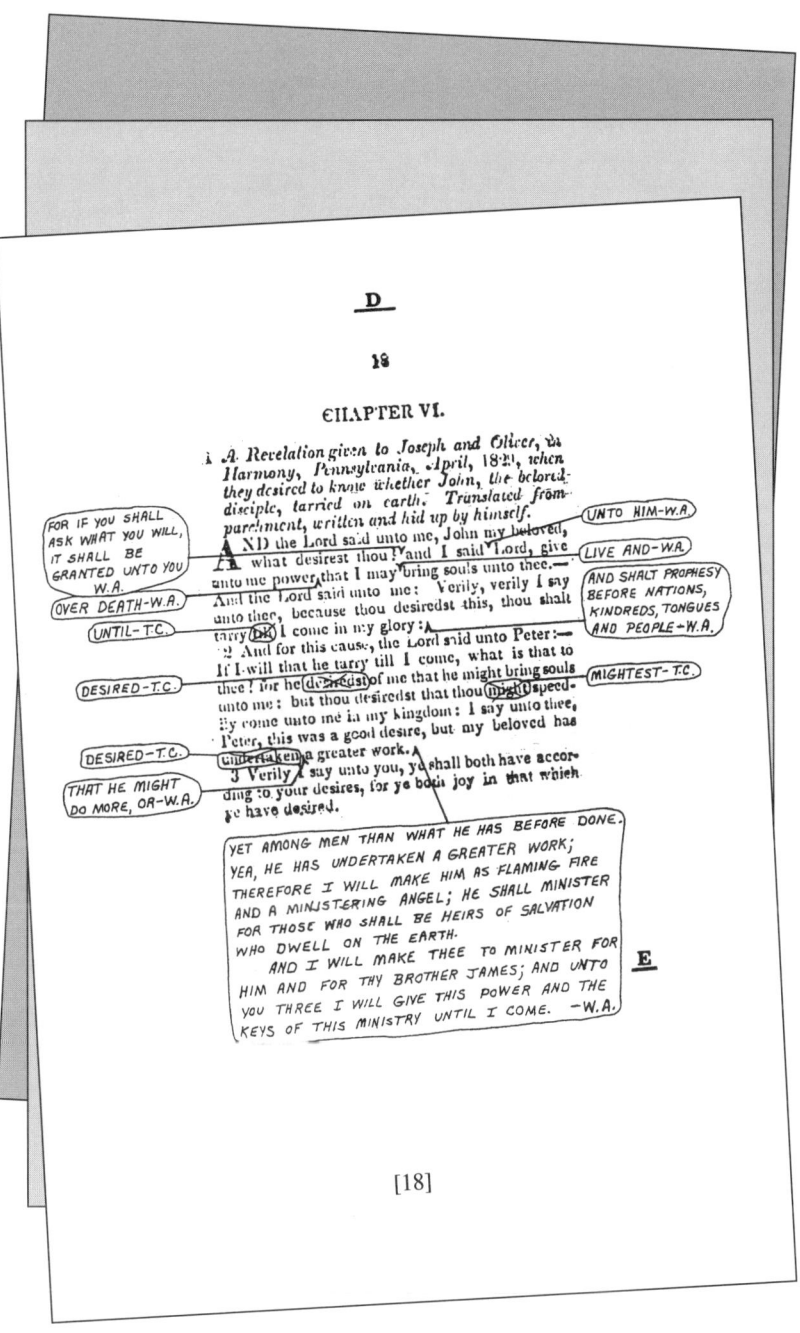

[18]

87

CHRISTIANITY & MORMONISM

19

CHAPTER VII.

1 *A Revelation given to Oliver, in Harmony, Pennsylvania, April, 1829.*

OLIVER, verily, verily I say unto you, that as surely as the Lord liveth, who is your God and your Redeemer, even so surely shall you receive a knowledge of whatsoever things you shall ask in faith, with an honest heart, believing that you shall receive a knowledge concerning the engravings of old records, which are ancient, which contain those parts of my scripture of which has been spoken, by the manifestation of my Spirit; yea, behold I will tell you in your mind and in your heart by the Holy Ghost, which shall come upon you and which shall dwell in your heart.

2 Now, behold this is the Spirit of revelation:— behold this is the Spirit by which Moses brought the children of Israel though the Red sea on dry ground; therefore, this is thy gift; apply unto it and blessed art thou; for it shall deliver you out of the hands of your enemies, when, if it were not so, they would slay you and bring your soul to destruction.

3 O remember, these words and keep my commandments. Remember this is your gift. Now this is not all, for you have another gift, which is the gift of working with the rod: behold it has told you things: behold there is no other power save God, that can cause this rod of nature, to work in your hands, for it is the work of God; and therefore whatsoever you shall ask me to tell you by that means, that will I grant unto you, that you shall know.

4 Remember that without faith you can do nothing.

Annotations:
- COWDERY – W.A.
- WHO – T.C.
- SURELY – T.C.
- HAS – T.C.
- THY GIFT – W.A.
- ARRON – T.C.
- MANY – W.A.
- GIFT OF AARON TO BE WITH YOU – W.A. THEREFORE, DOUBT NOT. – W.A. HAVE KNOWLEDGE CONCERNING IT. T.C.
- THE POWER OF W.A.
- W.D.
- AND YOU SHALL HOLD IT IN YOUR HANDS, AND DO MARVELOUS WORKS; AND NO POWER SHALL BE ABLE TO TAKE IT AWAY OUT OF YOUR HANDS, FOR IT IS THE WORK OF GOD. – W.A.
- GIFT – T.C.
- AND – T.C.

[19]

The Mormon Bondage to Changing Revelation

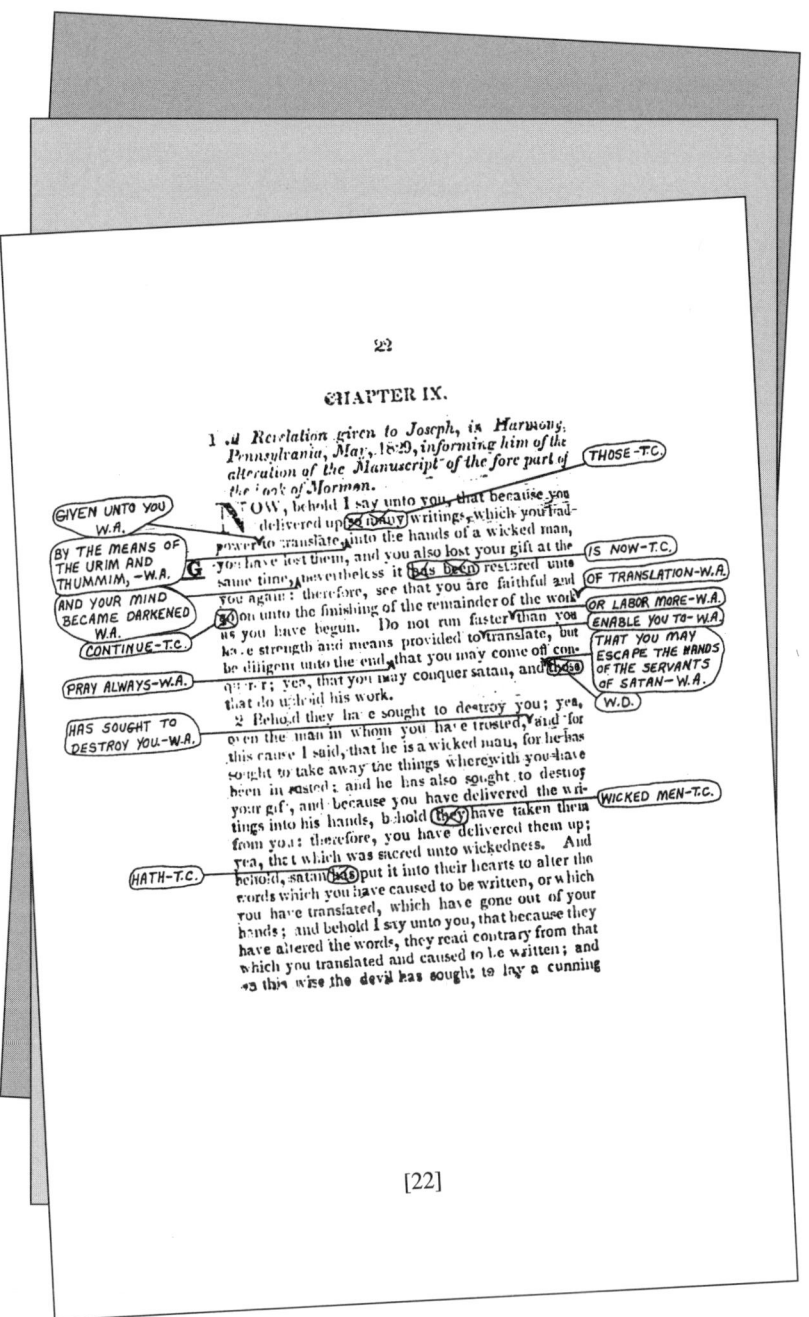

23

plan, that he may destroy this work; for he ~~has~~ put
it into their hearts to do this, that by lying they may
say they have caught you in the words which you
have pretended to translate.

3 Verily I say unto you, that I will not suffer that
satan shall accomplish his evil design in this thing;
for behold he ha~~s~~ put it into their hearts to tempt the
Lord ~~their~~ God; ~~&~~ behol I they sa~~y~~ in their hearts,
We will see if God has given him power to translate, if so, he will also give him power again; and
if God giveth him power again, or if he ~~translate~~
again, or in other words, if he bringeth forth the
same words, behold we have the same with us, and
we have altered them: Therefore, they will not
agree, and we will say that he has lied in his words,
and that he has no gift, and that he has no power:
therefore, we will destroy him, and also the work,
and we will do this that we may not be ashamed in
the end, and that we may get glory of the world.

4 Verily, verily I say unto you, that satan has
great hold upon their hearts; he stirreth them up to
do iniquity against that which is good; that he may
lead their souls to destruction, and thus he has laid
a cunning plan to destroy the work of God; yea, he
stirreth up their hearts to anger against this work;
yea, he saith unto them, Deceive and lie in wait to
catch, that ye may destroy: behold this is no harm,
and thus he flattereth them and telleth them that it
is no sin to lie, that they may catch a man in a lie,
that they may destroy him, and thus he flattereth
them, and leageth them along until he draggeth their
souls down to hell; and thus he causeth them to
catch themselves in their own snare; and thus he
goeth up and down, to and fro in the earth, seeking
to destroy the souls of men.

(HATH — T.C.)
(GET THEE TO W.A.)
(W.D.)
(THY — T.C.)
(AND THINK — W.A.)
(IN ASKING TO TRANSLATE IT OVER AGAIN. AND THEN, — W.A.)
(TRANSLATES T.C.)
(AND THEIR HEARTS ARE CORRUPT, AND FULL OF WICKEDNESS AND ABOMINATIONS; AND THEY LOVE DARKNESS RATHER THAN LIGHT, BECAUSE THEIR DEEDS ARE EVIL; THEREFORE THEY WILL NOT ASK OF ME. SATAN STIRRETH THEM UP, W.A.)
(W.D.)
(THINKING W.A.)
(BUT I WILL REQUIRE THIS AT THEIR HANDS, AND IT SHALL TURN TO THEIR SHAME AND CONDEMNATION IN THE DAY OF JUDGMENT. — W.A.)

[23]

The Mormon Bondage to Changing Revelation

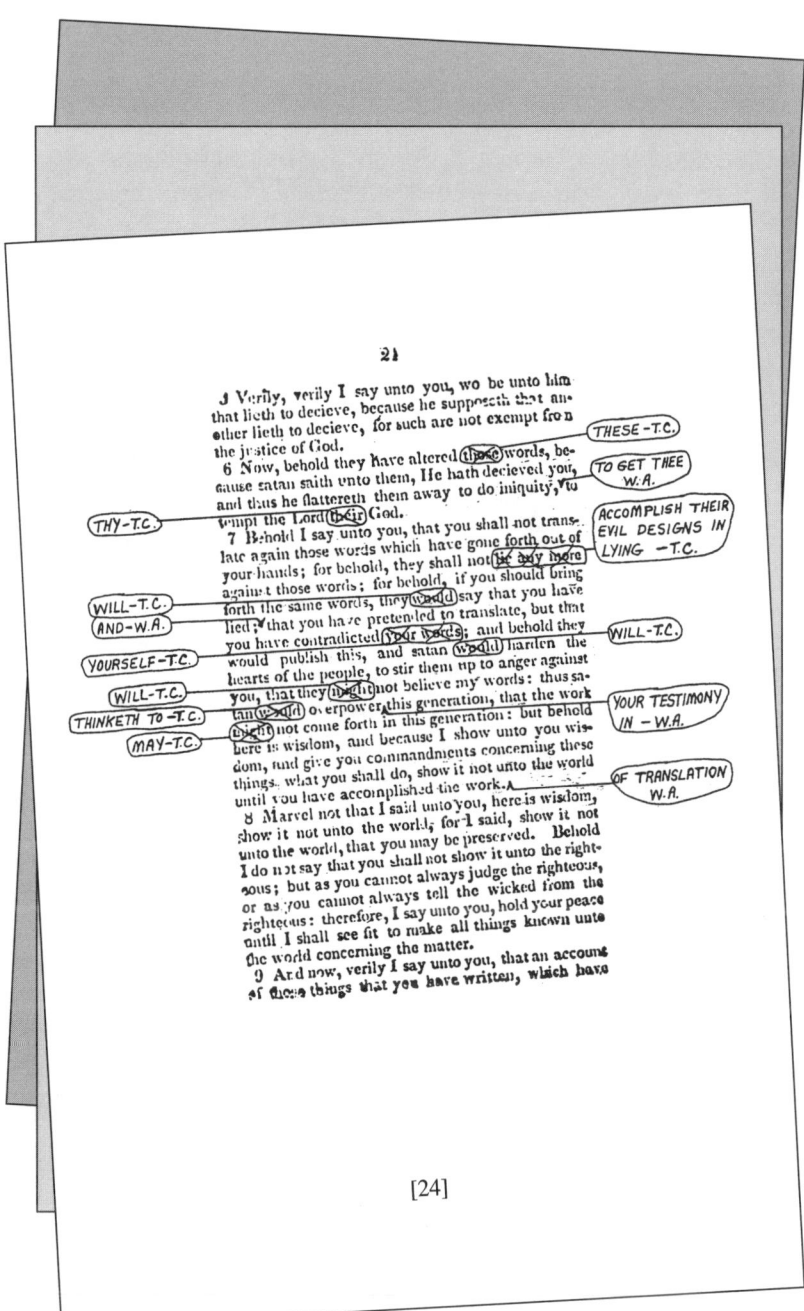

[24]

35

Spirit in many instances, that the things which you have written are true:

3 Wherefore you know that they are true; and if you know that they are true, behold I give unto you a commandment, that you rely upon the things which are written; for in them are all things written, concerning my church, my gospel, and my rock.

4 Wherefore if you shall build up my church, and my gospel, and my rock, the gates of hell shall not prevail against you.

5 Behold the world is ripening in iniquity, and it must needs be, that the children of men are stirred up unto repentance, both the Gentiles, and also the house of Israel:

6 Wherefore as thou hast been baptized by the hand of my servant, according to that which I have commanded him:

7 Wherefore he hath fulfilled the thing which I commanded him.

8 And now marvel not that I have called him unto mine own purpose, which purpose is known in me:

9 Wherefore if he shall be diligent in keeping my commandments, he shall be blessed unto eternal life, and his name is Joseph.

10 And now Oliver, I speak unto you, and also unto David, by the way of commandment:

11 For behold I command all men every where to repent, and I speak unto you, even as unto Paul mine apostle, for you are called even with that same calling with which he was called.

12 Remember the worth of souls is great in the sight of God:

13 For behold the Lord your God suffered death

[35]

Annotations:
- THE FOUNDATION OF — W.A. (H)
- UPON THE FOUNDATION OF — W.A. (H)
- W.D.
- HANDS — T.C.
- JOSEPH SMITH, JUN. — W.A.
- W.D.
- WHITMER — W.A.
- COWDERY — W.A.
- REDEEMER — T.C.

92

The Mormon Bondage to Changing Revelation

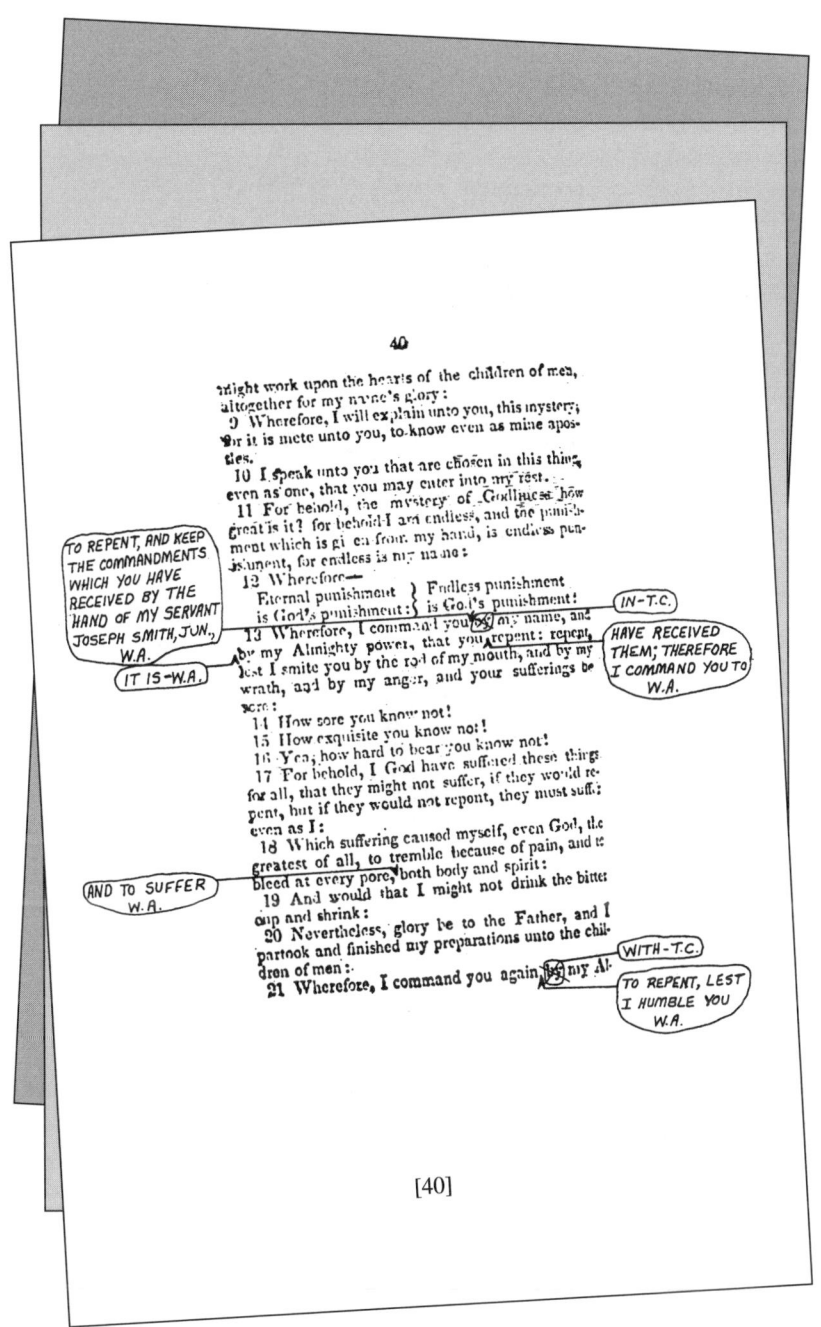

CHRISTIANITY & MORMONISM

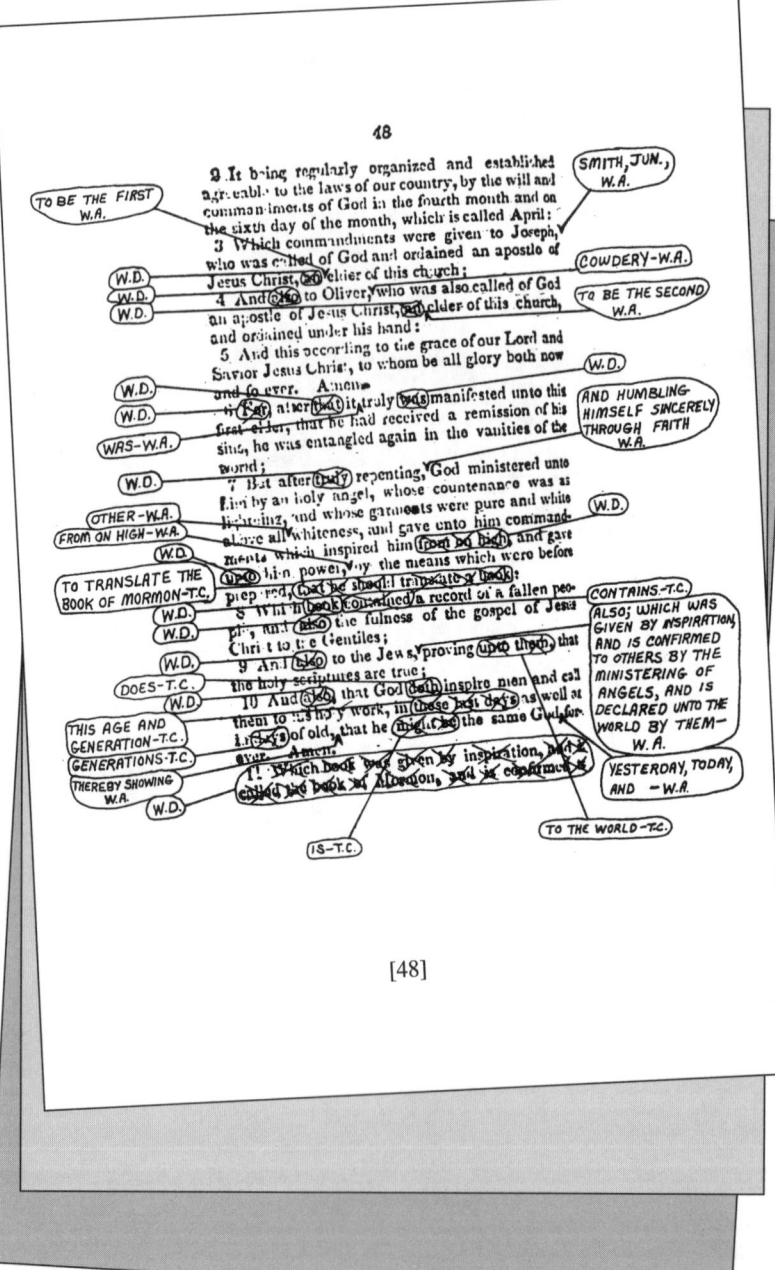

The Mormon Bondage to Changing Revelation

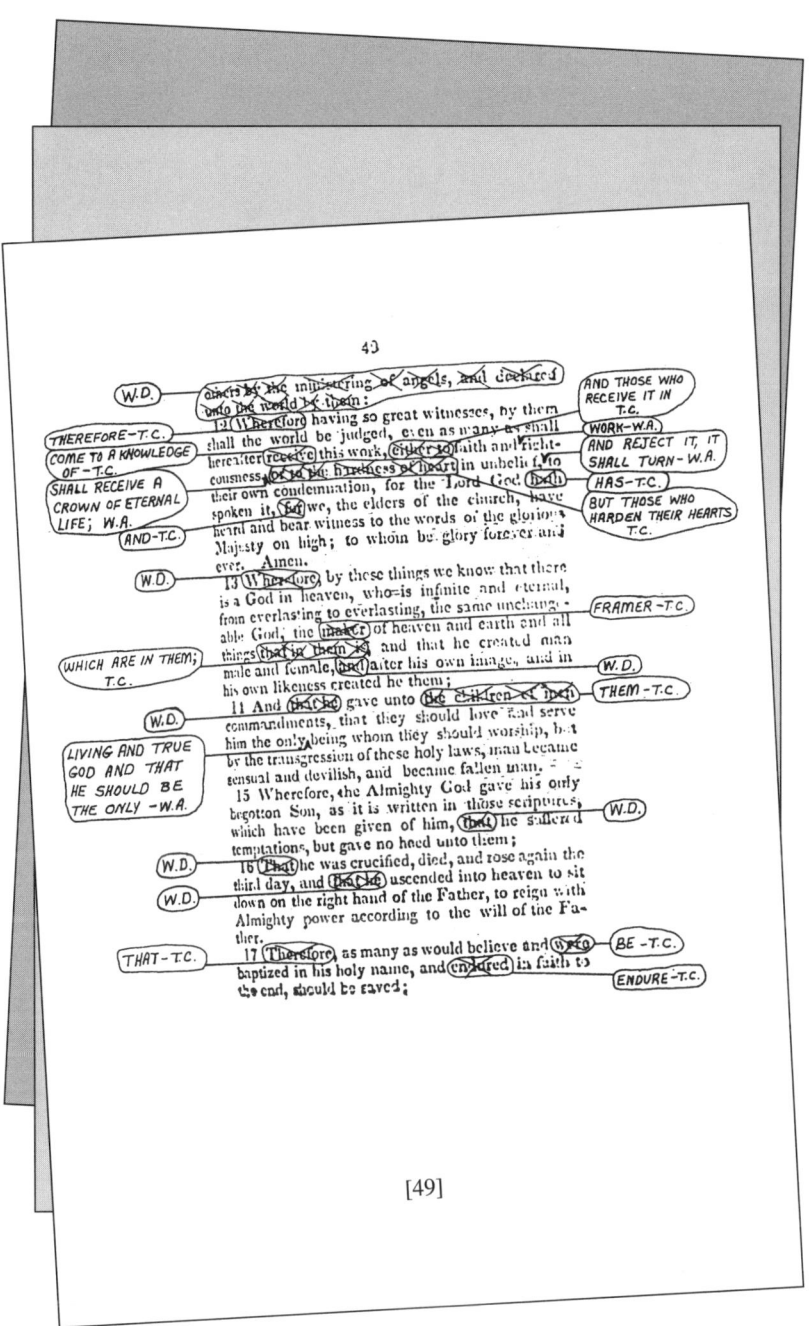

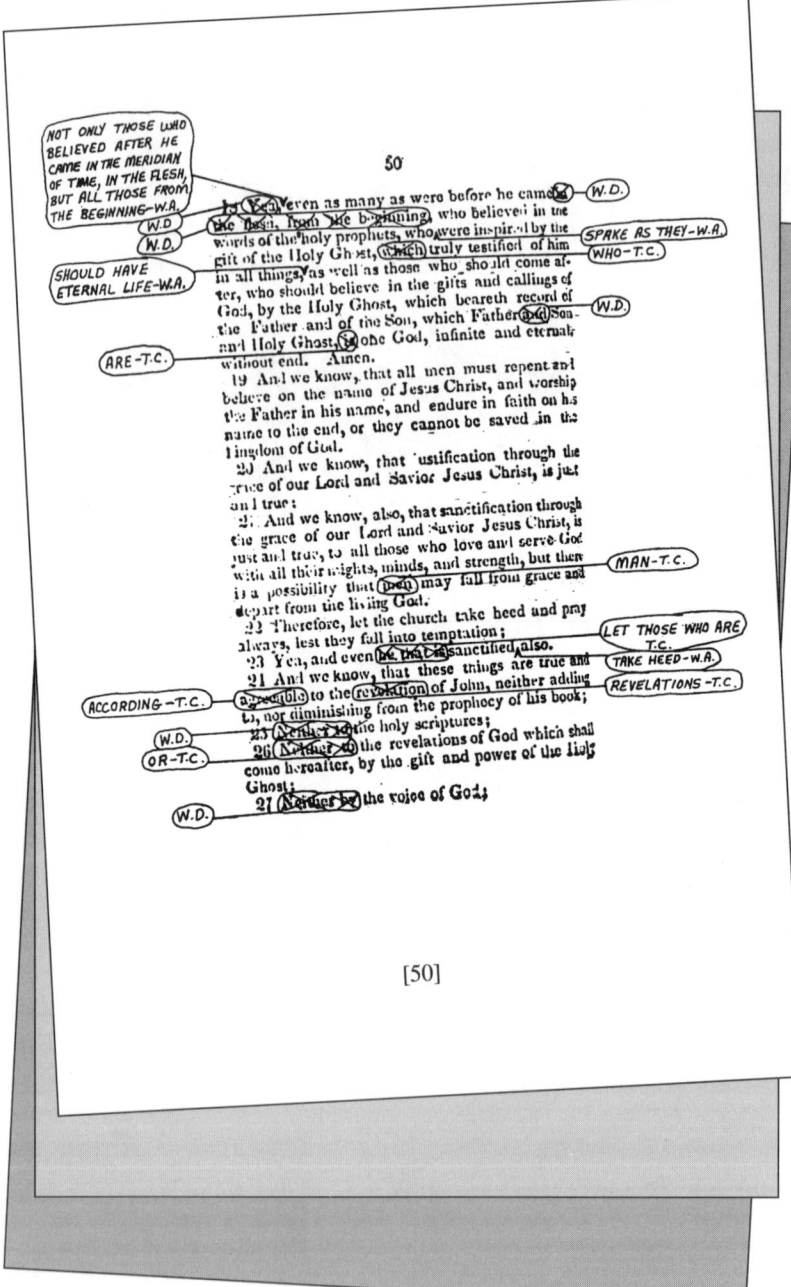

The Mormon Bondage to Changing Revelation

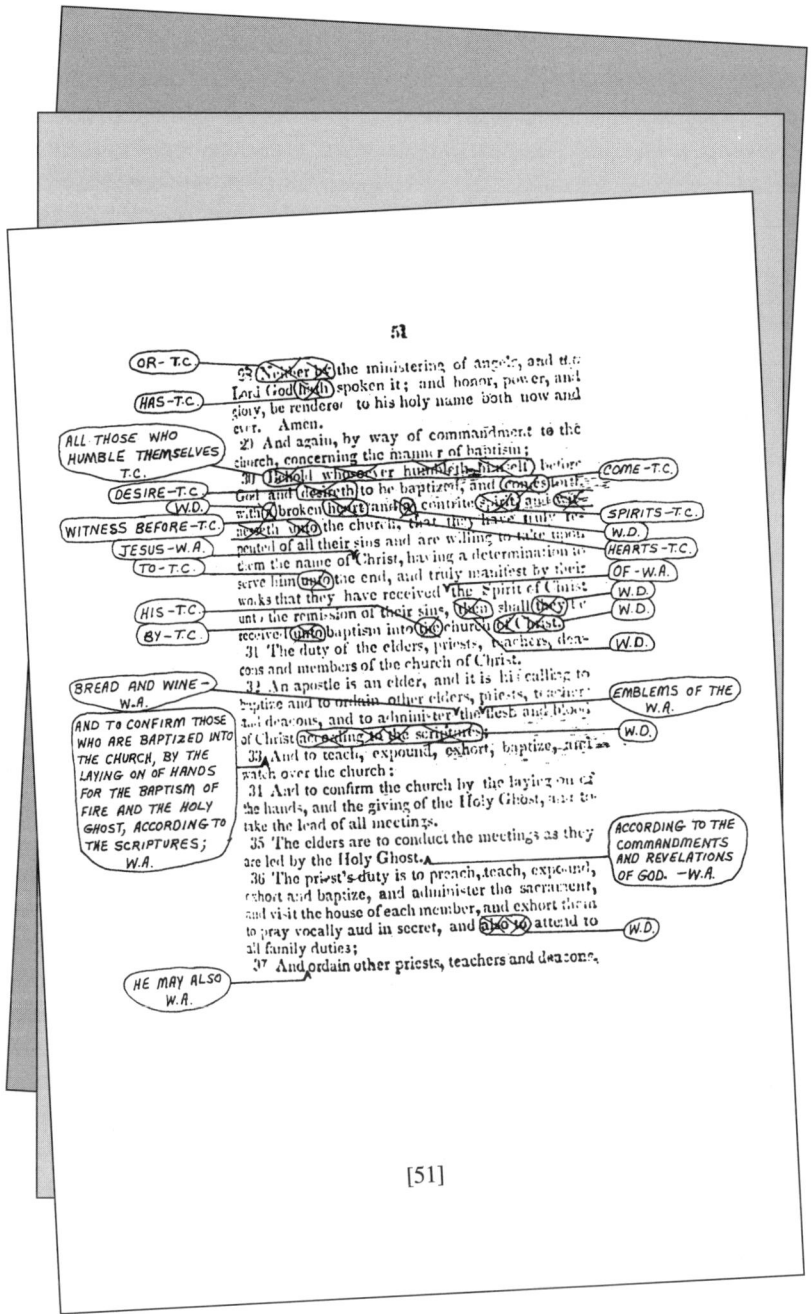

CHRISTIANITY & MORMONISM

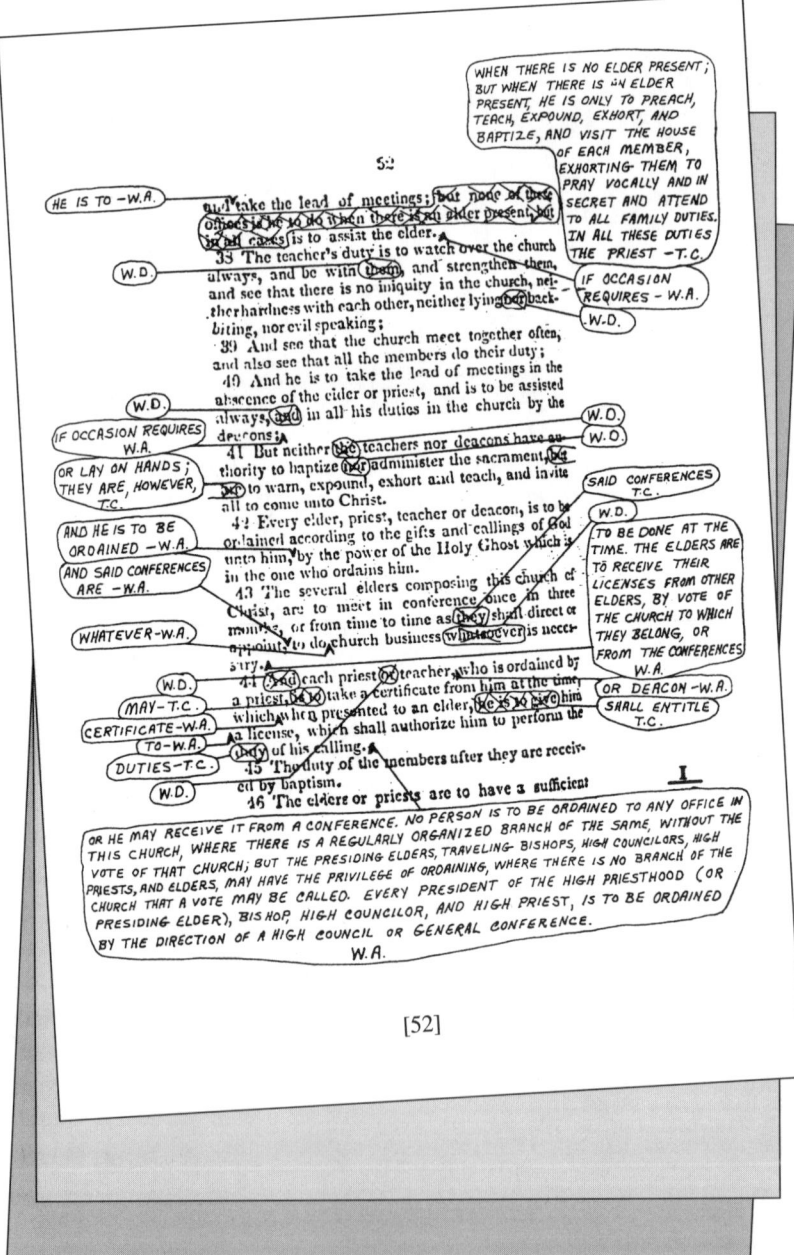

[52]

The Mormon Bondage to Changing Revelation

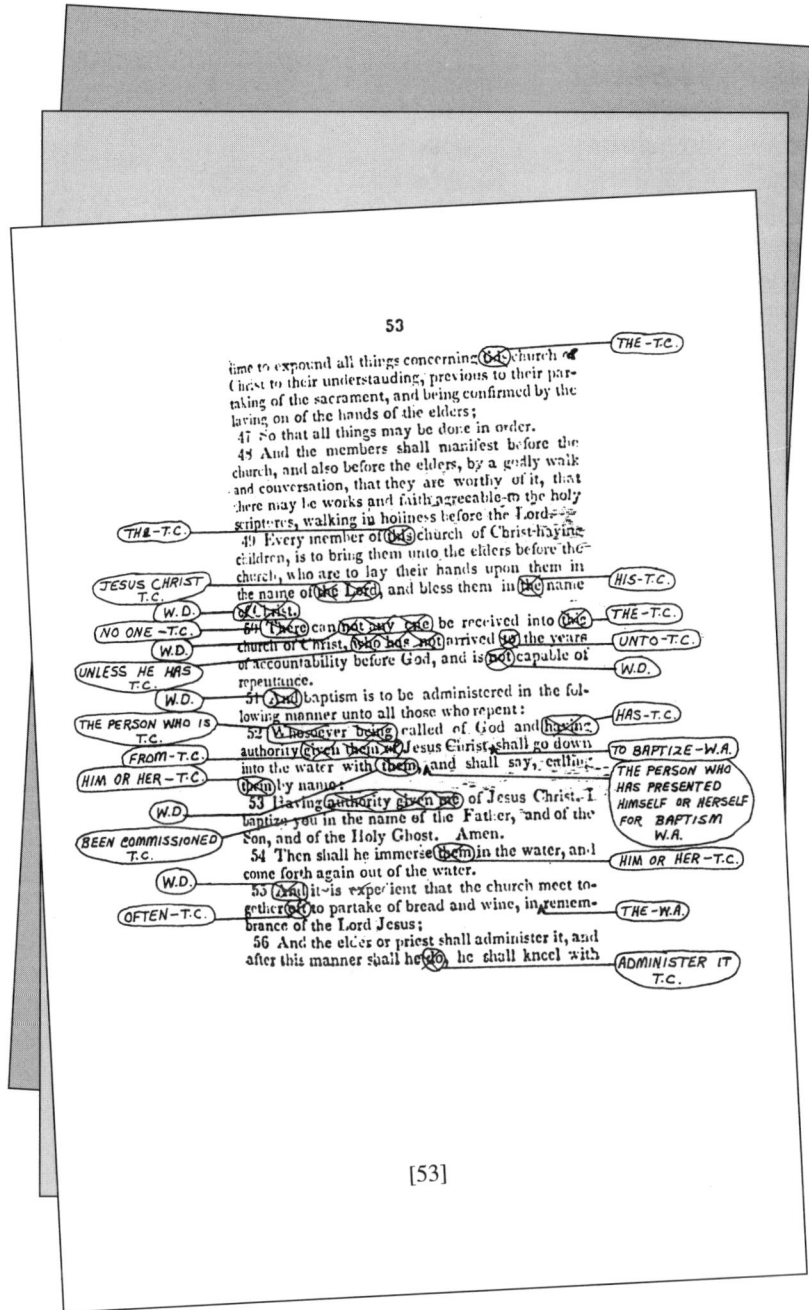

CHAPTER XXVI.

1 A Revelation to Emma, given in Harmone, Pennsylvania, July, 1830.

EMMA, my daughter ~~by Zion~~, a revelation I give unto you, concerning my will: 2 Behold thy sins are forgiven thee, and thou art an elect lady, whom I have called.

3 Murmur not because of the things which thou hast not seen, for they are withheld from thee, and from the world, which is wisdom in me in a time to come.

4 And the office of thy calling shall be for a comfort unto my servant Joseph, thy husband, in his afflictions with consoling words, in the spirit of meekness.

5 And thou shalt go with him at the time of his going, and be unto him for a scribe, that I may send Oliver whithersoever I will.

6 And thou shalt be ordained under his hand to expound scriptures, and to exhort the church, according as it shall be given thee by my spirit:

7 For he shall lay his hands upon thee, and thou shalt receive the Holy Ghost, and thy time shall be given to writing, and to learning much.

8 And thou needest not fear, for thy husband shall support thee ~~from~~ the church:

9 For unto them is his calling, that all things might be revealed unto them, whatsoever I will according to their faith.

10 And verily I say unto thee, that thou shalt lay aside the things of this world, and seek for the things of a better.

11 And it shall be given thee, also, to make a selection of sacred Hymns, as it shall be given thee;

[58]

Annotations:
- HEARKEN UNTO THE VOICE OF THE LORD YOUR GOD, WHILE I SPEAK UNTO YOU, — W.A.
- W.D.
- SMITH — W.A.
- FOR VERILY I SAY UNTO YOU, ALL THOSE WHO RECEIVE MY GOSPEL ARE SONS AND DAUGHTERS IN MY KINGDOM. — W.A.
- AND IF THOU ART FAITHFUL AND WALK IN THE PATHS OF VIRTUE BEFORE ME, I WILL PRESERVE THY LIFE, AND THOU SHALT RECEIVE AN INHERITANCE IN ZION. W.A.
- SMITH, JUN., W.A.
- WHILE THERE IS NO ONE TO BE A SCRIBE FOR HIM, — W.A.
- MY SERVANT W.A.
- COWDERY W.A.
- J (IN -T.C.)

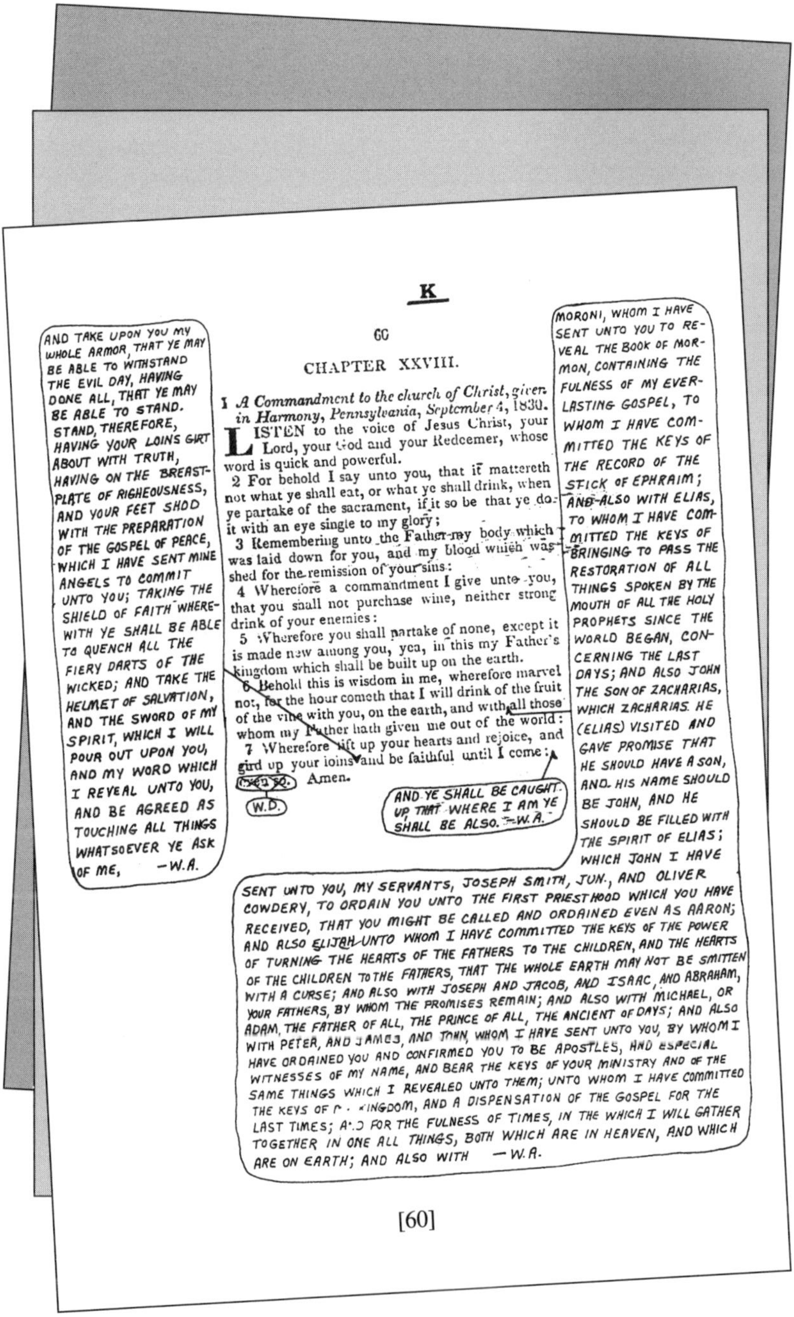

The Mormon Bondage to Changing Revelation

CHAPTER XXVIII.

1 *A Commandment to the church of Christ, given in Harmony, Pennsylvania, September 4, 1830.*

LISTEN to the voice of Jesus Christ, your Lord, your God and your Redeemer, whose word is quick and powerful.

2 For behold I say unto you, that it mattereth not what ye shall eat, or what ye shall drink, when ye partake of the sacrament, if it so be that ye do it with an eye single to my glory;

3 Remembering unto the Father my body which was laid down for you, and my blood which was shed for the remission of your sins:

4 Wherefore a commandment I give unto you, that you shall not purchase wine, neither strong drink of your enemies:

5 Wherefore you shall partake of none, except it is made new among you, yea, in this my Father's kingdom which shall be built up on the earth.

6 Behold this is wisdom in me, wherefore marvel not, for the hour cometh that I will drink of the fruit of the vine with you, on the earth, and with all those whom my Father hath given me out of the world:

7 Wherefore lift up your hearts and rejoice, and gird up your loins and be faithful until I come: Amen. (W.D.)

[Left margin annotation — W.A.:]
AND TAKE UPON YOU MY WHOLE ARMOR, THAT YE MAY BE ABLE TO WITHSTAND THE EVIL DAY, HAVING DONE ALL, THAT YE MAY BE ABLE TO STAND. STAND, THEREFORE, HAVING YOUR LOINS GIRT ABOUT WITH TRUTH, HAVING ON THE BREASTPLATE OF RIGHEOUSNESS, AND YOUR FEET SHOD WITH THE PREPARATION OF THE GOSPEL OF PEACE, WHICH I HAVE SENT MINE ANGELS TO COMMIT UNTO YOU; TAKING THE SHIELD OF FAITH WHEREWITH YE SHALL BE ABLE TO QUENCH ALL THE FIERY DARTS OF THE WICKED; AND TAKE THE HELMET OF SALVATION, AND THE SWORD OF MY SPIRIT, WHICH I WILL POUR OUT UPON YOU, AND MY WORD WHICH I REVEAL UNTO YOU, AND BE AGREED AS TOUCHING ALL THINGS WHATSOEVER YE ASK OF ME, —W.A.

[Center annotation — W.A.:]
AND YE SHALL BE CAUGHT UP THAT WHERE I AM YE SHALL BE ALSO. —W.A.

[Right margin annotation — W.A.:]
MORONI, WHOM I HAVE SENT UNTO YOU TO REVEAL THE BOOK OF MORMON, CONTAINING THE FULNESS OF MY EVERLASTING GOSPEL, TO WHOM I HAVE COMMITTED THE KEYS OF THE RECORD OF THE STICK OF EPHRAIM; AND ALSO WITH ELIAS, TO WHOM I HAVE COMMITTED THE KEYS OF BRINGING TO PASS THE RESTORATION OF ALL THINGS SPOKEN BY THE MOUTH OF ALL THE HOLY PROPHETS SINCE THE WORLD BEGAN, CONCERNING THE LAST DAYS; AND ALSO JOHN THE SON OF ZACHARIAS, WHICH ZACHARIAS HE (ELIAS) VISITED AND GAVE PROMISE THAT HE SHOULD HAVE A SON, AND HIS NAME SHOULD BE JOHN, AND HE SHOULD BE FILLED WITH THE SPIRIT OF ELIAS; WHICH JOHN I HAVE SENT UNTO YOU, MY SERVANTS, JOSEPH SMITH, JUN., AND OLIVER COWDERY, TO ORDAIN YOU UNTO THE FIRST PRIESTHOOD WHICH YOU HAVE RECEIVED, THAT YOU MIGHT BE CALLED AND ORDAINED EVEN AS AARON; AND ALSO ELIJAH UNTO WHOM I HAVE COMMITTED THE KEYS OF THE POWER OF TURNING THE HEARTS OF THE FATHERS TO THE CHILDREN, AND THE HEARTS OF THE CHILDREN TO THE FATHERS, THAT THE WHOLE EARTH MAY NOT BE SMITTEN WITH A CURSE; AND ALSO WITH JOSEPH AND JACOB, AND ISAAC, AND ABRAHAM, YOUR FATHERS, BY WHOM THE PROMISES REMAIN; AND ALSO WITH MICHAEL, OR ADAM, THE FATHER OF ALL, THE PRINCE OF ALL, THE ANCIENT OF DAYS; AND ALSO WITH PETER, AND JAMES, AND JOHN, WHOM I HAVE SENT UNTO YOU, BY WHOM I HAVE ORDAINED YOU AND CONFIRMED YOU TO BE APOSTLES, AND ESPECIAL WITNESSES OF MY NAME, AND BEAR THE KEYS OF YOUR MINISTRY AND OF THE SAME THINGS WHICH I REVEALED UNTO THEM; UNTO WHOM I HAVE COMMITTED THE KEYS OF MY KINGDOM, AND A DISPENSATION OF THE GOSPEL FOR THE LAST TIMES; AND FOR THE FULNESS OF TIMES, IN THE WHICH I WILL GATHER TOGETHER IN ONE ALL THINGS, BOTH WHICH ARE IN HEAVEN, AND WHICH ARE ON EARTH; AND ALSO WITH —W.A.

[60]

CHRISTIANITY & MORMONISM

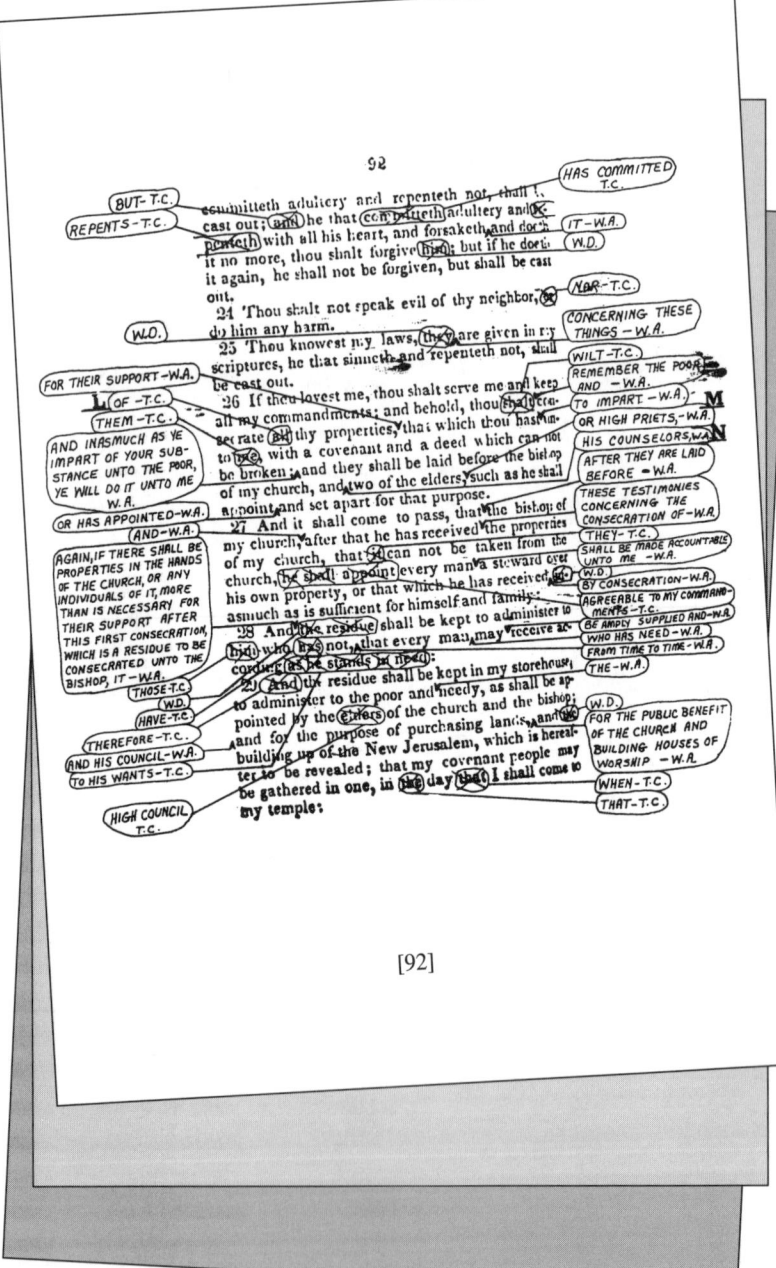

[92]

The Mormon Bondage to Changing Revelation

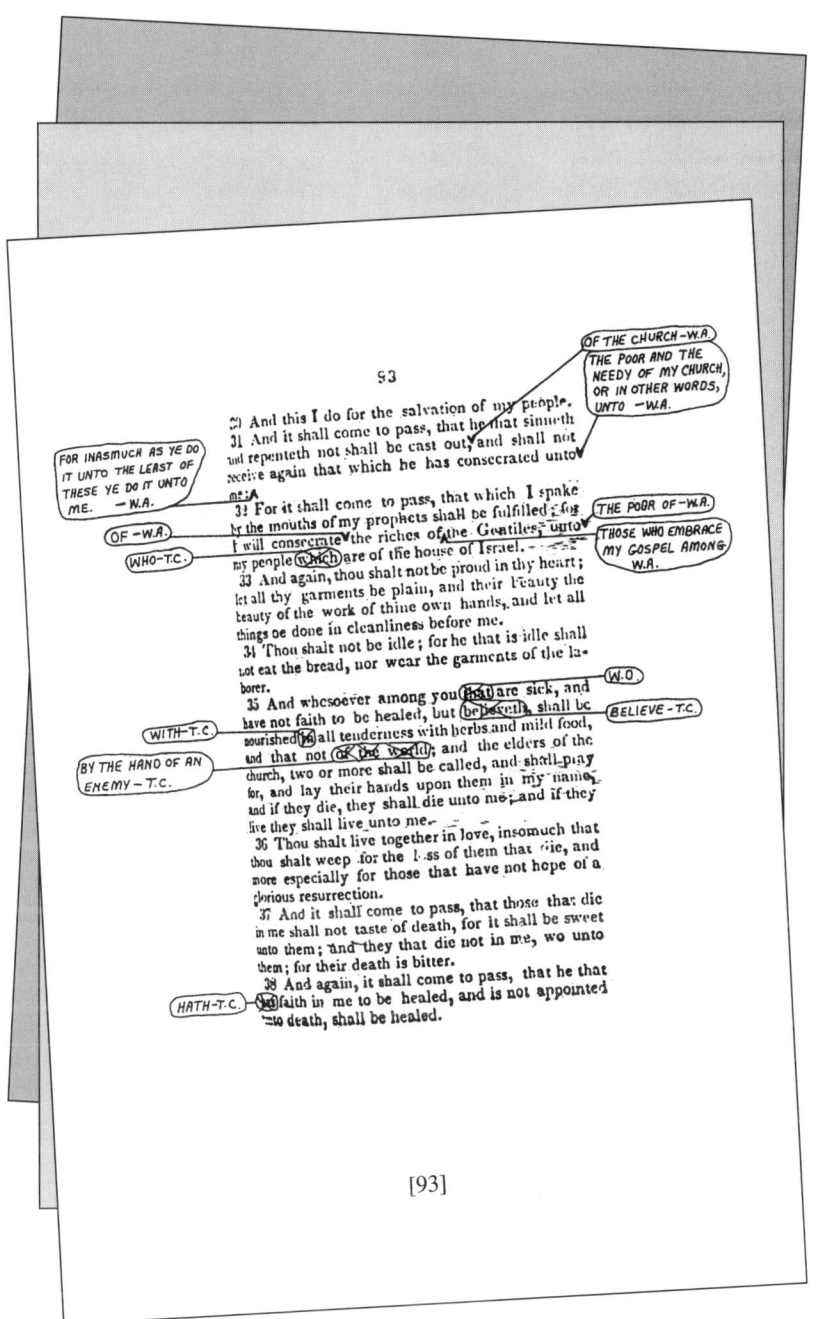

[93]

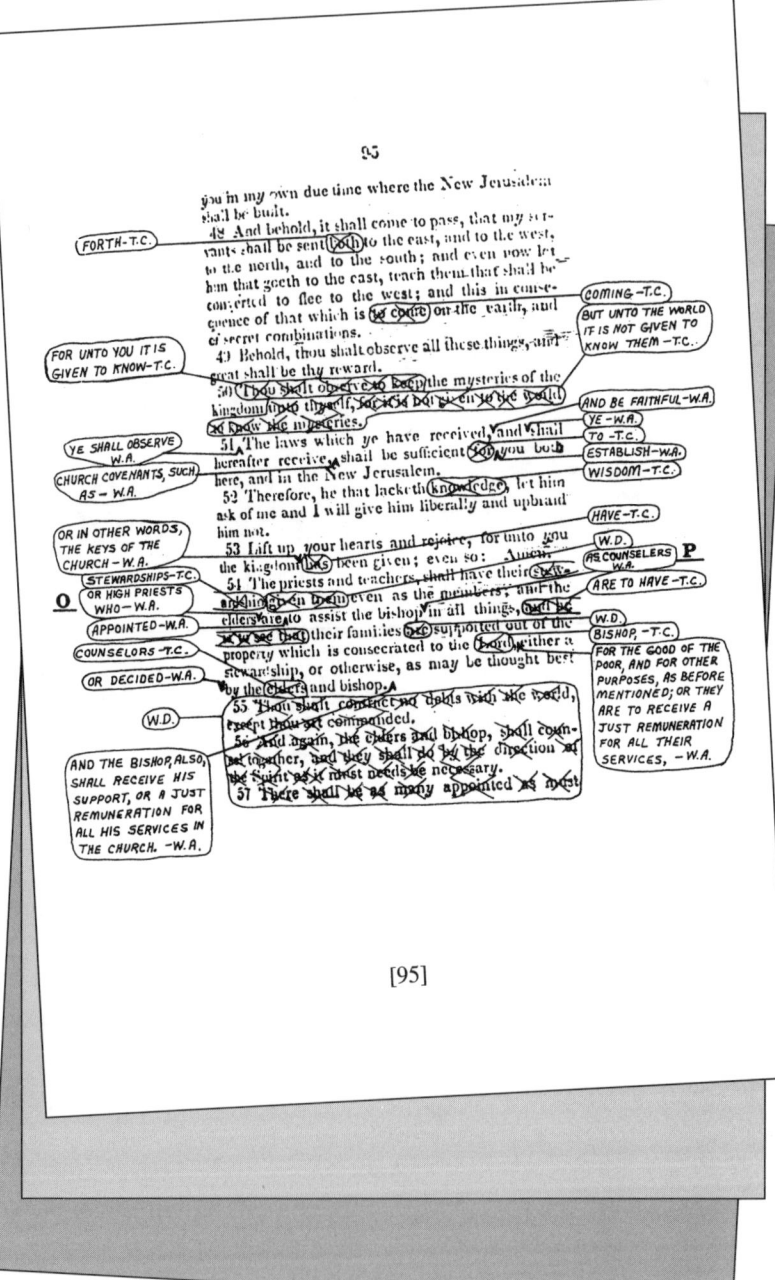

The Mormon Bondage to Changing Revelation

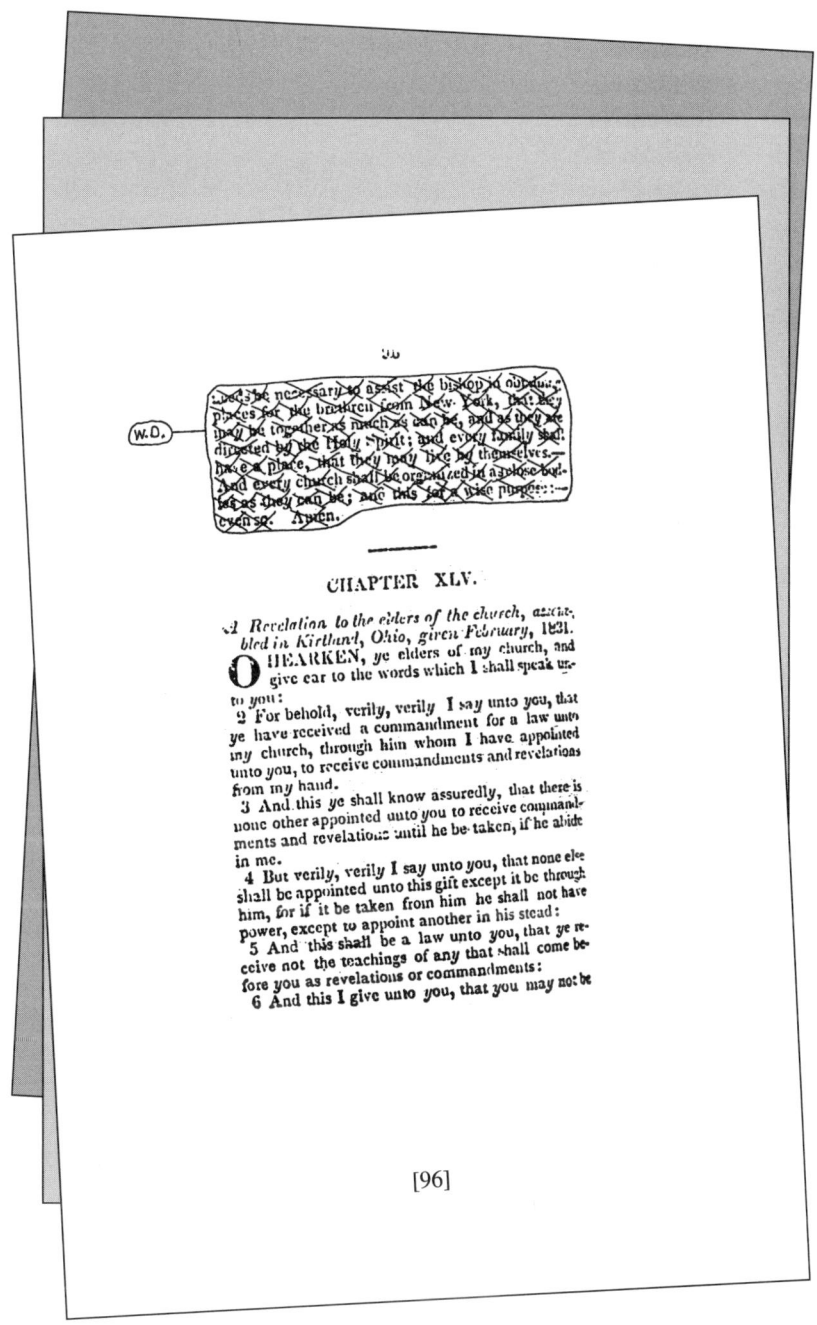

be it necessary to assist the bishop in obtaining places for the brethren from New York, that they shall be together as much as can be, and as they are directed by the Holy Spirit; and every family shall have a place, that they may live by themselves.—And every church shall be organized in as close bodies as they can be; and this for a wise purpose: even so. Amen.

CHAPTER XLV.

A Revelation to the elders of the church, assembled in Kirtland, Ohio, given February, 1831.

O HEARKEN, ye elders of my church, and give ear to the words which I shall speak unto you;

2 For behold, verily, verily I say unto you, that ye have received a commandment for a law unto my church, through him whom I have appointed unto you, to receive commandments and revelations from my hand.

3 And this ye shall know assuredly, that there is none other appointed unto you to receive commandments and revelations until he be taken, if he abide in me.

4 But verily, verily I say unto you, that none else shall be appointed unto this gift except it be through him, for if it be taken from him he shall not have power, except to appoint another in his stead:

5 And this shall be a law unto you, that ye receive not the teachings of any that shall come before you as revelations or commandments:

6 And this I give unto you, that you may not be

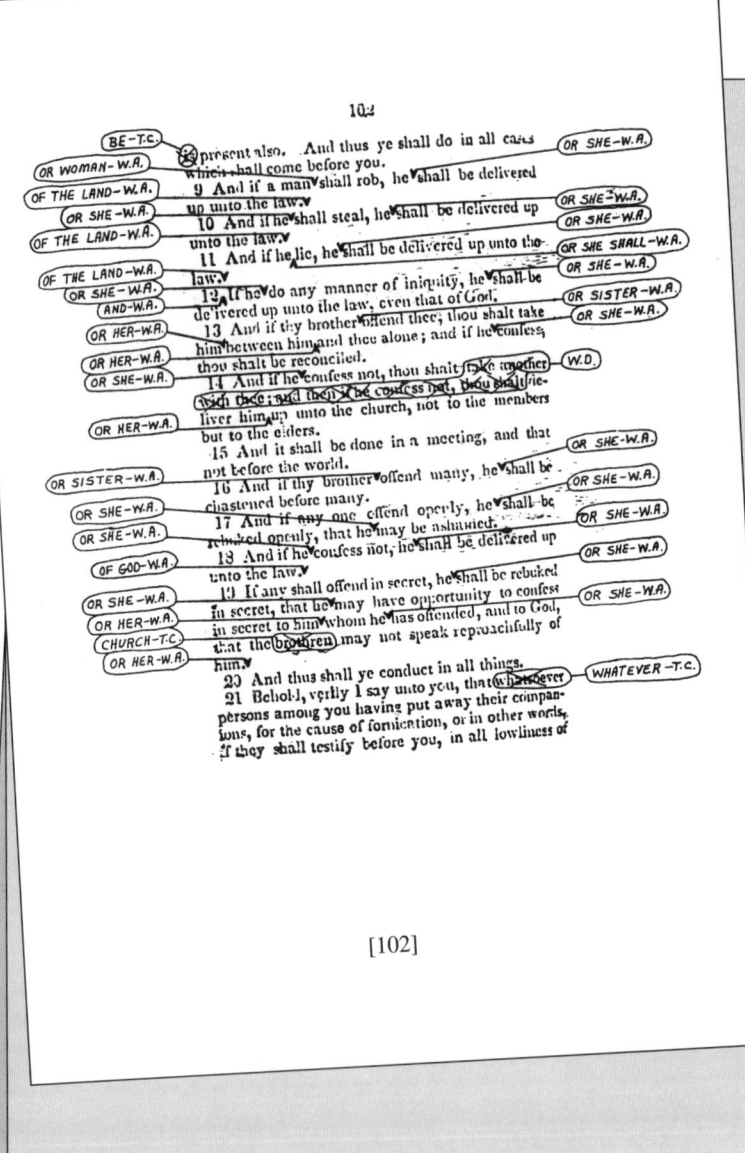

The comparison in these preceding photocopies will indicate the nature of other changed revelations. As mentioned previously, a thorough examination of all the textual variant readings in the Bible reveals not one doctrinal change. The nature of the variant readings is inconsequential: a missing phrase, an abbreviated word, or a fragmentary ending. But no respect is shown for the supposed unchanging Word of God with *The Doctrine and Covenants*. Rather, it is changed at will; if something proves inconvenient, just change it! The Bible has been preserved with great integrity over thousands of years, while *The Doctrine and Covenants* has been grossly revised in less than ten years.

Should we as thinking people not reject such changed and corrupt "revelations"? Certainly they were not from Almighty God. In the New Testament book of Revelation, God protected the "two witnesses," i.e., the Old and New Testament. If anyone threatened the "two witnesses" fire came out from their mouths and devoured them (Revelation 11:5).

The accusation that a revelation from God has been changed is a serious one. To prove that a revelation has been changed is to destroy the credibility of that work and those who changed it. If we could prove that the Bible has been changed by man, since God gave it, that proof would destroy its credibility. The Bible's accuracy has been established, while *The Book of Mormon* and *The Doctrine and Covenants* have been greatly changed, revised, and edited. The Bible has been proven to be a pure document, while the Mormon scriptures are corrupted. Other serious accusations will be made against *The Doctrine and Covenants*. Observe the following as examples of the types of problems found.

PROBLEMS WITH CONTENT IN *THE DOCTRINE AND COVENANTS*

The Word of Wisdom

No Coffee or Tea

The eighty-ninth section of *The Doctrine and Covenants* is commonly referred to as "The Word of Wisdom." The teaching that prohibits drinking of coffee or tea comes from this section. In reality it forbids drinking alcohol or *hot drinks*, not just coffee or tea. For years LDS church members did not drink cola drinks as well.

This is a rather ridiculous little document. This is a little blunt, but strictly the fact of the matter. The Mormon church does not go by all of its teachings, only the parts of it that suit their fancy. If it condemns the use of all hot drinks, why is little said against hot chocolate by the church? In times past cola drinks were condemned, but this teaching has now been

CHRISTIANITY & MORMONISM

reversed. Could this possibly be because U & I Sugar, a Mormon-owned company, sells large quantities of sugar to the cola drink producers?[36]

Sacrament, Water, or Grape Juice?
In verse five of this same section we are told what elements are to be used to observe the sacraments (Lord's Supper).

> That inasmuch as any man drinketh wine or strong drink among you, behold it is not good, neither meet in the sight of your Father, only in assembling yourselves together to offer up your sacraments before him. And behold this should be wine, yea, pure wine of the grape of the vine, of your own make (DC 89:5-6).

In spite of this clear statement, the Mormon church uses water in the communion cup. Why observe one part of the section that teaches against hot drinks and not observe the other that teaches how communion is to be served?

The Bible and Jesus make it clear that communion is to be observed with "the fruit of the vine" (Luke 22:18). This has been the practice from the beginning of the church. It is another way in which the LDS church needs to turn to mainstream Christianity: Obey Jesus' teaching on His Supper.

Tobacco to Treat All Sick Cattle?
Here is some advice for veterinarians about how to treat sick cattle: "And again, tobacco is not for the body, neither for the belly, and is not good for man, but is an herb for bruises and all sick cattle, to be used with judgment and skill" (DC 89:8).

Admittedly tobacco is not good for people, smoked or chewed. But, is tobacco to be used on all sick cattle? If a dairyman finds his cow has mastitis, is the recommended dosage an injection of tobacco into the udder? If your calf has a case of scours, a tonic of tobacco ought to finish it off. Medically this document is a joke! It clearly states, "tobacco is to be used for *all* sick cattle...."

Do LDS athletic trainers use tobacco for treating bruises? Why not, they have good "scriptural" basis for the practice. Or is this antiquated nonsense? Is it not in fact another form of bondage?

To Eat or Not to Eat Meat, that is the Question
The advice on eating meat is confusing and contradictory. It is hard

---

[36]What may have been an apocryphal rumor was that the church was warned, "If you knock our product we will not buy your sugar."

to tell if we are to eat meat or be vegetarians. Probably the intent was to teach people to eat meat only if there were no vegetables. But who can say for sure?

> Yea, flesh also of beasts and of the fowls of the air, I, the Lord, have ordained for the use of man with Thanksgiving; nevertheless they are to be used sparingly; And it is pleasing unto me that they should not be used, only in times of winter, or of cold or famine.... And these hath God made for the use of man only in times of famine and excess of hunger (DC 89:12-15).

Does the LDS church believe that meat is to be eaten only when there is famine? The teaching is very clear. It is to be used only in the winter or in times of famine. Is this the teaching of the church today? Not so, McDonald's, Burger King, Sizzler, and all the rest do a thriving business year-around due to the patronage of church members. Mormon leaders have treated me to T-bone steaks and ate them with me—yes, in the summer.

Why should the church enforce one part and neglect the other clear teachings? The conclusion must be that they only obey the parts of their scripture that suit them. Should not these old, antiquated teachings be repudiated? Isn't a church that enforces one verse and neglects the next a system of spiritual bondage? It is time for their prophet to turn them to the truth!

Polytheism in *The Doctrine and Covenants*—How Many Gods?

The Book of Mormon is purely monotheistic; teaching there is only one God and Father. It is *The Doctrine and Covenants* that introduces the teaching of polytheism. In section 121 we read, "A time to come in the which nothing shall be withheld, whether there be one God or many gods, they shall be manifest" (DC 121:28). A few verses later in the same chapter there is a further hint of the new doctrine's introduction. "According to that which was ordained in the midst of the Council of the Eternal God of all other gods before the world was, that should be reserved unto the finishing and the end thereof, when every man shall enter into his eternal presence and into his immortal rest" (DC 121:32).

This is the beginning of polytheism in the LDS church. There will be a more complete discussion later under the heading of Mormon doctrines. Can the LDS church in truth be called a Christian church with their doctrine of many gods?

CHRISTIANITY & MORMONISM

Polygamy in *The Doctrine and Covenants*—How Many Wives?

The Book of Mormon takes a strong stand against polygamy:

> And now it came to pass that the people of Nephi, under the reign of the second king, began to grow hard in their hearts, and indulge themselves somewhat in wicked practices, such as like unto David of old desiring many wives and concubines, and also Solomon, his son (Jacob 1:15).

> Behold, David and Solomon truly had many wives and concubines, which thing was abominable before me, saith the Lord.... Wherefore, I the Lord God will not suffer that this people shall do like unto them of old. Wherefore my brethren, hear me, and hearken to the word of the Lord: For there shall not any man among you have save it be one wife, and concubines he shall have none; For I, the Lord God, delight in the chastity of women. And whoredoms are an abomination before me; thus saith the Lord of Hosts (Jacob 2:24-28).

It is also *The Doctrine and Covenants* that introduces polygamy. It survives even today in Utah and other mountain states. Those living in Utah today have opportunity to meet polygamists. While living in Utah, I knew several. The main church does not sanction polygamy, but these people call themselves "fundamentalists."[37]

Section 132 of *The Doctrine and Covenants* deals extensively with this matter. Just as *The Book of Mormon* is very plain that polygamy is a grievous sin, *The Doctrine and Covenants* takes the opposite side, insisting that it is the only means of justification and attaining the "celestial glory." It even suggests that those who reject polygamy will be damned eternally.

> Verily, thus saith the Lord unto you my servant Joseph, that inasmuch as you have inquired of my hand to know and understand wherein I, the Lord, justified my servants Abraham, Isaac, and Jacob, as also Moses, David and Solomon, my servants, as touching the principle and doctrine of their having many wives and concubines.... Therefore, prepare thy heart to receive and obey the instructions which I am about to give unto you; for all

---

[37] Fundamentalists are those seeking to return to the fundamental teachings of the church, their scriptures.

those who have this law revealed unto them must obey the same. For behold, I reveal unto you a new and an everlasting covenant; and if ye abide not that covenant, then are ye damned; for no one can reject this covenant and be permitted to enter into my glory (DC 132:1; 3-4).

So polygamy is introduced as "a new and *everlasting* covenant" that must be obeyed by *all* that have it revealed to them. If they refuse to obey it they are to be damned. If this is the truth, what justification can there be for the LDS church submitting to the United States government and discontinuing the practice of polygamy? The words of Peter in Acts 5:29 ring clear, "We must obey God rather than men!" when the Sanhedrin forbid them to preach the gospel.

Nevertheless, it is not an issue of what the LDS church does, for we have already learned that they feel little compulsion to do what their scriptures say if they do not like it. In fact, why not just take these things out and rewrite it like they want? Well, that would fly in the face of Section One that says God's laws are never changing. It also presents a problem when polygamy is said to be an everlasting covenant.

Let's read on.

> David also received many wives and concubines, and also Solomon and Moses my servants, as also many other of my servants, from the beginning of creation until this time; and in nothing did they sin save in those things which they received not of me. David's wives and concubines were given unto him of me, by the hand of Nathan, my servant, and others of the prophets who had the keys of this power; and in none of these things did he sin against me save in the case of Uriah and his wife; ... I am the Lord thy God, and I gave unto thee, my servant Joseph, an appointment and restore all things. Ask what ye will, and it shall be given unto you according to my word (132:38-40).

Although the section is wordy and it appears that Joseph Smith is trying to appease his wife, Emma, about this matter; the thread is clear. Joseph is instituting polygamy. It was understood this way by the Latter-day Saints of his day, and was practiced until the United States forced them to quit years later. For the church today to deny this fact is dishonest. What this section says is clear, and what Joseph Smith, Brigham Young, and a long succession of Mormons practiced is a matter of recorded history.

In the same section Joseph's purpose can be further seen.

> And again, as pertaining to the law of the priesthood—if any man espouse a virgin, and desire to espouse another, and the first give her consent, and if he espouses the second, and they are virgins, and have vowed to no other man, then is he justified; he cannot commit adultery for they are given unto him; for he cannot commit adultery with that that belongeth unto him and to no one else. And if he have ten virgins given unto him by this law, he cannot commit adultery, for they belong to him, and they are given unto him; therefore is he justified (132:61-62).

No doubt can be left as to Joseph Smith's intentions in this section. It is the institution of polygamy. Is this God's plan for man? Was God ever really pleased with polygamy? Check every case of polygamy in the Bible. In every case it produced heartache and trouble for those involved and the generations to follow.

Genesis says, "For this reason a man shall leave his father and his mother, and be joined to his wife; and they shall become one flesh" (Genesis 2:24). The text says, "wife" not "wives." God created only one wife for Adam, not many. This was His plan for mankind: one man and one woman, companions. Did God ever command polygamy, or did He only permit it? The evidence points to the latter.

The fruits of polygamy still plague our world. Abraham took a second "wife," Hagar, because Sarah had been barren. Hagar bore a son and then later Sarah did. Abraham became the father of two nations and they have fought ever since.

Solomon's wives turned his heart away from God. It is no surprise that the New Testament instructs church leaders to have only one wife.

> An overseer, then, must be above reproach, the husband of one wife, temperate, prudent, respectable, hospitable, able to teach.... Deacons must be husbands of only one wife, and good managers of their children and their own households (1 Timothy 3:2, 12).

> For this reason I left you in Crete, that you would set in order what remains and appoint elders in every city as I directed you, namely, if any man is above reproach, the husband of one wife, having children who believe, not accused of dissipation or rebellion (Titus 1:5-6).

So polygamy is condemned in both the New Testament and *The Book of Mormon* (Jacob 2:24-27); yet *The Doctrine and Covenants* endorsed and commanded it. Is God that confused about the matter? It is difficult to accept such contradictory "revelations" as having their origin in Jehovah God.

Polygamy has brought terrible sorrow to women. It is humiliating and dehumanizing to suppose that a Christian man should have a whole harem of women. Brigham Young confessed that he had so many concubines over the years that he could not remember the number. Whose wives were these one-night stands to become? Think how this would have degraded and violated the women and defrauded their future husbands. How could God's plan for marriage be fulfilled under such a system? The purpose of marriage was to provide help and companionship. It is difficult to accept such contradictory "revelations" as having their origin with God. The LDS prophet has a lot of work to do before they can claim they are a Christian religion. It is hard to imagine a more cruel bondage for women than what has been taught and practiced in the LDS church. Come, come you saints ... back to the freedom of Christ!

THE BONDAGE OF *THE PEARL OF GREAT PRICE*

The Pearl of Great Price is a small volume made up of three parts: the books of Moses, Abraham, and Joseph Smith. This volume presents the most damaging evidence against Joseph Smith. In this volume we have positive proof that Joseph Smith was not capable of translating any foreign document.

The Book of Abraham begins with a few comments in the heading above the text that says,

> A Translation of some ancient Records, that have fallen into our hands from the catacombs of Egypt–The writings of Abraham while he was in Egypt, called the Book of Abraham, written by his own hand, upon papyrus.[38]

This would be fantastic information, if it were true. Can you imagine having the very own handwriting of Father Abraham? It would be the only such instance of an original handwritten document of any Bible writer. We are immediately skeptical, since Abraham lived so long ago, and we do not have any other Bible author's original manuscript, called a "signature" copy.

Several things make one skeptical about the possibility for such a

---

[38]*The Pearl of Great Price*, Preface to the Book of Abraham.

document to exist. First, papyrus is durable, but not durable enough that it could last for nearly four thousand years in an "alligator" skin, which is where the archaeologist who sold the manuscript to Joseph Smith is said to have found it. Yet this is the claim that Joseph made for the document.

When Joseph Smith "translated" the document into the Book of Abraham, he made a handwritten copy. He placed the Egyptian character in the left-hand column and then explained what it meant on the right side of the paper. For years this handwritten copy has been available by photo reprint, but the original Egyptian papyrus was lost. The great Chicago fire of 1871 supposedly destroyed it.

In 1967 the papyrus was found and presented to the LDS church by The Metropolitan Museum of Art in New York. Thinking that Joseph Smith couldn't possibly have made a mistake, or lied, the church allowed it to be photographed and published in *Dialogue Magazine*. The cat was out of the bag, for this photocopy was submitted to three different Egyptologists for them to independently translate. Each translated it into about seventy words, with almost identical meanings, and agreed that it was a quite common type of document that had to do with funerals in Egypt.

Joseph Smith came nowhere close to its real meaning, when he wrote his Book of Abraham. In fact, Joseph Smith made it into over four thousand words. This means some characters had to be translated into seventy-five to one hundred or more words, and this from just one Egyptian letter.[39]

We must conclude that Joseph Smith could not translate a foreign document. After many years we now have proof that he was a fraud. We do not have the gold plates. If there were gold plates, and Joseph Smith did seek to translate them, you can be sure he made a mess of their "translation."

The Book of Abraham is a partial basis for the doctrine that an African could not hold the priesthood in the LDS church. A white boy of twelve could hold the priesthood but a black man, of the finest character, could not.[40] In *The Pearl of Great Price*, Book of Abraham we read,

> Now, Pharaoh being of that lineage by which he could not have the right of Priesthood, notwithstanding the Pharaohs would fain claim it from Noah through Ham, therefore my father was led away by their idolatry (1:2).

---

[39] For a complete treatment of this subject, see Chapter 22 in Tanner, *Mormonism–Shadow or Reality?* (1972).

[40] A more complete study of this subject will be given in Chapter 7, "Supposed Cursed Races." Some southern slaveholders had taught that the Bible placed a curse on black people.

The Bible teaches that all people are equal in Christ regardless of the color of their skin or race. "There is neither Jew nor Greek, there is neither slave nor free man, there is neither male nor female; for you are all one in Christ Jesus. And if you belong to Christ, then you are Abraham's descendants, heirs according to promise" (Galatians 3:28-29).

SUMMARY

A close examination of *The Doctrine and Covenants* has shown many serious problems. While it makes a definite claim to being a direct revelation from God, never to pass away or be changed, we found that there are 2,786 changes, including more than twenty serious doctrinal changes. How could a thinking person accept it as Scripture? Probably it holds the record as the most changed book ever to have claimed to be Scripture.

There is such a vast difference between the integrity of the Bible and that of *The Doctrine and Covenants* that one is forced to conclude that it is not the work of God. Such ridiculous sections as the one on polygamy and the Word of Wisdom clearly prove that it is not a revelation from God.

The Pearl of Great Price supplies the most damaging evidence against Joseph Smith, the translator. His claim to have translated the Book of Abraham from some Egyptian papyrus has been completely proven false. One Egyptian scholar said if he had to grade his paper he would be forced to give him a zero, because he had not gotten even one thing right.

It is clear that the Bible is a book from God, divine in its origin, carefully preserved for us today. The Bible has passed every test. The critics have tried to destroy it but have not been able to find grounds to do so. The Bible has stood.

Yet Mormon scripture: *The Book of Mormon, Doctrine and Covenants,* and *Pearl of Great Price* have not stood the test. Investigation has destroyed them. People who know the truth about them should not cling to them. In the light of modern research and evidence it is likely that enlightened people, no longer in bondage, will eventually turn from them. When the system does fall it is probable that their scriptures will be a major factor in this fall.

The challenge is extended to our LDS friends, to your LDS church leaders, to your prophet: Stop attacking those who love you enough to tell you the truth. If in fact the church wants to be known as a mainstream Christian religion there is a lot of work to do. Why not begin by repudiating Joseph Smith as a prophet and discarding your bogus scripture?

CHRISTIANITY & MORMONISM

FROM BONDAGE TO FREEDOM

The Bars of Bondage
1. Based on your personal opinion, list five of the most significant changes to *The Doctrine and Covenants*.
2. Why do Mormon prophets need to change their scriptures? How does this affect the claim that their writings came from God?
3. Which books provide the most damaging evidence against Joseph Smith?
4. What is the most damaging evidence against the Book of Abraham (in *The Pearl of Great Price*)?

The Keys to Freedom
1. Research and compile a list of Mormons in your community. Add them to your prayer list! Invite a Mormon friend to your church activities and worship times.
2. Pray for teaching opportunities with a Mormon friend to point out how *The Book of Mormon* does not support their doctrine. Then offer to study the Bible and discover together the freedom in God's revealed Word.

CHAPTER FIVE
The Mormon Bondage to False Prophets

"For there shall arise false Christs, and false prophets, and shall shew great signs and wonders; insomuch that, if it were possible, they shall deceive the very elect" (Matthew 24:24, KJV).

JOSEPH SMITH—A FALSE PROPHET

Of the nearly sixty prophecies of the future that Joseph Smith put into print, none were fulfilled as prophesied, and only one partly came to pass. Put another way, Joseph was a prophet .00166 % of the time. Here are five examples of his false prophecies.

Brigham Young to Be President of the United States

"The Church and kingdom to which we belong will become the kingdom of our God and his Christ, and brother Brigham Young will become President of the United States…. You may think that I am joking; but I am perfectly willing that brother Long should write every word of it; for I can see it just as naturally as I see the earth and the productions thereof."[41]

Civil War Will Not Free Slaves

"Ham will continue to be the servant of servants, as the Lord has decreed, until the curse is removed. Will the present struggle free the slaves? No."[42]

---

[41] Joseph Smith, *The Journal of Discourses*, vol. 5, p. 219.
[42] Ibid., vol. 10, p. 250.

Temple to Be Built in Independence, Missouri

"The day is near when a Temple shall be reared in the Center Stake of Zion, and the Lord has said his glory shall rest on that House in this generation, that is in the generation in which the revelation was given, which is upwards of thirty years ago."[43]

"A revelation of Jesus Christ unto his servant Joseph Smith... Verily this is the word of the Lord, that the city New Jerusalem shall be built by the gathering of the saints, beginning at this place, even the place of the temple, which temple shall be reared in this generation. For verily this generation shall not all pass away until an house shall be built unto the Lord" (DC 84:1,4). The promised temple has not yet been built.

Joseph Smith Will Live till Christ Returns

"Among the number, my father presented himself, but before I washed his feet, I asked of him a father's blessing, which he granted by laying his hands upon my head, in the name of Jesus Christ, and declaring that I should continue in the Priest's office until Christ comes."[44]

Jesus Would Return in Fifty-Six Years

"President Smith then stated that the meeting had been called, because God had commanded it; and it was made known to him by vision and by the Holy Spirit ... the coming of the Lord, which was nigh—even fifty-six years should wind up the scene."[45]

Other False Prophecies

Space does not permit an examination of all of Joseph's prophecies. However, we could mention Joseph Smith's teaching that the inhabitants of the Moon dressed like Quakers and lived to be 1,000 years old. Or his prophecy of the Civil War: He got it partly right, but mostly wrong as he predicted that the Civil War would become a worldwide war and usher in the return of Christ. On several occasions he predicted certain people would become famous and their names would remain household names forever, which never occurred.

Biblical prophets were 100% correct 100% of the time. If a person

---

[43] Ibid., p. 344.
[44] Joseph Smith, *History of the Church*, vol. 1, p. 323.
[45] Joseph Smith, *History of the Church*, vol. 2, p. 182.

missed one prediction, he was a false prophet. In the light of the Bible's teaching about the coming of many false prophets, we have been fairly warned not to follow the false prophet Joseph Smith.

A Comparison of Bible Prophecies with Those in *The Book of Mormon*

The text of the Bible contains many hundreds, possibly even thousands, of prophecies. These prophecies are found from Genesis to Revelation. There are over 330 prophecies about Christ found in the Old Testament. These prophecies about Christ have been proven to be genuine predictive prophecy, since we have the Dead Sea Scrolls that predate Christ's birth.

Examples from the Bible

"Therefore the LORD Himself will give you a sign: Behold a virgin will be with child and bear a son, and she will call His name Immanuel" (Isaiah 7:14).

> For a child will be born to us, a son will be given to us;
> And the government will rest on His shoulders;
> And His name will be called Wonderful Counselor, Mighty God,
> Eternal Father, Prince of Peace.
> There will be no end to the increase of His government or of
>   peace,
> On the throne of David and over his kingdom,
> To establish it and to uphold it with justice and righteousness
> From then on and forevermore.
> The zeal of the LORD of hosts will accomplish this (Isaiah 9:6-7).

Isaiah gives quite a detailed prophecy about Christ. This prophecy says,

> He was despised and forsaken of men,
> A man of sorrows and acquainted with grief;
> And like one from whom men hide their face
> He was despised, and we did not esteem Him.
> Surely our griefs He Himself bore,
> And our sorrows He carried;
> Yet we ourselves esteemed Him stricken,
> Smitten of God, and afflicted.
> But He was pierced through for our transgressions,
> He was crushed for our iniquities;

> The chastening for our well-being fell upon Him,
> And by His scourging we are healed.
> All of us like sheep have gone astray,
> Each of us has turned to his own way;
> But the LORD has caused the iniquity of us all
> To fall on Him (Isaiah 53:3-6).

There is something that can be observed about these Messianic prophecies. They are not clear enough that a person could have fulfilled them intentionally at a later date. Rather, they speak in guarded terms, in somewhat symbolic language. After looking back at them, when the prophecy has been fulfilled, it is very clear that they were actual prophecies and that these prophecies were fulfilled. Yet, there is always a certain ambiguity about Old Testament prophecy that leaves it rather obscure. The prophetic writer himself often did not understand what he was speaking about until after the event had been fulfilled. This is a rule that is true of all Old Testament prophecies. Were they prophecies? Absolutely. Were they given years in advance? Certainly. They range from 400 to 4,000 years before Christ!

Is prophecy similar in *The Book of Mormon*? No! The prophecies in *The Book of Mormon* are so fantastic and clear. But here is where the problem lies. They tell too much. They say too much. For example, Jacob 6:6-9 says,

> Yea, today, if ye will hear his voice, harden not your hearts; for why will ye die? For behold, after ye have been nourished by the good word of God all the day long, will ye bring forth evil fruit, that ye must be hewn down and cast into the fire? Behold, will ye reject these words? Will ye reject the words of the prophets; and will ye reject all the words which have been spoken concerning Christ, after so many have spoken concerning Him; and deny the good word of Christ, and the power of God, and the gift of the Holy Ghost, and quench the Holy Spirit, and make a mock of the great plan of redemption, which hath been laid for you? Know ye not that if ye will do these things, that the power of the redemption and the resurrection, which is in Christ, will bring you to stand with shame and awful guilt before the bar of God?

This particular prophecy was given between thirty and fifty years before the time of Christ. Isn't it remarkable that many of the main details of the life of Christ, including His name, His resurrection, the Holy Spirit, and redemption are mentioned in this one, brief passage? It leads one to

The Mormon Bondage to False Prophets

believe, in comparing it with the Bible, that this was a prophecy written after the event, not before, as is claimed. It is very easy to "prophesy" *after* the fact. Only God knows the future.

Whenever a prophecy is too detailed, names are given and all the details about the life of the person and events to come are given, then it is wise to be suspicious of that prophecy. This elaborate and detailed type of prophecy is given throughout *The Book of Mormon*. Such things as "baptism and the remission of sins" are often spoken of as being preached in the days of Christ. This is compelling textual evidence showing that *The Book of Mormon* really is not a book of prophecy at all as is claimed. It is "prophecy" written after the event, often anachronistically by hindsight, not foresight.

These prophecies also bear too much resemblance to the terminology and language of the King James Version. We thus are able to trace them to their real source, which was in fact a direct quotation from the King James Version of the Bible. They were inserted into *The Book of Mormon* framework to simulate prophecy.

If *The Book of Mormon* is true, then certainly the words of Ephesians 3:8-10 are not true:

> To me, the very least of all saints, this grace was given, to preach to the Gentiles the unfathomable riches of Christ, and to bring to light what is the administration of the mystery which for ages has been hidden in God who created all things; so that the manifold wisdom of God might now be made known through the church to the rulers and the authorities in the heavenly places.

If *The Book of Mormon* is true, then the Bible is not true, because the Bible makes it very clear that these mysteries had been hidden in ages past. The ancients would not have had such details until Christ came.

EIGHT BIBLE PASSAGES ON TRUE OR FALSE PROPHETS

The claim that is made for Joseph Smith is that he is a prophet from God. It is an easy matter to make such a claim; it is harder to substantiate that claim with the Scriptures. Does Joseph Smith bear the marks or signs of a true prophet of God? Does he measure up to the Biblical qualifications for what a prophet should be? Does the Bible teach that there are to be prophets today? Let's give our attention to these questions.

If you were to take a tour of the beautiful, new Visitors Information Center at Temple Square in Salt Lake City, Utah, as a part of that tour you would be told about all the great prophets of old. Such men as Enoch,

Noah, Abraham, Moses, and Isaiah would likely be mentioned.[46]

This is done in the setting of the most lavish surroundings of fine architecture and beautiful paintings. An articulate, well-educated, and well-dressed guide will lead the visitor. He or she will point out that in times past God raised up John the Baptist, then Paul, and each because of the great need. Later in history when there was a great need, men like Martin Luther, John Wesley, and Calvin were raised up. After one has gotten in the habit of saying "yes, yes, yes," it is affirmed that in just such a way God raised up Joseph Smith, Jr., to bring the people back to God. In the surroundings of the expensive Visitors Information Center and with a polished guide who can make Mormonism sound so wonderful, many people are baptized into the Mormon church before they continue their journey from Salt Lake City. One must give them credit for doing a superb job of selling their religion. Yet, what does the Bible really say about this matter of modern-day prophets?

Deuteronomy 13

Moses answers the first question, "Do signs and wonders prove that a prophet is of God?" The answer is "No." Even if a person can work notable signs and wonders, yet if he instructs us to go contrary to the instructions we already have from Jehovah God, we are *not* to follow that prophet. The devil, too, can work notable miracles.

> "If a prophet or a dreamer of dreams arises among you and gives you a sign or a wonder, and the sign or the wonder comes true, concerning which he spoke to you, saying, 'Let us go after other gods (whom you have not known) and let us serve them,' you shall not listen to the words of that prophet or that dreamer of dreams; for the LORD your God is testing you to find out if you love the LORD your God with all your heart and with all your soul. You shall follow the LORD your God and fear Him; and you shall keep His commandments, listen to His voice, serve Him, and cling to Him. But that prophet or that dreamer of dreams shall be put to death, because he has counseled rebellion against the LORD your God who brought you from the land of Egypt and redeemed you from the house of slavery, to seduce you from the way in which the LORD your God commanded you to walk. So you shall purge the evil from among you" (Deuteronomy 13:1-5).

---

[46] The tour content is changed from time to time. I am describing what the tour was during the 1970s and early 1980s.

The instruction is quite clear. Miracles, signs, or dreams are not enough to prove that one is a prophet. If the prophet does not teach and keep the commandments that have *already* been given by God, then he is to be rejected. Even if the prophet can predict the future, he is not to be received.

Today, someone who seems to be able to work some sign or wonder has often led people to false teaching. If a supposed prophet can predict the future with some sort of accuracy, or "speak in tongues," then people are inclined to listen to whatever he or she has to say as the gospel truth.

In establishing a rule to deal with supposed prophets, we should first ask, "Does the prophet follow the proven commands of God?" If he does not, then he is to be rejected as a prophet.

Zechariah 12 & 13

A second passage of Scripture is even more forceful and comes from the Prophet Zechariah. In order to understand this passage it is helpful to read what comes before and after before reading the text itself. In the twelfth chapter we have what are recognized as definite predictions about Jesus Christ.

> I will pour out on the house of David and on the inhabitants of Jerusalem, the Spirit of grace and of supplication, so that they will look on Me whom they have pierced; and they will mourn for Him, as one mourns for an only son, and they will weep bitterly over Him like the bitter weeping over a firstborn (Zechariah 12:10).

In the light of the context of the twelfth and thirteenth chapters, it is clear that this is talking about Jesus. The one who would be pierced was to be of the house of David. The event would take place in Jerusalem. They did not pierce Zechariah. The mourning was for an only Son. Without a doubt it is a prediction about Jesus Christ and His death since Jesus applied this context to Himself (Matthew 26:31). (Also worthy of note is that some modern translations capitalize the personal pronouns.)

In Zechariah 13 we have another prediction about Jesus, "Awake, O sword, against My Shepherd, And against the man, My Associate," Declares the LORD of hosts. "Strike the Shepherd that the sheep may be scattered; And I will turn My hand against the little ones" (Zechariah 13:7).

Christ Himself indicated that this passage was talking about His being taken away from among the apostles. There can be no doubt that Jesus Himself considered this a Messianic prophecy.

In the middle of such clear predictions we have another prophecy about Jesus Christ.

> "In that day a fountain will be opened for the house of David and for the inhabitants of Jerusalem, for sin and for impurity.
>
> "It will come about in that day," declares the LORD of hosts, "that I will cut off the names of the idols from the land, and they will no longer be remembered; and I will also remove the prophets and the unclean spirit from the land. And if anyone still prophesies, then his father and mother who gave birth to him will say to him, 'You shall not live, for you have spoken falsely in the name of the LORD'; and his father and mother who gave birth to him will pierce him through when he prophesies" (Zechariah 13:1-3).

This isn't one of the easiest passages of Scripture to understand. A further explanation might be helpful. A fountain or spring in Israel was a great blessing. For the most part the land is dry. Wells and springs have always been at a premium. So he speaks of Christ's coming as a fountain. It is a spiritual fountain. This fountain was to be of the house of David; we know that Jesus came from the house and lineage of David. This would happen in Jerusalem; Jesus was crucified just about 150-200 yards beyond the walls of Jerusalem. This fountain was to be for sin and uncleanness; Christ came to save His people from their sins; He washed our sins away. The conclusion is that this passage is talking about the day of Christ's life and sacrifice.

It says, "in that day... I will cause the prophets ... to pass out of the land." The question needs to be answered as to whether this was a twenty-four hour day or a longer period of time. It is clear from observing the period under discussion that the prophet Zechariah did not mean a literal twenty-four hour day but a period of time, probably the lifetime of Jesus and His apostles.

So with Christ's generation passing, we would expect that there should be no more prophets. A look at church history shows that when those that received the special gifts of the Holy Spirit passed off the scene and the Bible was completed, there were no more prophets, except false ones. This was what Zechariah predicted.

In the words of Zechariah, "if anyone still prophesies...." they speak "falsely in the name of the LORD." So when those last ones to whom were given special gifts by the apostles passed off the scene, there would be no more prophets.

Have we understood this passage correctly? If not, then who after the apostolic day were prophets? There have been none but false prophets. None came for centuries. Then comes Joseph Smith, must we not take an extra good look at him since there have been no others for almost 2,000 years? Let's not rest our case entirely on this passage, but see what other Scriptures have to say about prophets.

Matthew 7

Jesus had a lot to say about the matter of prophets. In our third passage, the Sermon on the Mount, He warned about false prophets coming and leading many astray.

> "Beware of the false prophets, who come to you in sheep's clothing, but inwardly are ravenous wolves. You will know them by their fruits.... Not everyone who says to Me, 'Lord, Lord,' will enter the kingdom of heaven, but he who does the will of My Father who is in heaven will enter. Many will say to Me on that day, 'Lord, Lord, did we not prophesy in Your name, and in Your name cast out demons, and in Your name perform many miracles?' And then I will declare to them, 'I never knew you; depart from Me, you who practice lawlessness.' Therefore everyone who hears these words of Mine and acts on them, may be compared to a wise man who built his house on the rock. And the rain fell, and the floods came, and the winds blew and slammed against that house; and yet it did not fall, for it had been founded on the rock. Everyone who hears these words of Mine and does not act on them, will be like a foolish man who built his house on the sand. The rain fell, and the floods came, and the winds blew and slammed against that house; and it fell— and great was its fall" (Matthew 7:15-27).

Jesus warns us that just because a person says that he is a prophet is not enough proof. We must observe his or her fruits. Of course the Mormon people point to the fruit of Joseph Smith's teachings and say that it is good. Yet, it is not enough that one has a few good works. One must do the will of the Father in heaven. Those who built on the sand heard the words of Jesus and did not do them. There are many instances in which Joseph Smith directly violated the very clear teachings of Jesus. (A later section will give more detail about how Joseph Smith departed from Jesus' teachings.)

At the present it is being stressed that Jesus warned that there would be false prophets. Jesus told us how we could determine who was a false prophet and who was not. Those who hear His words and do not do them definitely are false prophets. When one claims to have good fruit and yet does not obey the teachings of Jesus, his claim is false. Disobedience to Jesus is an open indication that one is not a prophet of God.

Matthew 24

Jesus again warns of false prophets in our fourth reference by saying, "For false Christs and false prophets will arise and will show great signs and wonders, so as to mislead, if possible, even the elect" (Matthew 24:24).

The question is, "Who have been the false prophets?" Jesus said they would come. Jesus certainly would not make an idle threat. Jesus warned that they would show great signs and wonders and deceive many people. We are not surprised when we see divergent movements, led by "prophets," each claiming to be from God, yet teaching contrary and conflicting doctrines. Jesus said it would be so. We certainly need to ask ourselves, "Is it possible that Jesus had Joseph Smith in mind?" We will want to examine the Bible's teaching to be sure that Joseph Smith has not led us away from the pure teachings of Jesus and His apostles.

Galatians 1

The Apostle Paul often warned about the danger of false prophets. Paul realized that the Devil was powerful and actively at work seeking to lead the people away from God. If it took religion to lead the people astray, then the Devil would raise up false prophets. We are not surprised, then, when Paul says in this fifth passage,

> I am amazed that you are so quickly deserting Him who called you by the grace of Christ, for a different gospel; which is really not another; only there are some who are disturbing you and want to distort the gospel of Christ. But even if we, or an angel from heaven, should preach to you a gospel contrary to what we have preached to you, he is to be accursed! As we have said before, so I say again now, if any man is preaching to you a gospel contrary to what you received, he is to be accursed! (Galatians 1:6-9).

Paul minces no words. The test of a preacher or a prophet is, Does he preach the same Biblical message? If he, even if an angel, comes with a different gospel, he is to be rejected. The test that needs to be applied to Joseph Smith is whether he proclaims the same gospel message. Does he teach the same doctrine about God, Christ, the Holy Spirit, the Lord's Supper, the Virgin Birth, revelation, and such matters? If he does not, we cannot accept him as a true prophet.

The burden of proof rests upon those who claim to have a modern-day prophet. They must show that they teach the same things Jesus and the apostles did. If it can be demonstrated that they proclaim a different gospel, then they must be rejected.

The Mormon Bondage to False Prophets

1 Timothy 4

Many Christians today believe that we are in the last days. We know that we live in the last dispensation of time and probably in the last days of that dispensation. We are warned by the Holy Spirit in our sixth passage to be extra careful in these last days. "But the Spirit explicitly says that in later times some will fall away from the faith, paying attention to deceitful spirits and doctrines of demons, by means of the hypocrisy of liars seared in their own conscience as with a branding iron...." (1 Timothy 4:1-2).

Since we are warned that many of these false teachers will come, then we should give special care not to be taken in by them. Every effort must be expended to examine the teachings of the Bible thoroughly and compare them carefully with anyone claiming that he is a prophet of God.

1 John 4

The Apostle John gives good advice about discerning who is of God and who is not of God. Often when we begin to question the claims of another religion, someone will say, "Judge not that you be not judged," or "I don't talk about politics or religion." Because of such poor reasoning we have error running rampant through our world. Would we use the same logic about dirty food, or drugs? In fact, we have an inspired apostle telling us in this seventh passage to examine closely anyone who claims to be a prophet.

> Beloved, do not believe every spirit, but test the spirits to see whether they are from God, because many false prophets have gone out into the world. By this you know the Spirit of God: every spirit that confesses that Jesus Christ has come in the flesh is from God; and every spirit that does not confess Jesus is not from God; this is the spirit of the antichrist, of which you have heard that it is coming, and now it is already in the world. You are from God, little children, and have overcome them; because greater is He who is in you than he who is in the world. They are from the world; therefore they speak as from the world, and the world listens to them. We are from God; he who knows God listens to us; he who is not from God does not listen to us. By this we know the spirit of truth and the spirit of error (1 John 4:1-6).

We have the command of the beloved Apostle John to examine those who claim to be prophets. It is not an un-Christian attitude that makes one do this, but rather obedience to apostolic instruction. Truth is not hurt by examination; it is helped by it.

The apostle explains that we must submit our lives to their teachings if we are to prove we are of God. John affirms that "we are of God" (1 John 4:4). This is speaking about "we apostles." He says that if we hear them, then we are of God. If we do not hear them we are not of God. We can tell the spirit of truth and the spirit of error by whether we hear them or not.

We must examine the teachings of the Latter-day Saints church by the teachings of Christ's apostles. If they measure up, fine; if they do not, we cannot accept their teachings.

Revelation 22

One last Scripture comes from the very last few verses of the Bible. Most Latter-day Saints have been taught that this verse of Scripture only applies to the book of Revelation. If any holds this view, they should think about these questions. If it is wrong to add to the book of Revelation, would it be any safer to do so with Romans? If it is wrong to take away from the book of Revelation would it be any better to do so with Matthew? Of course not! Therefore the truth expressed must apply to the whole Bible.

> I testify to everyone who hears the words of the prophecy of this book: if anyone adds to them, God will add to him the plagues which are written in this book; and if anyone takes away from the words of the book of this prophecy, God will take away his part from the tree of life and from the holy city, which are written in this book (Revelation 22:18-19).

What a solemn warning! It stands as a sentinel at the very close of the Scriptures, reminding us that we are to hear and obey its words. We are to be careful to protect and uphold its teachings, to observe and preserve them.

Moses came as a lawgiver from God. Exodus and Deuteronomy give the laws that were given by God through him. All the prophets in subsequent generations, until the time of Christ, turned people back to Moses. Not one new doctrine was ever added to the teachings of Moses. Why? Because *God* gave the laws and commands. It only stands to reason that such laws should be preserved and observed. So the later prophets did not introduce new teachings. Some of what they said was new, since they were predictions of the future, but not even one change of doctrine came through the later prophets.

So it was with Jesus Christ. He came as the Divine lawgiver. He set up His church and instituted its laws and rules that were for all time. If anyone claims to be a prophet from God, he must only point people back to the lawgiver, Jesus. When one does any more or less than that, he has

The Mormon Bondage to False Prophets

proven beyond a shadow of a doubt that he is a false prophet.

SUMMARY

Since the Bible teaches that after Jesus' and His apostles' day there would be no more prophets, except false prophets, we cannot accept Joseph Smith as a true prophet of God. Since the Bible warns us over and over again to not accept anyone who teaches a different doctrine, we must reject Joseph Smith. Since he introduced many new doctrines, changed existing doctrine, and contradicted the clear teachings of Jesus and His apostles, we must not consider or accept him as a prophet. (Later in the book we will discuss the many doctrinal changes brought by Joseph Smith.)

FROM BONDAGE TO FREEDOM

The Bars of Bondage
1. Discuss what it means to Mormonism if Joseph Smith is not God's prophet. How does this relate to the foundation of the LDS church?
2. Name two of your favorite false prophecies made by Joseph Smith.
3. Which Old Testament passage about prophecy is the most damaging to the Mormon belief that Joseph Smith was a prophet of God?
4. Which New Testament passage has the sharpest warning to modern would-be "prophets"?
5. Summarize the contents of this chapter in one paragraph.

The Keys to Freedom
1. Add the summary of this chapter that you wrote for #5 above to your notebook. If you have not already, designate one section of the notebook for other chapter summaries from this book.
2. Search the Internet and other resources for mission organizations actively working with Mormons. Share the information with others in your group or church. Pray about how you can help them minister.

CHAPTER SIX
The Mormon Bondage to Fourteen False Doctrines, Part One

"But an hour is coming, and now is, when the true worshipers will worship the Father in spirit and truth; for such people the Father seeks to be His worshipers" (John 4:23).

Often today people wonder why religious people are so concerned about the teachings of the church. In our permissive, politically correct society, where almost anything goes except intolerance, the attitude is, why be concerned about what the church teaches? Should not Christians just love each other and do as they please? What difference does it make what we believe as long as we are sincere?—*It makes a lot of difference!*

Why should we be concerned? First, pure doctrine is as important as pure food, water, or medicine. When we do not have pure food we have sick people. When we do not have pure doctrine we have hurt people. People can become emotionally and spiritually sick because of false teaching. Error always hurts people. False teaching will ultimately hurt those who hold those untruths. The same is true with ignorance. Besides, we should want to know what is right, simply because it is right. Jesus said, "… and you will know the truth, and the truth will make you free" (John 8:32).

One Mormon leader excused the many theological and doctrinal problems in the Mormon church by saying, "Every church has its doctrinal problems and I'm not surprised that we do, too." This is a real "cop out," to use a modern expression. Can we just shrug our shoulders and say, "Everyone else has problems so I might as well have some too"? It would be as reasonable to say, "Since one-third of the earth is hungry, I won't feed my children either." Or, "Many people are dirty so I'll not take a bath either." "The rest of the world has inflation, so America might as well have it, too." This is the very attitude that brings decay in governments and churches. Let us therefore compare fourteen important doctrinal departures from the Bible that are taught by the Mormon church. We will cover the first seven of these false doctrines in this chapter. An honest review of these Biblical departures would be a good beginning point to turn their church to mainstream Christianity.

THE DOCTRINE ABOUT GOD

If there is a false doctrine about God we are in trouble from the start. Just as a house that does not have a good foundation cannot be sound no matter how many stories one might add, so a religion that has a false doctrine about God can never be sound. We have already hinted at this in the previous chapter.

What is the LDS doctrine of God? It can be summed up in a little poem of unknown origin.

> As man now is, God once was;
> As God now is, man may be.
> A son of God, like God to be
> Would not be robbing deity.[47]

To the Christian, and even to some Mormon folk, this statement sounds repugnant, yet it is an actual statement of LDS church doctrine. It is often quoted by Mormon church leaders and is their current doctrinal position. This statement is normally phrased: "As man now is, God once was; as God now is, man may become." This is a part of the doctrine of "eternal progression." Briefly stated, man has lived before and is now what he is because of what he did in his previous existence. He will become in the next life what he has prepared himself to become by his preparation in this life. Man progresses until he reaches "Godhood."

God Himself once was a man, now is God; man will also have this opportunity. This doctrine is a doctrine of many gods. In short, Mormons

---

[47]Having heard the above poem quoted many times, and in an effort to substantiate it, I called the church offices and asked concerning its source. I was told that Lorenzo Snow, prophet and revelator of the Latter-day Saint church, had first put this doctrine in print in 1919, in the June issue of the Improvement Era. I was told that Brigham Young stated the same doctrine at Joseph Smith's funeral. It is generally conceded that these "truths" are in *The Doctrine and Covenants*, Section 121, verses 28 and 32. During this telephone conversation, the authorities at the LDS church office readily agreed that this is a fair statement of their position and an often-quoted poem.

are not monotheistic, but polytheistic. They believe in many galaxies over which elevated men now rule. This doctrine conceives of God as having body, parts, and passions.

Brigham Young, a Mormon prophet, revelator, and seer, said of Adam: "He is our Father and our God, and the only God with whom we have to do."[48]

Another oft-quoted statement, attributed to Joseph Smith:

> God himself was once as we are now, and is an exalted man ... if you were to see him today, you would see him like yourselves, in all the person, image and very form of man, and you have got to learn how to be Gods yourselves ... the same as all Gods have done before you.[49]

And again:

> First, God himself, who sits enthroned in yonder heavens, is a man like unto one of yourselves, that is the great secret ... God himself; the Father of us all dwelt on an earth the same as Jesus Christ himself did.... You have got to learn how to be gods yourselves.... No man can learn you more than what I have told you.[50]

Is this a true Christian doctrine? Is this taught in the Bible? Did Christ teach this doctrine? Here are a few verses of the Bible that should make the answer clear.

> "You are My witnesses," declares the LORD,
> "And My servant whom I have chosen,
> So that you may know and believe Me
> And understand that I am He.
> Before Me there was no God formed,
> And there will be none after Me" (Isaiah 43:10).

The Bible teaching is in direct contradiction to LDS church teaching. There is a direct contradiction between Isaiah and Lorenzo Snow, Joseph

---

[48]G.D. Watt, ed., *Journal of Discourses*, by Brigham Young, 26 vols., (Liverpool: F.D. & S.W. Richards, 1854; reprint, Salt Lake City: Deseret News Publishing Co., 1966) 1:50.

[49]Franklin D. Richards and James A. Little, eds., *A Compendium of the Doctrine of the Gospel*, 2nd ed. (Salt Lake City: Deseret News Publishing Company, 1884), p. 238.

[50]Joseph Smith, *Times and Seasons*, vol. 5, pp. 613-614, quoted in Tanner, Mormonism–Shadow or Reality? (1964), p. 137.

CHRISTIANITY & MORMONISM

Smith, and Brigham Young. Further, Isaiah says, "Is there any God besides Me, Or is there any other Rock? I know of none" (Isaiah 44:8b). If God didn't know of any other God, our trio of prophets certainly should not have known of any. Isaiah makes the matter even more clear:

"I am the LORD, and there is no other;
Besides Me there is no God.
I will gird you, though you have not known Me;
That men may know from the rising to the setting of the sun
That there is no one besides Me.
I am the LORD, and there is no other...." (Isaiah 45:5-6).

Apparently God wanted men to know this fact clearly, for He had it recorded repeatedly. Probably the clearest of these passages is this one:

"Remember the former things long past,
For I am God, and there is no other;
I am God, and there is no one like Me,
Declaring the end from the beginning,
And from ancient times things which have not been done,
Saying, 'My purpose will be established,
And I will accomplish all My good pleasure.'" (Isaiah 46:9-10).

If, in truth, God does know the end from the beginning, then He would know for sure if there were any other gods.

Jesus only knew there to be one God. "And Jesus said to him, "Why do you call Me good? No one is good except God alone" (Mark 10:18). "This is eternal life, that they may know You, the only true God, and Jesus Christ whom You have sent" (John 17:3).

The Apostle Paul said, "Therefore concerning the eating of things sacrificed to idols, we know that there is no such thing as an idol in the world, and that there is no God but one" (1 Corinthians 8:4).

Mormon teaching says man can become God, and God once was a man. The Bible says there is but one God. There is none else, never has been, and never will be. If you can be polytheistic, then you can be a Mormon. If you accept this doctrine "As man now is, God once was; as God now is, man may become," you do not believe in the Christian God, the God of the Bible.

No more serious accusation could be made against a religious movement than that it did not believe in *one* Supreme Being, one God who rules everything throughout the entire universe. This is the whole basis of

Christianity. Almost all religious bodies claiming to be Christian, throughout the world, believe in one Supreme Being. The Mormons are the exception. This is one good, clear reason why it is not reasonable to accept the claims of the LDS church. If the church wants to be accepted as "Christian" this is a doctrine they need to correct. This is religious darkness and bondage.

THE DOCTRINE ABOUT JESUS CHRIST

According to universal Christian teaching, it is absolutely necessary that we know Jesus Christ to be saved. "And there is salvation in no one else; for there is no other name under heaven that has been given among men by which we must be saved" (Acts 4:12).

If a movement dishonors Jesus Christ, it has to be operating under a spirit other than the Holy Spirit. One of the things that can be said about several of the cults is that they seek to "humanize" Jesus, reducing Him to an ordinary man. This is the problem with the Jehovah's Witnesses. Since Mormons have the doctrine of eternal progression, it simply means that Jesus was a *created being*. He was once a man; but now has become God. He has gotten ahead of us in the eternal progression. Not only does the doctrine of eternal progression affect God; it also affects Jesus Christ.

The Bible clearly teaches that Jesus is God. This is the basis of the "Trinity" doctrine, that there are three Beings (God, Jesus, the Holy Spirit) that work together in unity. These Beings are eternal and one.

Looking more closely at the Mormon doctrine, we discover it teaches that God created a large group of spirits at the very beginning of the earth. Among the spirits were the Devil and Jesus Christ. All men were spirit beings, gathered around God. God asked the spirits how He could safely usher them all into heaven. The Devil spoke up and said, "If I were given authority over one-third of them I would force them to serve you God." Jesus said, "Oh, no, Father. I would teach them to love and worship you." At this point Jesus began to get ahead of the other spirits in the eternal progression.

There are several serious doctrinal problems here. Can we believe, and does the Bible teach, that Jesus is the same age spiritually as all other men? Does the Bible teach that Jesus and the Devil are really brothers? Did Jesus become God just because He was a little smarter than the Devil? Is it true that Jesus is a created god? What does the Bible say?

First, the Bible says that Jesus created all things. "In the beginning was the Word, and the Word was with God, and the Word was God. He was in the beginning with God. All things came into being through Him, and apart from Him nothing came into being that has come into being" (John 1:1-3). The Bible teaches that Jesus was God from the very beginning, not that He became God later. In fact, it says that Jesus created everything that has been made. In Colossians it says,

> For by Him all things were created, both in the heavens and on earth, visible and invisible, whether thrones or dominions or rulers or authorities—all things have been created through Him and for Him. He is before all things, and in Him all things hold together. He is also head of the body, the church; and He is the beginning, the firstborn from the dead, so that He Himself will come to have first place in everything (Colossians 1:16-18).

On the basis of such Scripture, is it possible to believe a story that says God created a mass of spirits and Jesus was among them? It is clearly stated that Jesus created all things that are in heaven and earth. It also makes clear that Jesus was before all things. Some have argued that since Colossians 1:15 says Jesus was the firstborn of all creation, this meant that Jesus was a created being. This is not the meaning. The passage says Christ created all things.

Here again not only do they have an incorrect view of God, but also they seek to anthropomorphize Jesus (that is, limiting God to being just a man). When a religious body has done such, they have violated the spirit and words of John: "so that all will honor the Son even as they honor the Father. He who does not honor the Son does not honor the Father who sent Him" (John 5:23).

The church is built upon Jesus Christ as the Divine Son of God. Mormonism denies this basic doctrine and contradicts clear Bible teaching. The Mormon prophet must accept Christ's deity if he wants the LDS church to be a Christian religion, to turn his people from bondage to freedom in Christ.

THE DOCTRINE OF CHRIST'S VIRGIN BIRTH

The doctrine of eternal progression also complicates the virgin birth of Christ for the LDS church. Since the whole order of creation, for the Mormon, is based upon the act of procreation, they must somehow involve Christ in this process.

Their doctrine brings Jesus down to man's level. Brigham Young, the second president of the Mormon church said, "Now, remember from this time forth, and forever, That Jesus Christ was not begotten by the Holy Ghost."[51] Yet the Bible says, "Now in the sixth month the angel Gabriel

The Mormon Bondage to Fourteen False Doctrines, Part I

was sent from God to a city in Galilee called Nazareth, to a virgin engaged to a man whose name was Joseph, of the descendants of David; and the virgin's name was Mary" (Luke 1:26-27).

When the angel told Mary that she would carry a baby, she replied, "'How can this be, since I am a virgin?' The angel answered and said to her, 'The Holy Spirit will come upon you, and the power of the Most High will overshadow you; and for that reason the holy Child shall be called the Son of God.'" (Luke 1:34-35).

With the exception of the place of Christ's birth (Bethlehem), *The Book of Mormon* agrees with the Biblical account. "And behold, he shall be born of Mary, at Jerusalem which is the land of our forefathers, she being a virgin, a precious and chosen vessel, who shall be overshadowed and conceive by the power of the Holy Ghost, and bring forth a son, yea, even the Son of God" (Alma 7:10).

Yet Joseph Fielding Smith, the recent "prophet and revelator" of the Mormon church said,

> They tell us the *Book of Mormon* stated that Jesus was begotten of the Holy Ghost. I challenge that statement. *The Book of Mormon* teaches no such thing. Neither does the Bible. It is true that there is one passage that states so, but we must consider it in the light of other passages with which it is in conflict.[52]

The Mormon Apostle Orson Pratt said,

> The fleshly body of Jesus required a mother as well as a father. Therefore, the father and mother of Jesus, according to the flesh, must have been associated together in the capacity of husband and wife; hence the Virgin Mary must have been, for the time being, the lawful wife of God the Father; we must use the term lawful wife, because it would be blasphemous in the highest degree to say that He overshadowed her or begat a Savior unlawful.... He had a lawful right to overshadow the Virgin Mary in the capacity of a husband, and begat a son, although she was espoused to another; for the law which He gave to govern men and women was not intended to govern Himself, or to prescribe rules for His own conduct. It was also lawful in Him, after having dealt thus with Mary to give

---

[51] Young, *The Journal of Discourses*, 1:15.
[52] Joseph Fielding Smith, *Doctrines of Salvation*, 3 vols., comp. by Bruce B. McConkie (Salt Lake City: Bookcraft, 1956) 1:19.

her to Joseph her espoused husband. Whether God the Father gave Mary to Joseph her espoused husband, for time only or for time and eternity, we are not informed. Inasmuch as God was the first husband to her, it may be that He only gave her to be the wife of Joseph while in the mortal state, and that He intended after the resurrection to take her as His wife in eternity.[53]

How can we accept such teaching when we read in Matthew 1:24-25, "And Joseph awoke from his sleep and did as the angel of the Lord commanded him, and took Mary as his wife, but kept her a virgin until she gave birth to a Son; and he called His name Jesus"?

Yet, Brigham Young explained the birth of Christ as follows: "The birth of the Savior was as natural as are the birth of our children: It was the result of natural action. He partook of flesh and blood—was begotten of His Father, as we were of our fathers."[54]

It is quite evident that there is a drastic contradiction between what the Bible says and what the Mormon church teaches. We know that God is not a God of confusion, so we must conclude that the supposed prophets of the LDS church are not prophets at all, but rather are imposters.

In a sermon at the Tabernacle in Salt Lake City, on April 9, 1852, Brigham Young said,

> I have given you a few leading items upon this subject, but a great deal more remains to be told. Now remember from this time forth, and forever, that Jesus Christ was not begotten by the Holy Ghost. I will repeat a little anecdote. I was in conversation with a certain learned professor upon the subject, when I replied, to this idea—"If the Son was begotten by the Holy Ghost, it would be very dangerous to baptize and confirm females, and give the Holy Ghost to them, lest he should beget children, to be palmed upon the Elders by the people, bringing the Elders into great difficulties."[55]

Such teachings verge on blasphemy, if they are not actually such. Here is another reason for the modern LDS prophet to apologize to mainstream Christianity.

Some might wonder if the church today still holds such ideas. A

---

[53]Orson Pratt, *The Seer*, p. 158, quoted in Tanner, *Mormonism—Shadow or Reality?* (1972), p. 261.
[54]Young, *The Journal of Discourses*, 8:115.
[55]Ibid., 1:51.

quotation from a recent news article confirms this to be true.

> Outburst after outburst of delighted laughter filled the Tabernacle Saturday afternoon as the fourth session of the 143rd annual Conference of the Church of Jesus Christ of Latter-day Saints drew to a close.
>
> ### Apostle LeGrand Richards
> The speaker was Elder LeGrand Richards of the Council of Twelve Apostles, well known for his missionary activities. Describing an experience he once had in the mission field, Elder Richards told of speaking to a large gathering of clergymen.
>
> ### Addresses Gathering
> "I explained to them the difference between reformation and restoration," Elder Richards said. "Then, when I finished my remarks, one of them stood up and said, 'Mr. Richards, we've been told you believe God had a wife. Would you please explain this?'"
>
> "I think he thought he had me," said Elder Richards. The audience in the Tabernacle began to chuckle. "I retorted that I didn't see how God could have a Son if He didn't have a wife."
>
> ### Proper Answer?
> The Tabernacle audience's chuckle grew to a full roar of laughter as Elder Richards turned to President Harold B. Lee, seated near the podium, to ask if this was a proper answer.
>
> President Lee nodded.[56]

So, still today, the Mormon church persists in teaching that Jesus was not born of the virgin Mary, but that God came down and slept with her. It is sickening to think that God would come down and so encroach upon the rights of Joseph. Such teachings are outright blasphemy. According to Jesus, Joseph and Mary would have been living in adultery. Mary would have been the wife of God, who could visit her when He pleased. To teach this is paganism in the extreme. Even pagans have a higher concept of their gods than to suggest that their morals were lower than man's.

The very basis of Christianity is the virgin birth and the deity of Christ. To deny these two foundational doctrines leaves Jesus an ordinary man—in fact, an illegitimate son of God—born from an illicit relationship with

---

[56] "Apostle's Humor Draws Laughter," *The Salt Lake Tribune* (April 8, 1973).

CHRISTIANITY & MORMONISM

another man's espoused wife. Here again is not only a false doctrine, but also a disgustingly corrupt doctrine that belittles Jesus and His Father. Mr. president and prophet, if you want to be recognized as a Christian church, you must accept the virgin birth of Jesus.

THE DOCTRINE OF LORD'S SUPPER ELEMENTS

Christian baptism is one of the issues that LDS missionaries often raise. The Mormon teaching insists upon the strict adherence to the Bible teaching of baptism by total immersion in water for the remission of sins. They base their argument on the clear commands of Christ and His apostles as well as their repeated example. The missionaries are quick to point out such passages as Mark 1:9-10 and Matthew 28:19, and they are right. They are absolutely correct about the *mode* of baptism.

The question that comes to mind, though, is what about the Lord's Supper? Matthew says, "But I say to you, I will not drink of this fruit of the vine from now on until that day when I drink it new with you in My Father's kingdom"(Matthew 26:29). Here, when Jesus instituted the Lord's Supper, He used the fruit of the vine. The Apostle Paul, while teaching about the Lord's Supper in 1 Corinthians, said Jesus commanded us to observe this simple feast. The Mormons do not use the fruit of the vine, but use water in the communion cup. Is it consistent to insist on obedience in baptism and not on obedience in the Lord's Supper? Of course this puts the Mormons on the spot; how can they explain the need for following the example and command of Jesus in baptism and ignoring it in communion?

The Doctrine and Covenants says in the Word of Wisdom:

> That inasmuch as any man drinketh wine or strong drink among you, behold it is not good, neither meet in the sight of your Father, only in assembling yourselves together to offer up your sacraments before him. And, behold, this should be wine, yea, pure wine of the grape of the vine, of your own make (DC 89:5-6).

Here is another instance of the LDS church neither following the Bible nor their own scriptures. They are condemned out of their own mouths. It shows how totally inconsistent their teachings really are.

Many excuses have been given for this change of doctrine. It has been said that when the Mormons first came to Utah their enemies polluted their wine that was used for communion so as to make them afraid to use it. Some said they were afraid it was poisoned. That might have been a good excuse for a year or two, but grapes grow in Utah today, and it is possible to buy pure grape juice from many of their own stores.

One of Jesus' last wishes was that we do these simple things in His memory. To willingly violate His wish could seem to indicate a lack of concern for His will. Again, we find one of the very basic teachings of Jesus and the Bible violated. Can we believe that this is really the restored church? Is it not one of the most doctrinally corrupt churches of today? The president and prophet must examine church teaching on the Lord's Supper if they are to become truly a Christian church.

THE DOCTRINE OF THE HIGH PRIESTHOOD

In the Mormon church many can hold the office of "high priest." The basis of their theology of having thousands of high priests is baffling. In the Old Testament there was only one high priest at a time. Aaron was the first High Priest and his sons, after him. It would have been unthinkable for there to have been more than one. At the time of Christ there were two, but one was an impostor. Having two would be like having two presidents of the United States. There were many priests, but only one held the high priesthood at a time. Another did not take over until the previous high priest had died.

Today, in the church we read about in our Bible, we find a High Priest:

> Now the main point in what has been said is this: we have such a high priest, who has taken His seat at the right hand of the throne of the Majesty in the heavens, a minister in the sanctuary and in the true tabernacle, which the Lord pitched, not man (Hebrews 8:1-2).

Jesus is the High Priest of the church. To have another claim the office, whether by his own decision or to be given the office by another, is to usurp the position that is held today by Jesus Christ. Such high priests are impostors.

Every high priest was to offer sacrifices for the sins of the people. "For every high priest taken from among men is appointed on behalf of men in things pertaining to God, in order to offer both gifts and sacrifices for sins...." (Hebrews 5:1). The high priest's job was to offer sacrifices for sins. The question to be asked of the Mormon high priests is, "What sacrifices do they offer for sins?" The Bible says that every high priest is to offer sacrifices for sins. The Bible's statement is very clear and easily understood; that is, Jesus paid for *all* sins, He offered *the* sacrifice for our sins. What other sacrifice for sins is needed? What work is there for any other high priest to do, that has not already been done once for all?

Here is another serious theological problem. It is evident that the LDS church is teaching a doctrine contrary to the Bible. Quite apparently the church has taught thousands to usurp this office. Many men are claiming to hold an office that belongs only to Jesus Christ.

THE DOCTRINE OF BAPTISM FOR THE DEAD

In the days of Joseph Smith there were many live issues that were heatedly discussed in the churches. When sermons from this era are read, some of those issues arise. "Baptism for the dead" was one of these subjects, along with others, such as "preaching to the spirits in prison," and "how many heavens" there really were.

Since Joseph Smith was a prophet, and prophets have all the answers, he began to teach that a person could be baptized by proxy for someone that had already died. He based this teaching upon the *single* verse of Scripture in 1 Corinthians, "Otherwise, what will those do who are baptized for the dead? If the dead are not raised at all, why then are they baptized for them?" (1 Corinthians 15:29).

It would be incorrect to say that this Scripture was easy to understand. Many church leaders have offered their interpretations of it. The question needing to be asked is, does it teach that we can be baptized for dead people by proxy?

Examination shows that the text says, "*they* do," not "*we* do." If Paul had been practicing baptism for dead people, he would have said, "we," not "they." It is apparent then that Paul was not practicing it. However, the very people who taught that there was *no* resurrection were also teaching that someone who had died could be baptized by proxy. Or they were baptizing, but baptism only has meaning in the light of confession of sin and forgiveness, death and the resurrection. Paul's point was the foolishness of such a practice. "Why baptize if there is no resurrection, as baptism is a picture of death and resurrection?"

Another explanation could also be given. We are baptized because of death. If we didn't ever die, we would not need to be baptized at all. Baptism pictures not only a death, but also a resurrection. Since these folks didn't believe in the resurrection, Paul points out that people are really baptized because of death. If there is no resurrection from death, why be baptized?

One rule of interpretation of Scripture is that we cannot interpret a hazy passage of Scripture in such a way as to contradict a clear passage of Scripture. Such would be the case here, if we were to understand that

Paul is teaching that people who have died in sin can still be saved by a proxy baptism. This would contradict such passages as, "And inasmuch as it is appointed for men to die once and after this comes judgment, so Christ also, having been offered once to bear the sins of many, will appear a second time for salvation without reference to sin, to those who eagerly await Him" (Hebrews 9:27-28). Jesus clearly taught in the parable of the rich man and Lazarus that after death one's state was sealed.

> "Now there was a rich man, and he habitually dressed in purple and fine linen, joyously living in splendor every day. And a poor man named Lazarus was laid at his gate, covered with sores, and longing to be fed with the crumbs which were falling from the rich man's table; besides, even the dogs were coming and licking his sores. Now the poor man died and was carried away by the angels to Abraham's bosom; and the rich man also died and was buried. In Hades he lifted up his eyes, being in torment, and saw Abraham far away and Lazarus in his bosom. And he cried out and said, 'Father Abraham, have mercy on me, and send Lazarus so that he may dip the tip of his finger in water and cool off my tongue, for I am in agony in this flame.' But Abraham said, 'Child, remember that during your life you received your good things, and likewise Lazarus bad things; but now he is being comforted here, and you are in agony. And besides all this, between us and you there is a great chasm fixed, so that those who wish to come over from here to you will not be able, and that none may cross over from there to us.'" (Luke 16:19-26).

This would have been a wonderful time for Jesus to tell the world about the second chance, proxy baptism for the dead. But no, Jesus does not say a word. Why? It is apparent that after death comes the judgment.

The most crushing blow comes to this false doctrine from the Mormons' own scripture, *The Book of Mormon*. One of the reasons it is so difficult to believe Joseph Smith wrote *The Book of Mormon* is his apparent unfamiliarity with it. Joseph Smith's later revelations contradict his earlier ones, seeming to indicate he was not familiar with them. Here is a good example, for *The Book of Mormon* says,

> For behold, this life is the time for men to prepare to meet God; yea, behold the day of this life is the day for men to perform their labors. And now, as I said unto you before, as ye have had so many witnesses, therefore, I beseech of you that ye do not

CHRISTIANITY & MORMONISM

procrastinate the day of your repentance until the end; for after this day of life, which is given us to prepare for eternity, behold, if we do not improve our time while in this life, then cometh the night of darkness wherein there can be no labor performed. Ye cannot say, when ye are brought to that awful crisis, that I will repent, that I will return to my God. Nay, ye cannot say this; for that same spirit which doth possess your bodies at the time that ye go out of this life, that same spirit will have power to possess your body in that eternal world. For behold, if ye have procrastinated the day of your repentance even until death, behold, ye have become subjected to the spirit of the devil, and he doth seal you his; therefore, the Spirit of the Lord hath withdrawn from you and hath no place in you, and the devil hath all power over you; and this is the final state of the wicked (Alma 34:32-35).

So *The Book of Mormon* clears up the matter quite well for the Mormons. When a person dies outside of Jesus he is sealed to Satan for all eternity and that is the final state of the wicked.

This is another evidence that the LDS church neither abides by the Bible nor *The Book of Mormon*. According to the teaching of their own books, all the genealogy work that they do and their temple baptisms are a useless waste of time. It is not uncommon for Mormons to have been baptized thirty, forty, or even fifty times for their dead relatives. It is a shame that they have wasted so much time studying genealogies and getting wet for nothing. Perhaps it is because baptism for the dead is of no value that Paul warns about wasting time on endless genealogies. "But avoid foolish controversies and genealogies and strife and disputes about the Law, for they are unprofitable and worthless" (Titus 3:9).

Certainly Paul could not have made such a statement if baptism for the dead were valid. So again we have found that the Mormon church doctrine just does not measure up to the close examination that we must give spiritual teachings. There are inconsistencies, contradictions, and outright falsehood throughout this doctrine of hope for those who have whiled away their day of grace until it is too late. The Mormon prophet needs to free their members from yet another point of bondage.

THE DOCTRINE OF HEAVENLY MARRIAGE

Two doctrines help to keep the LDS people in bondage. These are the doctrines of "celestial marriage" and "sealing of families together for time and eternity." If you do not perform these works in one of their temples you are taught that you may lose your families for all eternity. For a Christian this is a frightening thought.

Unless a Mormon keeps his life in line with church doctrines he cannot get into the temple to perform these works for eternity. It is a real mark of social attainment, as well as spiritual attainment, to be married in the temple. In order to get into the temple one must have a "Temple Recommend" from his bishop, who is the equivalent of the preacher in the Christian congregation. The bishop is not to give this recommendation if the person drinks coffee, tea, or alcoholic beverages, smokes, is not faithful, does not have his tithing paid up to date, and so forth. Therefore, it is a way to keep the people in bondage under the subjugation of the church. A Mormon will think twice about being separated from his wife; maybe someone else will have her, or they will be separated from their children for eternity. So the bondage rests upon them.

The sorrow about this doctrine is that the Bible teaches that there will be no marriage in heaven. This is clearly stated in three of the four Gospels, and by Christ Himself. "For in the resurrection they neither marry nor are given in marriage, but are like angels in heaven" (Matthew 22:30; Mark 12:25 and slightly different in Luke 20:35).

We will not be married, like people; but will be like angels, not married at all. Isn't it strange how distorted things can get when people seek to play god?

Yes, in heaven we will know our loved ones. The Bible teaches that it will be so. But we will leave behind many of the things we know in this earthly state, and one of those things that will be left behind is marriage. I suppose that to a sex-oriented religion this is a tragic thought!

The remaining seven of the fourteen false doctrines will be addressed in the next chapter.

SUMMARY

Mormon doctrine is not just a little different from mainstream Christian teaching. From God, to Jesus, the virgin birth, the Lord's Supper, high priesthood, baptism for dead people and eternal marriages, all are vastly different from the rest of Christianity.

Each of these doctorines leaves people believing falsehoods and fosters hope based on fiction. This is a cruel bondage. Their labors are fruitless like those in slavery.

CHRISTIANITY & MORMONISM

FROM BONDAGE TO FREEDOM

The Bars of Bondage

1. In your opinion, which of the false doctrines in this chapter most bizarre? Why?
2. Which of these is the most foundational to the structure Mormonism?
3. Explain the doctrine of "eternal progression."
4. How does the Mormon view of high priesthood differ from Bible's teaching about Jesus' High Priesthood?
5. Choose any two of these doctrines and discuss how they reveal the real differences between Mormonism and mainstream Christianity.

The Keys to Freedom

1. Prayerfully consider asking a Mormon friend to a social activity with your family. Go to a sports event or backyard barbecue. Look for opportunities to talk about your personal faith in Jesus.
2. Although it would be considered blasphemous to Mormons, you could use a highlighter to mark passages in *The Book of Mormon* mentioned in this book.
3. Invite your Mormon friends to your small group Bible study.

CHAPTER SEVEN
The Mormon Bondage to Fourteen False Doctrines, Part Two

"There is neither Jew nor Greek, there is neither slave nor free man, there is neither male nor female; for you are all one in Christ Jesus" (Galatians 3:28).

THE DOCTRINE OF THE GOSPEL OF JESUS

At first this may seem like a rather harmless doctrine. Adam, Enoch, Noah, Abraham, and others supposedly preached this gospel. Yet is falsehood ever really harmless? The real question is, "Does it measure up to the truth?" Did the Old Testament people understand and preach the same clear gospel story that we preach? Were these folks saved in exactly the same way we are?

The Book of Mormon teaches in this eighth false doctrine that the people immigrating to America "preached Jesus Christ" and baptized people who believed.

> And he commandeth all men that they must repent, and be baptized in his name, having perfect faith in the Holy One of Israel, or they cannot be saved in the kingdom of God. And if they will not repent and believe in his name, and be baptized in his name, and endure to the end, they must be damned; for the Lord God, the Holy One of Israel, has spoken it (2 Nephi 9:23-24).

A similar statement is made again by Nephi:

> And now, if the Lamb of God, he being holy, should have

need to be baptized by water, to fulfil all righteousness, O then, how much more need we, being unholy, to be baptized, yea, even by water! And now, I would ask of you, my beloved brethren, wherein the Lamb of God did fulfill all righteousness in being baptized by water? (2 Nephi 31:5-6).

The problem with these passages from *The Book of Mormon* is that they were supposedly written about 550 BC. Are we to believe that they had the same message to preach then that we do now? What does the New Testament Scripture say about this matter?

The New Testament teaches quite clearly that the prophets did not receive the same promises that we do.

> As to this salvation, the prophets who prophesied of the grace that would come to you made careful searches and inquiries, seeking to know what person or time the Spirit of Christ within them was indicating as He predicted the sufferings of Christ and the glories to follow. It was revealed to them that they were not serving themselves, but you, in these things which now have been announced to you through those who preached the gospel to you by the Holy Spirit sent from heaven—things into which angels long to look.
>
> Therefore, prepare your minds for action, keep sober in spirit, fix your hope completely on the grace to be brought to you at the revelation of Jesus Christ (1 Peter 1:10-13).

Paul puts the matter even more clearly when he says,

> To me, the very least of all saints, this grace was given, to preach to the Gentiles the unfathomable riches of Christ, and to bring to light what is the administration of the mystery which for ages has been hidden in God who created all things.... (Ephesians 3:8-9).

We have absolutely no record of it being preached, other than the prophets looking ahead and prophesying that it would come some day in the future. The mystery of the gospel was not fully known before Jesus came to earth.

The book of Romans also indicates that Jesus' salvation was not fully understood till *after* His death. Even the apostles didn't know what was going on until after the Holy Spirit came upon them. "Now to Him who is able to establish you according to my gospel and the preaching of Jesus Christ, according to the revelation of the mystery which has been kept secret for long ages past...." (Romans 16:25).

So there we have it again. The mystery of salvation through Jesus was not preached until after His resurrection. Even the work of John the Baptist was only one of a "way-preparer."

Here again is an indication that *The Book of Mormon* was not really written as early as it claims to have been. It is really easy to know all the details of events after they have happened. It would have been an easy thing to have written *The Book of Mormon* after the events had taken place, pretending that it was really an ancient book. This is very good evidence that the book is not nearly as old as Joseph Smith said it was.

Beyond this, the Bible clearly shows that this doctrine of salvation being preached in the name of Jesus in the Old Testament days is false. It is another proof that the Mormon system is not of God. It is another problem of bondage that their prophet needs to get straightened out if they are in truth to be a Christian religion.

THE DOCTRINE OF SUPPOSED CURSED RACES

The doctrine of "cursed races" was a part of Mormon teaching from the beginning of the LDS church until June 9, 1978. At that time a pronouncement was made by president Spencer W. Kimball which said, "... all worthy male members of the church may be ordained to the priesthood without regard for race or color."[57]

Below is a refutation of this absurd doctrine, so long held by the church, and how it came to be changed. There remains the problem for the church because two of their supposed scriptures indicate that certain races could not ever hold the priesthood.

Their doctrine had its roots in *The Pearl of Great Price*, Book of Abraham, and statements from *The Book of Mormon*. According to these sources the African-American and American Indian had dark skin because of their sins in the preexistence (2 Nephi 5:21-22; Alma 3:6; Abraham 1:21-27). This is a very serious accusation because it places a slur upon every dark-skinned person. It creates another serious problem for the church in that if their scriptures teach that people's skin color is an indication of their basic sinful nature, then how can the prophet change their scripture just because of social pressure put upon the church?

Their doctrine had its origin in the idea that people were sinful in the

---
[57]*Deseret News* (June 9, 1978), p. 1A.

preexistence, God thus placed them in black or dark skins on earth as a punishment. This would lead one to have serious doubts about a black person's trustworthiness. In fact, this doctrine had been interpreted so as to not let one African-American have a place of leadership in the Mormon church, until 1978. A white boy of twelve years of age could hold a higher office than a grown Native American or African-American. The Book of Abraham says, "Now, Pharaoh being of that lineage by which he could not have the right of Priesthood, notwithstanding the Pharaohs would fain claim it from Noah, through Ham, therefore my father was led away by their idolatry" (Abraham 1:27). This passage has been interpreted by the prophets of the church to mean African-Americans were cursed by God. Joseph Fielding Smith, recent prophet of the church stated,

> Not only was Cain called upon to suffer, but because of his wickedness he became the father of an inferior race. A curse was placed upon him, and that curse has been continued through his lineage, and must do so while time endures.[58]

In another place he says,

> There is a reason why one man is born black and with other disadvantages, while another is born white with great advantages. The reason is that we once had an estate before we came here, and were obedient, more or less, to the laws that were given us there. Those who were faithful in all things there received greater blessings here, and those who were not faithful received less.[59]

In a letter dated April 10, 1963, Joseph Fielding Smith said,

> According to the doctrine of the Church, the Negro because of some condition of unfaithfulness in the spirit—or pre-existence, was not valiant and hence was not denied the mortal probation, but denied the blessing of the priesthood.[60]

Brigham Young, second prophet of the church stated,

---

[58]Joseph Fielding Smith, *The Way to Perfection* (Salt Lake City: *Deseret Book Press*), p. 101.
[59]Joseph Fielding Smith, *Doctrines of Salvation*, 1:61.
[60]Tanner, *Mormonism–Shadow or Reality?* (1964), p. 296.

Cain slew his brother. Canaan might have been killed, and that would have put a termination to the line of human beings. This was not to be, and the Lord put a mark upon him, which is the flat nose and black skin....[61]

Can the Bible substantiate these serious accusations, directed towards a whole race of people? Since the race problem continues to the present day, it seems helpful to present what the Bible actually says about this matter.

So often the Bible has been used as a crutch to keep the black race down. People have looked within its pages to find sanction for slavery, racial injustices, and discrimination. This doctrine, still taught in Mormon scripture, and so long held by some churches, is a terrible bondage for many worthy people. Their doctrine is a relic of the past ignorance, a definite indication that they do not have a true prophet in their midst.

Two passages of Scripture have been used as prooftexts to support their contention that the black race is inferior, due to an act of God. These two passages of Scripture are Genesis 4:15 and Genesis 9:20-27. Because of hazy and faulty interpretation of these two passages, "Christians" have thought themselves justified in keeping the black race in bondage; at least they sought to justify their doing so.

The first passage deals with the "mark of Cain." It does not say what the mark was, but it has been affirmed by many religious leaders of various faiths that God turned Cain black as a curse for his sin of murder. A program was aired on the Salt Lake City radio station KSXX, discussing this very issue. At times the words were quite heated on the call-in show. Finally a lady called in who was apparently an older black woman. She said, "We think God turned Cain white." She had a very good point; at least she had as much proof for her view as there is for the Mormons'. It could have as easily been that God turned Cain white, rather than black. In truth, this passage does not prove God turned Cain any color, it only says, "a mark in his flesh."

The second passage mentions the curse that Noah put on his grandson, Canaan, because his father Ham saw Noah's nakedness. The obvious fault in reasoning here is that Ham is said to mean "black skinned," but basically the word in Hebrew, "Ham" means "father-in-law." It is very doubtful that Ham's name meant "black skinned." As a Bible scholar, I would hate to insist that it did mean such. Beyond this, the curse was not placed on Ham at all, but upon his son, Canaan.

---

[61]Young, *The Journal of Discourses*, 7:290-291.

The evidence seems to indicate that the African-American races are not of Canaan. T.B. Maston says,

> It is generally agreed that the Canaanites, descendants of Canaan, were not black. In the main, they moved into Asia Minor and at least as far east as the Tigris and Euphrates valley. Other descendants of Ham went south into Africa, but not the Canaanites, upon whom the curse was at least specially pronounced. Ryle suggests that "the application of this clause to the African races is an error of interpretation." Similarly, Marcus Dods concludes, "Canaan being thus selected, the fulfillment of the curse must not be looked for in the other descendants of Ham, and still less in the Negro races." Pieters likewise says that even if the Negroes be conceded to be the sons of Ham, they are certainly not descendants of Canaan, and these only are under the curse.[62]

We must conclude that God never has cursed black people at all. Ignorant Protestants, mostly in a southern culture, sought to justify their keeping other humans in bondage by Scripture passages of doubtful meaning at best. The Mormons, while in Missouri, picked up this teaching. While most Protestants have opened their eyes to the truth, the Mormon scripture continues to spread this error.

If there had ever been a curse placed on any race it would have been removed in Christ, for the Bible says,

> For all of you who were baptized into Christ have clothed yourselves with Christ. There is neither Jew nor Greek, there is neither slave nor free man, there is neither male nor female; for you are all one in Christ Jesus. And if you belong to Christ, then you are Abraham's descendants, heirs according to promise (Galatians 3:27-29).

Nationalities are bridged, races and social distinctions are spanned, and economic and servitude lines are crossed when one comes into Christ. This passage is so clear that it must of necessity take preference over ones of such doubtful interpretation as those in Genesis cited above.

The Colossian letter speaks even more clearly about this matter when it says,

---

[62]T.B. Baston, *The Bible and Race* (Nashville: Broadman, 1962), p. 112.

> ... and have put on the new self who is being renewed to a true knowledge according to the image of the One who created him—a renewal in which there is no distinction between Greek and Jew, circumcised and uncircumcised, barbarian, Scythian, slave and freeman, but Christ is all, and in all (Colossians 3:10-11).

This passage makes it very clear that Christ breaks down all barriers of race and culture. Even in the church of the first century there were almost certainly people from the black race. This has been almost entirely overlooked by those who reject their black brothers. What about Simeon who was called Niger (Acts 13:1)? It seems likely, or much more so, that he was black rather than Cain and Canaan were. Yet he was prominent in the church at Antioch. It is also likely that the Ethiopian Eunuch was of a dark-skinned race. Phillip the Evangelist received him into the church without question (Acts 8:26-39). Men from "every nation under heaven" (Acts 2:5) were received into the church on the Day of Pentecost. We can remember the words of God to Peter when Peter was told to "Get up ... kill and eat!" (Acts 10:13). Peter didn't want to touch the unclean animals, but God told him to do so. Peter later said in reference to this revelation from God, "... I most certainly understand now that God is not one to show partiality, but in every nation the man who fears Him and does what is right is welcome to Him" (Acts 10:34-35).

Another passage of Scripture that speaks clearly about the race issue is found in Acts: "... and He made from one man every nation of mankind to live on all the face of the earth, having determined their appointed times and the boundaries of their habitation...." (Acts 17:26). Was the apostle speaking the truth? Has God made all nations one in Christ? It would certainly appear so. Christ died for all mankind. God has not placed any biological blocks between the races for they can marry and raise children. The Bible repeatedly stresses that anyone who wishes may be saved. That God does not want any to perish is a clear teaching of Scripture. Those who are in Christ Jesus are one body, His church.

Jesus spoke directly about racial prejudice in His ministry. The Jews were very prejudiced against the Samaritans. They would travel around their country rather than to pass through it. They would have no social interaction with them. They preferred not even to do business with them. Their racial pride was very similar to what we still, unfortunately, see in some parts of America.

When a certain lawyer asked Jesus what he should do to inherit eternal life, Christ answered with another question:

CHRISTIANITY & MORMONISM

And He said to him, "What is written in the Law? How does it read to you?" And he answered, "YOU SHALL LOVE THE LORD YOUR GOD WITH ALL YOUR HEART, AND WITH ALL YOUR SOUL, AND WITH ALL YOUR STRENGTH, AND WITH ALL YOUR MIND; AND YOUR NEIGHBOR AS YOURSELF." And He said to him, "You have answered correctly; DO THIS AND YOU WILL LIVE." But wishing to justify himself, he said to Jesus, "And who is my neighbor?" (Luke 10:26-29).

Jesus then told the story of the man who was injured and both a priest and a Levite passed by, while the despised Samaritan stopped and helped the man who was hurt. Jesus here pictures the despised race as being more acceptable than those they counted worthy of honor. Jesus presents the Samaritan as being the one pleasing to God. Might it be so today? Could it be that those who feel they are the elect of God, the special favored race, are not as acceptable as those sometimes considered inferior?

This rather lengthy explanation has been given because racial prejudice has had too slow a death in America. Especially those who call themselves Christian should have no place in their hearts for prejudice against any brother or sister in Christ. Many supposed Christians have continued to hold ill will and malice against those for whom Christ died. This is no credit to Christian or Mormon.

It is commendable that the LDS church has allowed those long considered cursed people to now hold the Priesthood. It is time for them to learn that all Christians are priests and it is not the churches' prerogative to give or withhold it. Now it is time for them to get *The Book of Mormon* and Book of Abraham cleaned up to reflect truth, rather than American rationalization.

THE DOCTRINE OF POLYGAMY

The LDS church asserts that "polygamy" is not a current issue with them, and has not been since the declaration by Wilford Woodruff, president of the church, on October 6, 1890, now over 100 years ago. This is not entirely true. I lived in Salt Lake City for many years and during those years knew several polygamists.

The church has not actively encouraged it, nor has it actively sought to stamp it out. When an individual makes an issue of someone being a polygamist, then the polygamist is put out of the church. This has happened many times. Yet, today it is estimated that there are thousands in the church practicing polygamy. The group most actively promoting polygamy call themselves "fundamentalists."

A *Ladies Home Journal* article in 1967 found from their research an estimated "30,000 Cases of Polygamy in Utah."[63] Polygamy's greatest growth has taken place since that time so this number has conceivably doubled. The author of this article went to Utah and lived among the people, agreeing not to name names or disclose his sources. After working under those conditions for a year he came to the above figure. Now, if polygamy has doubled in Utah since 1970, you can begin to see the extent of the problem today.

Polygamists do not have to hide their polygamy, for they are not prosecuted. The excuse for not enforcing the law is that it would flood the welfare rolls beyond endurance. (Utah already has an unusually high rate of welfare recipients.)

In counseling with polygamists you discover all kinds of family problems that arise because of jealousy and multiple wives under the same roof. A young woman became a member of a Christian church in Utah without revealing the fact that she was the wife of a polygamist. The husband of the family felt duty bound to practice polygamy and used, as his reason, the 132nd section of *The Doctrine and Covenants*. He said it was a terrible burden to have to have so many wives. In order for him to take another wife, he had to have the permission of his current wives. His "Christian" wife would not give this permission, so he resorted to physical force, during which she received a black eye and a severely swollen lip. Later she left him, while he took the wife that he was wanting. He insisted that "it was a terrible burden," although his words did not have the ring of credibility to them. It is unlikely that his motives were as pure as he would have had people think.

Another well-known incident involved a man who had several wives. Each of these wives was young and pretty. Not one of them was the sort of person one might imagine them to be, possibly unattractive, lacking in personality, or deficient in some way. They were not people who couldn't get another husband, but were convinced that they were keeping the commandments of God.

Near the mouth of Little Cottonwood Canyon, near Salt Lake City, lived a man who also had seven wives and more than twenty children. It was common knowledge among the people of the whole area that this family practiced polygamy. Several children attended public school, were about the same ages, brothers and sisters, but no twins. They shared the

---

[63] Ben Merson, "Husbands with More Than One Wife," *Ladies Home Journal* (June 1967), pp. 78-79.

CHRISTIANITY & MORMONISM

same name and the same father, but different mothers.

At that time in Bountiful, Utah, there was a man with twelve wives and twenty-four children. This case of polygamy was widely known to exist, and nothing was done to seek to stop it.

The estimate is probably correct that suggests there are more people practicing polygamy today than there were in the days of Brigham Young, before polygamy was outlawed. If the Mormon church wanted to stop the progress and practice of polygamy they probably could, for they control the state, politically, economically, and socially.

One LDS church leader said he viewed practicing polygamy no worse than breaking the speed limit, it did not offend God; it was only breaking a human law. Some believe they must obey God rather than men. They feel bound by conscience to obey God.

The passages that endorse polygamy are

> Verily, thus saith the Lord unto you my servant Joseph, that inasmuch as you have inquired of my hand to know and understand wherein I, the Lord, justified my servants Abraham, Isaac, and Jacob, as also Moses, David and Solomon, my servants, as touching the principle and doctrine of their having many wives and concubines—Behold, and lo, I am the Lord thy God, and will answer thee as touching this matter. Therefore, prepare thy heart to receive and obey the instructions which I am about to give unto you; for all those who have this law revealed unto them must obey the same. For behold, I reveal unto you a new and an everlasting covenant; and if ye abide not that covenant, then are ye damned; for no one can reject this covenant and be permitted to enter into my glory . . . and he that receiveth a fulness there of must and shall abide the law, or he shall be damned, saith the Lord God (DC 132:1-4,6).

Joseph Smith is very wordy under normal circumstances, but seems a little more vague than usual. Could it be that he is trying to mollify Emma Smith, his wife? He needs to be definite, but wants to be a little ambiguous at the same time. A little later in the same section he says,

> Go ye, therefore, and do the works of Abraham; enter ye into my law and ye shall be saved. But if ye enter not into my law ye cannot receive the promise of my Father, which he made unto Abraham. God commanded Abraham, and Sarah gave Hagar to Abraham to wife. And why did she do it? Because this was the

law; and from Hagar sprang many people. This, therefore, was fulfilling, among other things, the promise (DC 132:32-34).

The message is clear that Joseph is commanded to do the works of Abraham and that was that God commanded Abraham to be a polygamist. Could it be read differently? Yet there is more to be said.

> David also received many wives and concubines, and also Solomon and Moses my servants, as also many others of my servants, from the beginning of creation until this time; and in nothing did they sin save in those things which they received not of me. David's wives and concubines were given unto him of me, by the hand of Nathan, my servant, and others of the prophets who had the keys of this power; and in none of these things did he sin against me.... I am the Lord thy God, and gave unto them, my servant Joseph, an appointment, and restore all things (DC 132:38-40).

Ultimately Joseph Smith says,

> And again, as pertaining to the law of the priesthood—if any man espouse a virgin, and desire to espouse another, and the first give her consent, and if he espouse the second, and they are virgins, and have vowed to no other man, then is he justified; he cannot commit adultery for they are given unto him, for he cannot commit adultery with that that belongeth unto him and no one else. And if he have ten virgins given unto him by this law, he cannot commit adultery, for they belong to him, and they are given unto him; therefore is he justified (DC 132:61-62).

So there you have it: "a new and everlasting covenant" that lasted until the United States Militia put the pressure on a latter prophet of the Latter-day Saints church. Then that latter prophet received word to rescind this "everlasting covenant." But today, slowly but surely it is coming back, or should we say, has come back with renewed vigor.

How anyone could deny that the major emphasis of the 132nd section of *The Doctrine and Covenants* is polygamy is beyond imagination. It is very clearly taught.

In the beginning ... polygamy was not the rule. When God created Adam and Eve He didn't make many wives for Adam. If He had wanted people to multiply on the earth through polygamy, why did He not make Adam several wives? But the command was, "For this reason a man shall leave his father and his mother, and be joined to his wife; and they shall become one flesh" (Genesis 2:24). Man was to cleave to his wife, singular.

Later when polygamy became common it was usually associated with trouble. A little research will show that almost every case of polygamy in the Bible is attended with trouble. Abraham had a serious problem with Sarah and Hagar, even making it necessary to put Hagar out of his house. The two nations that came from this polygamist union have hated each other ever since. The Jews and the Arabs are still fighting. We read about this hatred in the Middle East almost daily.

David got himself into trouble, not only with Bathsheba, but also with his children hating each other, murdering each other, and one of his own sons defiling his wives upon Mount Zion—in the sight of all Israel.

Solomon's wives turned his heart away from God. Both David and Solomon died relatively young men, probably in their early sixties. It is not suggested that these men were lost, since they lived in a time when they didn't have as clear a revelation of God's will as we do today.

But today we have clear teaching in the Bible that church leaders are to have only one wife, not to be polygamists. "An overseer, then, must be above reproach, the husband of one wife, temperate, prudent, respectable, hospitable, able to teach.... Deacons must be husbands of only one wife, and good managers of their children and their own households" (1 Timothy 3:2,12). Most Bible scholars believe that there was some polygamy in the days of the early church, especially among Gentile converts, but none of these were to have places of leadership in the church.

A similar set of instructions is given to help Titus in choosing church leaders. "For this reason I left you in Crete, that you would set in order what remains and appoint elders in every city as I directed you, namely, if any man is above reproach, the husband of one wife, having children who believe, not accused of dissipation or rebellion" (Titus 1:5-6). There is no need for us to misunderstand, for the instruction is given twice. Elders, Bishops, and Deacons are to have only one wife.

Under the section of this book that deals with *The Book of Mormon*, it has already been pointed out that *The Book of Mormon* says no one is to have more than one wife. We must remember that God is not a God of confusion. He is unchanging, the same yesterday, today, and forever.

If there has been one doctrine that has brought bondage upon a rather large segment of the LDS church it has been this one. An investigation of a few accounts of Mormon polygamy reveals that a universal condition is very unhappy women and children. Human nature cautions that to put two wives under one roof is to create havoc, and such is the case with polygamy.

If the church wants to be considered Christian they need to distance themselves from their bogus scripture like *The Doctrine and Covenants*. At the same time they need to repudiate their doctrine of celestial polygamy, of being sealed to more than one wife in time and eternity. Is this a Christian doctrine? No! No! NO! It is the very worst of spiritual and social bondage. Think of the lives of depression, privation, and suffering so many women have endured because of Mormon bondage.

THE DOCTRINE OF JESUS' MARRIAGE

It is hard to pinpoint just what the official LDS doctrine is on "the marriage of Jesus." All that can be done is to quote influential leaders of the church and what they have said about their views. A few quotations from some of the leaders of the church on the matter of Christ's marriage and marriages will illustrate their view.

Keep in mind that marriage is necessary as a part of "eternal progression."

> It will be borne in mind that once on a time, there was a marriage in Cana of Galilee; and on a careful reading of that transaction, it will be discovered that no less a person that Jesus Christ was married, on that occasion. If he was never married, his intimacy with Mary and Martha and the other Mary also whom Jesus loved, must have been highly unbecoming and improper to say the best of it.
>
> I will venture to say that if Jesus Christ were now to pass through the most pious countries in Christendom with a train of woman, such as used to follow him, fondling about him, combing his hair, anointing him with precious ointment, washing his feet with tears, and wiping them with the hair of their heads and unmarried, or even married, he would be mobbed, tarred, and feathered, and rode not on an ass, but on a rail.[64]

This is a bit of plain blasphemy in print. It is painful even to record it. Yet, such has been the extent of the false doctrine of the LDS church.

The Mormon Apostle Jedediah Grant commented,

> The grand reason of the burst of public sentiment in anathemas upon Christ and his disciples, causing his crucifixion, was

---

[64]Orson Hyde, "Man the Head of a Woman–Kingdom of God–The Seed of Christ-Polygamy-Society in Utah," *The Journal of Discourses*, 4:259.

evidently based upon polygamy, according to the testimony of the philosophers who rose in that age. A belief in the doctrine of a plurality of wives caused the persecution of Jesus and his followers. We might almost think they were "Mormons."[65]

The church does not now actively teach that Jesus was married; however, the doctrines of the church imply He had at least one wife and possibly more. The highest degree a person can reach in heaven is called "exaltation" and this is not attainable by an unmarried person. A man and a woman must be sealed for time and all eternity by an authorized person in a temple ceremony before exaltation is possible. It would appear from this doctrine that Jesus would have to have been married in this manner to fulfill all requirements, to obtain His exaltation, and thus be worthy of returning to the presence of God the Father. The highest attainable goal that an unmarried person can reach is that of a ministering angel. The Mormon doctrine does not teach that Jesus is a ministering angel, but that He is a God second only to God the Father. A very high authority, Brigham Young, has taught that Christ was married.

> They have refused our brethren membership in their lodge, because they are polygamists. Who was the founder of Freemasonry? They can go back as far as Solomon, and there they stop. There is the king who established this high and holy order. Now was he a polygamist, or was he not? If he did believe in monogamy, he did not practice it a great deal, for he had seven hundred wives, and that is more than I have, and he had three hundred concubines, of which I have none that I know of. Yet the whole fraternity throughout Christendom will cry out against this order, "Oh dear, Oh dear, Oh dear," they all cry out; "I am in pain ... I am suffering at witnessing the wickedness there is in the land. Here is one of the relics of barbarism." Yes, one of the relics of Adam, of Enoch, of Noah, of Abraham, of Isaac, of Jacob, of Moses, David, Solomon, the Prophets, and Jesus and his apostles.[66]

On July 2, 1899, Apostle George Q. Cannon made the following statement followed by an answer by the president of the church, Lorenzo Snow. Cannon said,

---

[65]Jedediah M. Grant, "Uniformity," *The Journal of Discourses*, 1:346.
[66]Brigham Young, *Deseret News* (February 10, 1867), quoted in Ogden Kraut, Jesus Was Married (Dugway, UT: Ogden Kraut, 1970), p. 62.

There are those in this audience who are descendants of the old Twelve Apostles—and shall I say it, yes, DESCENDANTS OF THE SAVIOR HIMSELF, HIS SEED IS REPRESENTED IN THIS BODY OF MEN.

Following President Cannon, President Snow arose and said that what Brother Cannon had stated respecting the literal descendants among this company of the old apostles and the Savior Himself is true—that the Savior's seed is represented in this body of men.[67]

Finally, even Joseph Smith claimed that he was a blood descendant from Jesus Christ. The preceding quotations are only a small sampling of what is written upon the subject of Christ's having been married and a polygamist. Scripture will show the absurdity of such a doctrine. "He was oppressed, and he was afflicted, yet he opened not his mouth: he is brought as a lamb to the slaughter, and as a sheep before her shearers is dumb, so he openeth not his mouth. He was taken from prison and from judgment: and who shall declare his generation? for he was cut off out of the land of the living: for the transgression of my people was he stricken" (Isaiah 53:7,8, KJV).

With so much that is un-Christian (even anti-Christian) in the LDS church, just where will the prophet begin to clean things up so they can in truth be what they are trying tell the world they are, Christian? There is so much spiritual bondage. It will take a spiritual Abraham Lincoln and a spiritual Union Army to free all these slaves.

THE DOCTRINE OF THE NON-PAID MINISTRY

Volunteers do the work of the LDS church almost entirely. This holds true of the officers and leaders of the local wards right on up through the president of the church. (The president may head several of the large corporations of the church, for which he can receive a salary.) This is reported to be the case with the apostles as well. Yet the many thousands of people who work for the church, do so for free. We can admire their dedication. Yet is this really good, or is it really God's will? The point: How qualified, focused, and educated is the LDS church leadership?

What it means is that the leaders of the church all must have other occupations to support themselves and the heavy tithing they are expected

---

[67] *Journal of Pres. Rudger Clawson*, pp. 374-375, quoted in Kraut, *Jesus Was Married*, p. 97.

to give to the church. Therefore amateurs lead the whole movement. Seldom are people found who really know what they are talking about. The results are many instances of inadequate or clearly harmful counseling and unethical techniques. Many times this has not been an intentional effort to misdirect people, but it demonstrates the lack of appropriate training. One area of ministry that shows this lack of trained leadership is funerals. Those suffering grief often experience services in poor taste, appalling ineptitude, and inadequate solace.

It has been said that in all of Mormon history, they have not yet produced one real theologian who did not leave the church. This is probably true. Much of it is tied in with the unpaid leadership. It makes it impossible to produce and maintain a competent leadership. This basic ignorance of theology is experienced from the newest missionary up through the ranks, even to the apostles and prophet.

The Bible is quite clear about the reasons for paid ministry. Jesus had very good reasons for so directing. Paul shows the reasons in his letter to the Corinthian church.

> Who at any time serves as a soldier at his own expense? Who plants a vineyard and does not eat the fruit of it? Or who tends a flock and does not use the milk of the flock?
>
> I am not speaking these things according to human judgment, am I? Or does not the Law also say these things? For it is written in the Law of Moses, "You shall not muzzle the ox while he is threshing." God is not concerned about oxen, is He? Or is He speaking altogether for our sake? Yes, for our sake it was written, because the plowman ought to plow in hope, and the thresher to thresh in hope of sharing the crops. If we sowed spiritual things in you, is it too much if we reap material things from you? If others share the right over you, do we not more? Nevertheless, we did not use this right, but we endure all things so that we will cause no hindrance to the gospel of Christ. Do you not know that those who perform sacred services eat the food of the temple, and those who attend regularly to the altar have their share from the altar? So also the Lord directed those who proclaim the gospel to get their living from the gospel (1 Corinthians 9:7-14).

Paul also reminded the Galatian Christians, "The one who is taught the word is to share all good things with the one who teaches him" (Galatians 6:6). This is an obvious teaching that the ministry is to be paid.

Paul received wages to preach the gospel. "I robbed other churches by taking wages from them to serve you...." (2 Corinthians 11:8).

Can it be that a church with no paid leadership is the restored church of Jesus Christ? Wouldn't you rather be a part of a church that had competent, qualified, leadership? Remember, Jesus warned about the blind being led by the blind.

The church has robbed those who have worked hard and long for the church so they could build one of the largest financial empires in America today. Here is another bondage—financial bondage, from which the church needs to liberate those who work so hard for them.

THE DOCTRINE OF ELDERS AND DEACONS

The Bible gives clear guidelines as to the qualifications for the elders and deacons in the church. Yet the LDS church does not follow these qualifications for leadership. In fact, a twelve-year-old boy can be a deacon in the church, and a young man of sixteen can be an elder. In the light of clear Bible pronouncements on this subject, we wonder how the church can claim to have restored the New Testament church like Christ and His apostles established it?

Beyond this, the Mormon church makes a distinction between the elder and the bishop. The bishop is considered to be a higher office than the elder. The Bible teaches that the elder and bishop are one and the same person. Paul used these terms interchangeably.

> For this reason I left you in Crete, that you would set in order what remains and appoint elders in every city as I directed you, namely, if any man is above reproach, the husband of one wife, having children who believe, not accused of dissipation or rebellion. For the overseer must be above reproach as God's steward, not self-willed, not quick-tempered, not addicted to wine, not pugnacious, not fond of sordid gain.... (Titus 1:5-7).

The words "elder" and "bishop" are used interchangeably for one and the same office. It stipulates that an elder is to have a wife and children. This is a rather stringent requirement for a sixteen-year-old boy, hardly ready to shave yet. Of course, Paul didn't mean that sixteen-year-old boys should be elders. It is just another example of the false teachings of the LDS church.

The Bible teaches that a deacon is also to be married. Paul said, "Deacons must be husbands of only one wife, and good managers of

CHRISTIANITY & MORMONISM

their children and their own households" (1 Timothy 3:12). Aside from this, Scripture describes the ministry of deacons as one of *mature* service. Should twelve-year-old boys be deacons?

Is the Mormon church doctrinally sound? Certainly not, and the above thirteen false doctrines are only a sample of some of the larger and more obvious doctrinal errors. Few, if any, religious bodies, claiming to be Christian, have so many glaring errors of teaching. It runs through the whole fabric of the church. The errors are such a part of the whole nature of the church that when the church awakens to how grossly in error they are the question they will have to face is just where to begin in the process of restoring Biblical Christianity.

THE DOCTRINE OF SALVATION

Salvation by Works

The following observations come from Alex Wilson in a letter that was in response to an article I wrote for the *Christian Standard*. Mr. Wilson pointed out that the Mormon doctrine of salvation is one of their most basic errors. He is right and below is a portion of his letter.

> Charles Crane's "Is Mormonism Christian or a Cult?" August 13, 2000, was very helpful. Yet it omitted one of Mormonism's most basic errors, regarding salvation. The following quotations make their view clear and enable us to understand their basic legalism.
>
> "We believe that through the atonement of Christ, all mankind may be saved, by obedience to the laws and ordinances of the gospel" (*Articles of Faith*). "The gospel is a code of laws and ordinances given to men to enable them to assimilate themselves to those who are in heaven" (Joseph Smith). "The gospel is a system or plan of laws and ordinances and by strict obedience to which people are assured they may return again into the presence of the Father" (Brigham Young). "Some of our old traditions [meaning their pre-Mormon beliefs] teach us that a man guilty of atrocious and murderous acts may savingly repent on the scaffold. Upon his execution you will hear the expression, 'Bless God, he has gone to heaven ... through the all redeeming merits of Christ the Lord!' This is all nonsense. Such a character will never see heaven" (Brigham Young).[68]

---

[68]Portions of a letter to me from Alex Wilson, Louisville, KY, August 12, 2000.

The Mormon Bondage to Fourteen False Doctrines, Part II

The Mormon doctrine keeps their members in a terrible bondage of working their way ever upward on the ladder of good works, when the Bible is clear that salvation is not of our own good works.

The thoughtful LDS member must feel the despair of somehow becoming "worthy" on his own merit of God's presence. How liberating it is for Christians who understand that salvation is by the grace of God, not of our own doing. It is like walking out of a freezing fog into the sunlight of a spring day. It is like having the waters of the Red Sea part, to cross over on dry land, to freedom. It is like stepping out of the most awful servitude/slavery into total liberation and freedom.

Salvation by Grace

The Mormon doctrine is a salvation by works, which is Biblically, theologically, and rationally impossible. Biblical salvation is by faith and grace. Salvation is a gift, free; no person can deserve or earn it. God honors our faith in Him. We obey as an act of faith, we are baptized into Jesus' death, burial, and resurrection as an act of faith. We are immediately and fully saved from the first moment.

Jesus can save to the uttermost, yes, even a thief and a murderer. To suppose that any person can earn heaven for eternity on the basis of what they can do in a few years on earth is a philosophical absurdity. We could never earn even a few milliseconds of heaven.

Christians have been set free from the law and works, which have never saved anyone, and delivered into the marvelous grace of Jesus Christ. We are free. Mormons can be free at last. Beware of this system of bondage! We appeal to the leaders of the LDS church to free their members from bondage. It will take men of great character to make such a bold move. The person who has this courage will go down in history as a much greater person than Joseph Smith or Brigham Young or any other who has ever before been a part of the Mormon system.

SUMMARY

Doctrines tht are based on social prejudice or that belittle half of the human race are a spiritual bondage. Doctrines of polygamy and Jesus' marriage should be an embarrasment to LDS people everywhere.

With fourteen major false doctrines and numerous lesser ones the church cannot truthfully claim they are really Christian with a ring of truth to the claim.

CHRISTIANITY & MORMONISM

FROM BONDAGE TO FREEDOM

The Bars of Bondage
1. In your opinion, which of the false doctrines in Part Two is the most bizarre? Why?
2. Could the gospel of Jesus be preached in Old Testament times? Explain your answer.
3. Have you known any polygamists? If so, how did they justify their doctrine? If not, why do you think that there are polygamists today?
4. Choose any two of these false doctrines and discuss how they reveal the real differences between Mormonism and mainstream Christianity.

The Keys to Freedom
1. Invite a Christian college professor or former Mormon to speak to your small group on the subject of Mormonism.
2. Develop a plan for evangelizing the Mormons in your community. Share this strategy with members in your group or church. Schedule times to meet and to pray about implementing your plan.

CHAPTER EIGHT
From Mormon Bondage to Christian Freedom

"Now these were more noble-minded than those in Thessalonica, for they received the word with great eagerness, examining the Scriptures daily to see whether these things were so" (Acts 17:11).

MORMON BONDAGE

The Bondage of Suppressed Thinking

We have affirmed repeatedly that the Mormon religion is a form of bondage. Can we be more specific? In the scientific or physical realm the universe operates under established rules. There are rules of light and dark, hot and cold, gravity, genetic codes, electricity, and atoms. "For every action, there is an equal and opposite reaction." Whenever error is introduced to the various systems, there is damage. For example, insisting there is no gravity will not stop you from splattering on the ground if you jump off of a tall building. Not believing a stove is hot does not prevent the burn you receive from touching it. Not believing in radioactive waste does not preclude the damage that it will cause if you contact it.

Similarly, it is true in the emotional realm. There are rules and patterns that govern the emotions of human beings. With certain stimuli come predictable results. Deal with your marriage partner in an insensitive way and the results may not be too gratifyin—but they are predictable.

This is also true in the religious realm. In our modern day it is not uncommon to find people who are quite rational until it comes to reasoning about religion. Here common sense is cast aside and emotions take over. Unfortunately each of us has our own set of predisposed theological prejudices. Knowing true religion or theological truth is not always easy. This is why theology has been known as the "Prince of the Sciences." Here is where constant investigation should be welcomed, more so than with any of the other sciences. Yes, theology is in fact a science, the prince of the sciences. Few fields require more careful study or constant vigilance.

Yet, too frequently, when a theological position is questioned people are quick to say, "Judge not that you be not judged." This is like saying, "Just put your brains away and wing it." This allows them to retrench in their ignorance, rather than to seek the truth. In today's culture we have added another complication, "politically correct speech." Everything is tolerated but disagreement. Let people be in their comfort zones whether they are right or wrong, heaven or hell bound.

While I was studying with a Mormon stake president, I asked him if he ever doubted what their prophet said. He replied with a look of total incredulity on his face, "Question? Never!!! When the prophet speaks the thinking has already been done! My duty is to believe. Question the Prophet? Never!"

Think about it, if the church has a true prophet, then the stake president is right. In such cases you would have been punished for thinking about or questioning (blaspheming?) what was taught. But with the LDS church, your thinking has already been done for you. What you must do is fall in line, zip your lip, get into submission, and do the goose step. But is that attitude Biblical? "Now these were more noble-minded than those in Thessalonica, for they received the word with great eagerness, examining the Scriptures daily to see whether these things were so" (Acts 17:11).

True, some people like to have their thinking done for them. This kind of person is willing to let others lead them along like sheep. Frankly, what kind of mindless life is this if it is not carefully thought through? If thinking, checking, researching, is going to destroy it, then is it worth believing? Truth is consistent with truth. Research never hurts truth. The LDS people must be freed from the "lemming" mentality of following their leaders without rational examination.

The premise of this book is that Jesus is correct when He connects truth with freedom. "Know the truth and the truth shall make you free." The converse is true, "Be found in error and the error shall keep you in bondage." Error is never desirable. Falsehood ruins freedom and many other worthwhile parts of life and eternity.

The Bondage of Psychological Power

So much of the teaching of Jesus had to do with a proper understanding and obedience to the truth. He told the parable of the foolish man who built his house on the sand; he heard Christ's words and did not do them. Jesus warned that if blind people lead the blind, they both would fall into the pit. Jesus warned about false prophets who lead people astray. Yes, a person who does not obey Christ may *believe* he is saved while still being on the broad road to perdition.

Further, think again of the enormous sorrow of women who have suffered in polygamy. Did they not have the right to a caring relationship with a committed husband? Think of the days, months, and years of agony they endured, and all for a false doctrine. The deepest yearnings of their souls, placed there by God, were never fulfilled, to have a close, intimate relationship with a person of the opposite sex. Instead they were placed in a system where they were no more than another possession for a greedy, selfish man.

Think of all the people led into error by the missionaries that only had a few days of training in how to give their testimony. Their testimony is not their own, but a canned presentation with a Madison Avenue flare. They live under the dire warning of Scripture, "Let not many of you become teachers, my brethren, knowing that as such we shall incur a stricter judgment" (James 3:1). There are two victims: the teacher and the taught.

False theological teaching damages people far more deeply than dirty food or water. Physical things are only temporary; spiritual things are eternal. Only in knowing the truth does freedom come. Imagine all the years of service Mormon people have given to a false religion. All of these months and years of invested time are lost, all money invested is lost; and the efforts have not been for good, but to deceive and mislead people eternally. What a terrible bondage!

The Mormon doctrine of working one's way to their several heavens is unBiblical and bondage. Think carefully, can anyone work enough to earn eternity? Mormons are full of good works, but for false reasons and a false system. Isn't working for nothing slavery?

Many LDS people, when they learn the truth, feel grossly misled and suffer deep anger. In the movie *The God Makers*, Ed Decker and Dick Baer display their hostility because the church had so misled them and ended up destroying much of their lives. When they finally got their eyes open to the real Jesus then their families were broken apart. They were understandably angry. The church had helped destroy their marriages and broken parents and children apart. I visited with a daughter of one of these men and was shocked at the level of hostility in the family. Could this be described any other way than by bondage? The sweet grace of Jesus should have bound that family together in truth. Instead it was blown apart.

Mormonism is bondage because there is no salvation, grace, peace, or lasting joy in a cultist religious system. Peace comes in knowing Jesus on a personal heart-felt level. All manmade religions are false and metastasize in order to get psychological power over people's lives. This can only be described as bondage.

The Bondage of Finances

It is not only harder but also more expensive to be a Mormon than to be a Christian. It is astounding what LDS members give to their church in comparison with what Christians give to theirs. The Mormon member with whom I compared notes said the average Mormon will give 27% of his/her money and 27% of his/her time.

They will tithe to the church, pay benevolence offerings, give to building maintenance, help family members on missions, contribute to building funds, and give other offerings. It is not suggested that giving to the work of God is bad, but giving so generously to enlarge one of the falsest, yet wealthiest churches in the world, is financial bondage. It is an investment much like throwing gold coins off of the Golden Gate Bridge into San Francisco Bay. It is like loaning money to a drunk. There is no *eternal* benefit.

It might not be so bad if the loss was only personal finances, but there is the loss to the family, dad often working an extra job so he can tithe and secure his way to being the god of his own world. Mom may have to take extra work outside the home. They forego a much-needed vacation so they can make their church wealthier. They are building up the kingdom of this world, not the kingdom of heaven. It is financial bondage!

The Bondage of Women

This last example may very well be the lowest part of Mormon doctrine. The teachings of the Mormon church about women are relics from the past when men dominated women, body, mind, and soul. A Mormon woman cannot reach exaltation, or the highest glory, without her husband and she must be married to get to the top glory. They must submit to their husbands in everything. All of this servitude is without any eternal reward, since it is a cultist system.

The Mormon woman cannot hold the same priesthood that a Mormon boy of twelve can. They must await the call of their "sealed" husband to rise from the grave. Their role in heaven is to be eternally pregnant to help their husband move on more briskly toward godhood. A cartoon showed a picture of a very pregnant Mormon woman, with hundreds of spirit children around her, with two more in her arms. She is saying, "If this is heaven, I want to try hell for a while." Fortunately this view of heaven is not factual, only the fanciful view of Mormon theology.

Unfaithfulness and pornography are widespread among Mormon men. Do not deny this fact, because if you have lived closely with Mormon men, and I have, you know it is true. (I used to play golf with a Mormon group. Finally I had to give it up as the continual sexual jokes and innuendoes became intolerable.)

A stake president acquaintance kept pornography in his desk drawer. When questioned about it he replied, "Oh there is nothing wrong with this, I could even have a few concubines if I wanted. I enjoy beautiful women just like our prophets have over the years." At Christmas he gave two kinds of business calendars, one a picture of Jesus praying in the garden, the other a picture of a totally nude woman. This was rather symbolic of the schizophrenia of the system. Unfortunately this is terribly dehumanizing for women.

He explained that having a mistress was only a violation of civil law, not heavenly law. He saw this activity as a totally wholesome part of his life. But, what about his aging wife? What were her rights? Did this leave her feeling cherished? Is it any wonder that depression is a major problem among Mormon women?

Mormon women are second-class citizens of the Mormon kingdom. It is time for them to be freed from this spiritual bondage.

CHRISTIAN FREEDOM

A Lot of Good in the Mormon Religion

There is so much that is good in the LDS religion. If they would turn their considerable resources to the pursuit of the truth, rather than to defending error, the church could move back toward what they claim to be—Christian. This will require a wise and bold leader and the process may take many years of research and change. Let the change begin!

Their emphasis on restoring the gospel is good. Their standards of cleanliness, freedom from hurtful habits, like smoking and alcohol, are admirable. They have good management skills and know how to mobilize membership. They have vast financial resources and fine church properties around the world. They have a commendable communication network that could be put to good use in spreading the true gospel and proclaiming the real Jesus.

They have printing facilities, banking organizations, good business people able to lead major industry, and access to the highest level of political influence in America. Their emphasis on benevolence is commendable. So much could be done with their welfare farms, food processing, and dispensing network.

CHRISTIANITY & MORMONISM

Their membership is as highly motivated to work in the church as any church. These people serve and give sacrificially. If they did not have to promote such unreasonable doctrines, they could be great assets in the proclamation of the gospel message.

A Focus on Truth, Not Traditional Teaching

If they would redirect their resources and commitment from maintaining some bogus, false prophet to seeking and promoting the truth, they could begin to refine what is good and drop what is bad. It they would cast off their blindness, they could point their people to freedom and salvation. Their vast missionary organization could be directed toward proclaiming the real Jesus. Their vast wealth could be directed to feeding the poor and helping downtrodden nations.

This will take a bold high-level leader in the church. This leader will have to become a student of the Holy Bible, a true theologian. I do not mean a businessman turned church leader when he is too old to be an innovator and bold leader. This will require strong character in order to withstand all the abuse that will be directed toward him when change is made. This task may not be as hard as it may first appear, as many Mormons know their system is riddled with error. They remain loyal because of family ties or financial reasons, not because they believe all of the strange teachings. When the church member gets a breath of free air he or she will gladly accept truth. Certainly the Devil, the father of all lies and false religion, will not let many people go without creating all sorts of havoc.

The move to the truth will also need to be empowered by a grass-root groundswell of theology students, who will hold the church's feet to the fire of truth. Instead of running off those who are their finest scholars, the church will need to begin to listen to them, to encourage an open investigation of the issues and open dialogue with their friends who call out to them.

So there will need to be a church-wide movement, a new spirit that seeks restoration of the true *Church of Jesus Christ*. It is time to encourage thinking in the church. To encourage people to be like the Berean women (Acts 17:11). The church must recognize that research never hurts the truth, only spreads it.

The church must enter into open dialogue with those who they now view as their critics and enemies. In our day of access to information they can no longer escape from the searchlight of truth. Instead of destroying those who differ with them, they will be forced to interact, to discuss both openly and privately. Instead of burying their heads in the sand like the proverbial ostrich, they will have to face the issues.

A Call to Return to the Fold

As mentioned in the Introduction, we have witnessed in recent years a great example of cult transformation. The Worldwide Church of God with H.W. Armstrong and his son, Garner Ted Armstrong, had a great shake up when their worldview fell apart. People realized that their leaders were not godly men, but deceivers. People began to leave and in a short while the whole system fell apart. People spread out into Bible-teaching churches everywhere. It is refreshing that this erroneous system of religion is now defunct.

Rather than the Utah branch LDS church suffering a similar fate, it is suggested that they begin vigorous reform while there is time to indicate good faith and a real commitment to restoring the church. With so much error to correct it will take them years even if the task is begun immediately.

It will take more than a good advertising campaign and *claiming* to be truly Christian. The whole doctrinal system must be corrected. There is so much of their scripture that needs to be discarded as a relic of the unenlightened past. The organization of the church needs total overhaul to bring it into line with Biblical teaching.

Time is running out for the church to make this move. I have loved the LDS people and appealed to them kindly and from a heart of love. It may be that the next move should be to spell out their many errors clearly and publicly. It is time to give up the farce!

The time seems ripe for them seriously to begin church-wide reform, from top to bottom, from beginning to end; the game is over. They must either admit that they are a gross cult and be content to remain such, or immediately begin to clean out the bats and owls of false doctrine, to show good faith by wide reforms—if they in truth want to be a Christian church. They must give up their false doctrine about God, Christ, revelation, heaven, hell, conversion and salvation by works. If they will prove by their actions that they really do want the truth, then their claim to being Christian can at least have a beginning ring of sincerity to it. Otherwise it remains that they are a system of the Devil, the father of lies and liars, a cult. Without major change their claim of being mainstream Christian is a smoke screen and major subterfuge.

If they are Christian it is time to preach Jesus, not Joseph. It is time to get back to the Bible and forget *The Book of Mormon*, which has been proven a fraud beyond any possible doubt. It is time to place *The Doctrine and Covenants* where it belongs, on the trash heap of false prophets' works! No one who compares the Bible with Mormon teachings will be able to do more than retch spiritually when they hear their misleading and false claims of being Christian. It is time to give up the farce.

CHRISTIANITY & MORMONISM

A Foundation with Major Cracks

Cracks in their theological walls are showing up everywhere. One of the biggest cracks is their admission that they cannot answer the logic and searchlight of truth directed upon them by writers such as Dr. Walter Martin, Wesley P. Walters, Jerald & Sandra Tanner, Dick Baer, Dr. Fales, Dr. Smith, Ed Decker, along with a hundred others. Their attacks on these Christian men are an admission of their own guilt. The age-old diversionary tactic—to attack the messenger instead of dealing with the message—is over.

This change of method is an admission that they can no longer defend their position with reason and logic, thus they must resort to intimidation. The next step in this natural progression is to admit their error and begin to work out of it. The whole world is watching. The Christian community will welcome a change of direction back to Christianity.

Christians Have a Safe Guide in the Bible

The Holy Bible has withstood the most intense scrutiny of some of the world's finest scholars for thousands of years. When the Bible says it, you can count on it being true. The texts of both Old and New Testaments have been proven pure and unchanged. As Jesus said, "Not the smallest letter or stroke shall pass from the Law until all is accomplished" (Matthew 5:18) and "… the Scripture cannot be broken.…" (John 10:35). The Bible stands!

Check as carefully as you like, investigating till your heart is content, and you will discover that the Bible stands. When my fifty-year study of theology began it was admitted that there were about 90 "unanswerable" problems in the Bible. Over the years this number has declined, due to more evidence, to about fifty. Today there are but a very few unanswerable problems. As scholars learn more it is probable that the Scriptures will be totally vindicated in every detail.

Check the Bible from another direction. Check its commands and prohibitions in light of human experience. If the Bible prohibits something, it is only because that action is a hurtful type of bondage. Check all of its commands and you will see that they are intent upon good and freedom for humans. If the Bible says "don't do it" you can trust that it is for good reason. If it commands a particular action, it is only for our good. All commands and prohibitions follow logically what is good for people.

The problem with cults and religious dogmas is that people are bound to a creed, a system of religion, conceived by humans to control people by bringing them into and keeping them in bondage. Man's religion seeks power over people's lives and thinking. Christian religion frees people from bondage: mental, social, spiritual.

When people are bound to their cult, denomination, or dogma, that religion will then tell them what the truth is. The adherent must believe it, true or false. Members must fall in line with some human prophet or prophetess.

The Christian is only bound by what is true, never by man-made creeds and dogmas. If Christians learn that what they thought was true is not, all they have to do is turn to the truth. No Christian is ever fully correct on all doctrine. But as Christians they continue to grow, and as they grow, they are not bound by a religious creed that is more or less than the truth. Their allegiance is to Jesus who is the truth.

A reformer described false religions by the following parable. He said that the Roman Catholic Church discovered that a Christian was to be three feet tall. They made a metal bedstead with a roller and knife. If they found a Christian that was only twenty-nine inches tall they would use the roller on him till he measured three feet tall. If the person were four feet tall they used the knife to cut off a foot. Then came Luther who learned that Christians were four feet tall. He made his bedstead with roller and knife, cutting or rolling people as needed. Then came Wesley, he found Christians should be five feet tall, he made his bedstead with roller and knife. But the Bible teaches that each of us is to grow continually until we measure to the fullness of the stature of Christ (Ephesians 4:13).

The beauty of holding allegiance to Christ, not to some prophet, cult, denomination, or man-made religion is that the pursuit is only for truth. The Christian never has the embarrassing task of defending some church dogma drawn up by a false prophet or man. When truth is found it can be joyfully embraced, even if one becomes seven feet tall spiritually. It is tremendous to be freed from the "metal bedstead, roller, and knife" mentality.

Think about it: Who saves us? Jesus. Or is it Jesus *plus* someone else? False religion wants some man added to Jesus. Some say, Jesus plus the Pope; others, Jesus plus Ellen G. White; others, Jesus plus Pastor Russell; others, Jesus plus Joseph Smith. If it takes Jesus plus anyone else, Jesus cannot save. The Bible says there is salvation in no other name than that of Jesus Christ.

Think again, if merely claiming to be a Christian cannot save us, then what good would it be to be a particular type, brand, or kind of Christian? Why be a hyphenated Christian? Baptist-Christian, Mormon-Christian, Catholic-Christian; isn't Christian enough? If not, why not? Jesus adds the saved to His own church daily. Christ has but one church and His church is made up of all Christians of all time.

Christians Hold Only to What Is True

What a unique idea, but one espoused by Jesus and the apostles, "… examine everything carefully; hold fast to that which is good.… "

(1 Thessalonians 5:21). The biggest problem with Mormonism is what to do with all the problems.

What is to be done with the 4,000 mistakes in *The Book of Mormon*? What is to be done with the outlandish, unbelievable stories in it? What is to be done with the foolish teachings of *The Doctrine and Covenants*? What is to be done with racist teachings of *The Book of Mormon* and the Book of Abraham? What do you do when you learn that Joseph Smith lied about the gold plates?

Two approaches can be taken. One is to begin the seemingly endless task of cleaning out all the falsehood and lies. Start with *The Book of Mormon* and finish cleaning out all the problems. This process has been going on for 150 years. Try to discard the story about gold plates and seer stone translation. Throw out the questionable witnesses. Or, maybe it would make more sense to simply admit it isn't Scripture and never was.

Then try to figure out what God said and didn't say in *The Doctrine and Covenants*. Then try to evaluate all the present prophet's teachings and coordinate them with all the past. But realistically, why not save time by admitting they aren't Scripture, and never were? (Frankly, I am already getting pretty confused and depressed with all this work so far.) So why not turn to Jesus and let Him free us from man-made religion?

Why not submit to Jesus Christ and become a Christian only? Then each day as you travel the Christian pathway study the Scripture and become a champion of truth. When error is found cast it aside, but when truth is found, guard it like a precious jewel. Prove all things; hold fast to that which is true. This is a truly liberating concept that can only lead one more and more into the light of God's will and the joys of spiritual freedom.

Christians Are Urged to Think and Reason

What a refreshing idea, take both your Bible and brains to church with you each Lord's day. Without fear, check the Scriptures daily to see if what is taught is the truth. We are able to use both mind and Scripture and still have a growing faith and closer walk with the Lord. Christians need never be bound by denominational or cultist dogmas, oppressive leaders, or mind-controlling people. This is liberty!

As all of God's people move steadily toward truth, Christians will become more and more alike and united. This appeal is to all churches. Churches that pursue truth will become more and more alike. Denominationalism will become less and less important as all of God's children unite around His truth, the Holy Bible. God will be more and more honored; people will be more and more free in Christ. The world will see a united Christianity and believe our common witness. Revival will again come to our world when Jesus is presented as Lord of all and Savior of all who follow Him.

Christians Are Free to Give Generously

The Christian motivation for giving generously to Christ's work is not law, but grace. We are no longer bound by a man-made system of rules and good-old-boy regimen, but willingly bound by the marvelous love of God shed abroad in our hearts. We give all tithes and offerings totally out of love for Christ and commitment to His work. It well may be more than the Mormon average of 27%, given not out of works, but out of a loving heart for the Lord and His work.

The concept of Mormons earning their way to some ever-ascending higher glory, world after world, is cast away with one fell swoop. It is replaced by a system in which a person is instantly and gloriously saved, saved to the fullest, the uttermost, the very first moment in Christ. Now all of their "works of righteousness" spring up out of love, from the filling of the Holy Spirit and with a true companionship with the heavenly "Comforter" (*Paracl ētos*) in their lives.

For nobody can live, as the Mormons suggest, in a way that will make it possible for him to gradually make his own way to some sort of anthropomorphic salvation. Rather, Jesus saves us as a gift by His marvelous grace, saving us instantly, totally, finally, and completely. To know Christ is to know *real* freedom.

Christian Women Are Liberated

Christ liberated women, making them priests and fellow heirs with all the saints. The conditions for women before Christ's day were horrible. The Jewish man would pray, "Thank God I was not created a Gentile nor a woman nor an ass." (Today women should pray, "Thank God I was not created a Mormon woman.")

It is true that God gave men and women different roles in the family and in the church. But God gave women the better part every time. They are to be treated with love and respect. Men are to take the heavy and dirty jobs. Men and women are granted priesthood and can be assured direct access to our High Melchizedek Priest, Jesus. They are assured that in heaven men and women will have the same rewards. Yes, elders and preachers are to be men; this is because God must have loved women more than men!

No religion has ever elevated women to a higher place than did Christ. Mormon women need to be liberated from bondage to the freedom that is in Christ.

CHRISTIANITY & MORMONISM

SUMMARY

So there we have it. Bondage in contrast to the simplicity and freedom that Christians enjoy. It is time to emancipate those in slavery. The LDS people need a spiritual Abraham Lincoln, a prophet with the intellectual honesty and courage to call the Mormon church back to real Christianity. The time is ripe for such a great leader to rise up and lead these fine people from slavery to grace and salvation, like Moses led the Israelites out of Egyptian bondage.

FROM BONDAGE TO FREEDOM

The Bars of Bondage
1. How are Mormons limited in their scientific thinking?
2. Describe the psychological power Mormon leaders have over LDS members.
3. How are Mormon women especially in bondage?
4. Discuss what you think are the three most important steps in restoring Mormons to orthodox beliefs.
5. How are Christians free to think, give, and fulfill their roles as men and women?

The Keys to Freedom
1. Create a "scrapbook" of newspaper, Internet, and journal articles chronicling the changing world of Mormonism. You can find this information through your local library, college, or bookstore. You may subscribe to the newsletters from one of the various missions to Mormons.
2. Individually or as a group find ways to present the material in this book and your notebook with others. Organize a class or seminar, form a study group, or invite the author to speak on the subject of Mormonism.

Conclusion

"And for an entire year they met with the church and taught considerable numbers; and the disciples were first called Christians in Antioch" (Acts 11:26).

MORMONISM HAS A LOT OF WORK TO DO

Without a shadow of a doubt, the Latter-day Saints church has not restored the church, nor the Bible teachings about the church, nor its leadership. It will take much more than putting a new name on the same old doctrines and organization to change reality. Recent efforts to get away from the names that have been given to them to hide their true identity are more symbols than substance. Renaming a Chevrolet a Cadillac does not change the fact that it still is a Chevy. Trying to tack on the name "Christian" does not change all of the strange, non-Christian doctrines and weird scripture. Does the Mormon church in truth want to be Christian?

Do they really believe that mainstream Christianity will accept them as "Christian" along with all the bogus scripture? Teachings that label all other churches as of the Devil? Teaching that they are the *most correct church on earth*? They need to get rid of their unBiblical elders and deacons. Quit sending out boys with nametags that say they are "Elders," when a Biblical elder is to be older, "gray haired" (meaning of the word elder), married, with children. If they are unwilling to begin a total reformation, then they should admit they remain the most non- and anti-Christian of the cults. In the meantime they remain a stronghold of corrupt scripture, of perverted and wicked doctrines, that need to be exposed to the light of truth and then expunged from the church. Do they want to stay with all these things? Then they need to be honest and admit that they are a very strange cultist church that has totally remodeled Christianity into a church that in very few ways even vaguely resembles Christianity. Is Islam

CHRISTIANITY & MORMONISM

a Christian religion? Islam may have a more accurate view of God, Jesus, and revelation than the LDS church system.

My appeal to them is to turn to Christ, turn to the Bible, and turn to the one and only God, Jehovah. Turn to mainstream Christianity. Christians will rejoice with them as they purge out the error, and begin in reality to become the *Church of Jesus Christ*. It is painful to be so blunt, but this is true. These may sound like harsh words, but they are the truth in love. It has been my dream that in my lifetime the Mormon church might turn to mainstream Christianity. What a glorious day that will be for their members and for the truth. Armstrongism has awakened to its challenge and has blended back into mainstream Christianity. If they *want* to do the same, *they* can!

MORMONISM COULD BEGIN TO REFORM

The job before the church is so gigantic that the question is not so much, can it be restored, but rather, is it so totally corrupted that it would be easier to start from scratch? My opinion is that it *could* be restored, but not without a great leader, willing to go to the wall for truth. If the church is not willing to begin massive changes it will remain a cult.

If they are willing, they might begin with major changes in the following areas.

Their Doctrine of God

They must begin by turning to a Biblical doctrine of God, turning to monotheism from their polytheistic view of God as a created being, over which other gods rule. They must scrap their view of men progressing to being gods. They must return to the Biblical view of one, eternal, always existing, supreme Being, manifested to us as the Holy Trinity, Father-Son-Holy Spirit. They must turn to monotheism from pagan polytheism if they want to be Christian.

Their Doctrine of Jesus

They need to repudiate their doctrine that Jesus and the Devil are brothers. They must find the real Jesus instead of a fully human Jesus. They must deny that Jesus is a created being. They must deny their teaching that Jesus is just one of many gods. If the church wants to be Christian these doctrines must be changed. They must replace their hodgepodge of conflicting and unBiblical doctrines with the Christian view of Jesus as eternal God, as an eternal Being of the Godhead.

Conclusion

Their Doctrine of the Virgin Birth of Christ

Is the church willing to turn to the Biblical doctrine of the virgin birth? If they wish to truly become Christian it is time to repudiate the horrendous teachings of Brigham Young, Joseph Fielding Smith, Orson Pratt and others about Jesus' birth and polygamous marriages! Their doctrine of celestial polygamy requires a married, polygamist Jesus.

Their disgusting doctrine that Jesus was born because God, who has a body, parts and passion, came down and had intercourse with Mary must be disavowed. This is truly a non-Christian doctrine. If they want to be Christian then these things must go! They must return to the Biblical doctrine that Jesus was begotten of the pure and holy Mary by miraculous action of the Holy Spirit, that Mary remained a virgin until after Jesus was born.

Their View of Revelation

A good beginning would be to purge out all of the bogus scripture: *The Book of Mormon*, *Doctrine and Covenants*, and *Pearl of Great Price*. These are not Scripture, never have been and never will be. They have not stood investigation. Wouldn't their Christian work be much easier if they did not have to defend these extraneous books and teachings? What more do we need than the Bible to know the way to Christ?

The Bible

They must return to a realistic view of the Bible. That is, criticism in *The Book of Mormon* of the Bible along with their other statements that the Bible is full of errors. These teachings must be replaced with the truth that the Bible has been proven remarkably unchanged. They must disavow Joseph Smith's Inspired Version of the Bible with its over 4,000 changes to the Bible. His changes have been proven to be outrageous distortions of Scripture. They must repudiate their prophet's criticism of the Bible.

The Book of Mormon

The Book of Mormon has not stood up to investigation. This will be a bitter pill for them to swallow, but swallow they must. They must admit that it has been a fraud from the beginning. It is not Scripture, but an epic novel based upon an old, now disproved idea, that American Indians are really Jews. With its errors, plagiarism of the King James Bible, with its outlandish stories, and modern inventions, they must give it up. Textual Criticism has proven that it is a deception.

The Doctrine and Covenants

Mormonism can never rejoin mainstream Christianity while still claiming that *The Doctrine and Covenants* is Scripture. Its text has been so deceptively corrupted as to have over 2,786 changes to what Section One claims was the unchangeable word of God. With over twenty doctrinal changes, contradicting what was originally said, with its strange view of God, marriage, heaven and hell, it must go.

The Journal of Discourses

This twenty-six volume, encyclopedia-like set of many sermons and lectures by the church prophets and apostles must go. Although very few people have really studied these carefully, including me, reading excerpts from them shows how far from Christianity the LDS church has always been. A married, polygamous Jesus, a sexually active Jehovah, a pre-existent state for all humans, an anthropomorphic God (and Jesus), proud and arrogant prophets and apostles—all must go!

A casual reading indicates that these volumes are packed with twisted interpretations of the Bible, filled with superstition, errors of exegesis, and for the most part not worth the paper to publish them. They should be relegated to the library that is made up of American religious oddities. Certainly there is no place for them in a truly Christian religion. Their pose as "Christian" will have a lot more credibility if they will purge *The Journal of Discourses*. To clean up all these sermons of false, un-Christian ideas, and inaccurate theology would be almost impossible. Trash the whole work!

The Pearl of Great Price

With its books of Moses and Abraham, that have been proven to be pure deceptions, *The Pearl* must go! The Book of Abraham, supposedly translated from an ancient manuscript written by Abraham himself, has been totally and finally shown to be a Joseph Smith hoax. There is no doubt. It is not surprising that the LDS want to attack those who question them, rather than to try to defend such an outlandish, bizarre, and laughable book. The Book of Abraham must also be tossed because of its teaching that dark-skinned people could not hold the priesthood having sinned in the pre-existence.

Do they want the nations to accept them as Christian? They must purge those awful, dehumanizing racial slurs about Blacks, Egyptians, and Native Americans from their supposed scripture. These are unBiblical, and racially bigoted teachings. The Book of Abraham with its slur against the African, Native American and other races, that have a bit more skin pigmentation, should be expunged from all literature, and particularly from that of a supposed Christian religion.

Conclusion

> My object in going to inquire of the Lord was to know which of all the sects was right, that I should know which to join. No sooner, therefore, did I get possession of myself, so as to be able to speak, than I asked the Personages who stood above me in the light, which of all the sects was right—and which I should join. I was answered that I must join none of them, for they were all wrong; and the Personage who addressed me said that all their creeds were an abomination were all corrupt ... having a form of godliness, but they deny the power thereof (*Pearl* 2:18-20).

This must go! Why would the LDS church want to be recognized as mainstream Christianity if all Christian churches are corrupt?

Their Hundreds of Other Doctrinal Problems

Mormon prophets have thoroughly stirred false theological ideas throughout the church—from their view of God, Christ, the Holy Spirit, the Bible, heaven and hell, salvation—until much of true Christianity is out of focus, with few teachings really on Biblical target. Their doctrine of working one's way gradually to the highest heaven is an insult to the blood of Christ and His marvelous grace. Their teaching totally misses the key doctrine of salvation by faith and grace.

Will mainstream Christianity accept that Mormons are really "Christian" as long as polygamy is so widely practiced in Utah and a part of the scheme of salvation? Are they really *ready* to change? Why do they continue the chameleon ruse?

Do they want to be "The Church of Jesus Christ?" Then they should turn to the Biblical practice of Communion and do away with the water and light bread substitutions. They need to quit usurping Jesus' role as High Priest of the church and stop conferring this office on all sorts of non-priests.

They must do away with all the "secret rites" and rituals including celestial marriages and baptism for dead people. These doctrines are neither Biblical nor even in harmony with *The Book of Mormon*. This is but another of Joseph Smith's errors that cannot stand the light of investigation. If they want their identity "The Church of Jesus Christ" to ring true in practice, they must recant their heavenly marriages and get back to the clear teaching of Jesus that there will be no marriage or giving in marriage in heaven. Otherwise it appears hypocritical to thinking Christians. They have changed their scripture at will before, now is the time again to get out the scissors and paste.

Their Need to Cast Out Joseph Smith and Other Supposed Prophets

The proof that Joseph Smith was no prophet of God is so clear, voluminous, and conclusive as to conclude that *he* must go. Let us review some of his strange and conflicting accounts.

- Of seeing God, Jesus and others, yet with three conflicting published accounts of the first vision
- His story of gold plates, running through the woods and jumping a fence with about 1,200-plus pounds tucked under one arm
- Proof that someone else wrote *The Book of Mormon*
- Book of Abraham—proof that he could not translate a foreign language
- His wicked behavior, lies, immorality, and polygamy
- His erroneous prophecies in *The Doctrine and Covenants*

Wouldn't it be refreshing for the Mormon church if they no longer had to defend Joseph Smith? It would make their job of evangelization so much easier. It would help give the ring of credibility to their claim that they are truly Christian.

MORMONISM IS A SYSTEM OF BONDAGE BORROWED FROM MANY SOURCES

My lasting, lifetime impression from studying of The Church of Jesus Christ of Latter-day Saints (Utah branch), and working with their people, is that the Mormon people subsist in a system of bondage. They are not free to think. They live in a religion of superstition, closely related to the occult, the Masonic Lodge, and things borrowed from Christian Churches/Churches of Christ, as well as borrowed from Islam and the Roman Catholic Church. This is quite an accusation, but none-the-less true. Consider the sources.

- With Joseph Smith's seer stones, wedding garment amulets, and talking snakes there is the occult connection.
- Joseph was a Mason and borrowed many Masonic temple rites.
- The Sidney Rigdon connection brought strong influence from the Christian Church/Church of Christ Restoration Movement with Alexander Campbell and Barton Stone. Here they borrowed the emphasis of restoring the church and perverted baptism by immersion for the remission of sins.

- Joseph Smith and Muhammad were cut out of the same piece of cloth. Muhammad was basically uneducated, came with his own book of scripture, the Koran; was a polygamist, consummating the relationship with his youngest wife at a very early age; claimed he was God's prophet on earth; and borrowed heavily from the Old and New Testament. Joseph Smith was a carbon copy of Muhammad: poorly educated; writer of his own book of scripture, *The Book of Mormon*; a polygamist, consummating sexual relations with very young women; a claimant as God's prophet on earth; and a heavy borrower from the Old and New Testament. This is only the beginning of comparisons between Muhammad and Joseph Smith.
- The LDS church has borrowed its polity from the Roman Catholic Church (form of government patterned after the Roman Empire), with prophet/Pope, prelates/apostles, the succession argument, etc.

Is the LDS church Biblical? The answer is a definite "No!"

MORMONISM MUST EXAMINE THE ISSUES

Instead of attacking and condemning anyone who points out their doctrinal and theological errors, they could actually engage their minds and examine the issues. They could begin to move to the truth. They could then actually become what they claim they are—Christian.

Regrettably for the LDS church, when they have been unable to defend their many errors, rather than to change, they choose to defame and attack those who tell them the truth. If they want to be known as lovers of truth and Christians they must no longer stoop to muckraking and maligning good people who love them enough to speak the truth to them. If they believed they had the truth they would be ready to address the issues, rather than to assassinate peoples' characters.

Since inwardly they must know their church cannot be defended in an open argument, their only recourse is to change. They need a new spiritual Moses to lead their people out of the bondage of their newfound Egypt, to the promised land of truth.

The church has to discontinue trying to ruin whistleblowers in or out of the church. In times past those who have tried to expose errors have been suppressed and run out of the church. These people need to be encouraged to speak out and if the church's position cannot stand the light of investigation, to focus their resources on learning the truth. The church needs to make some public apologies to people whose reputations have been smirched and whose influence has been destroyed because of LDS members publishing lies against them. Vicious personal attacks on those who point out their errors must stop. The game is over! It is time for the myriads of inconsistencies, false history, twisted records, and corrupt and phony scripture, to be discarded. If they will come to the truth, return to mainstream Christianity, they will be liberated!

MORMONISM'S BEHAVIOR IS AN ADMISSION OF GUILT

The most pagan of the American cults has a gulf to cross before they can be recognized as Christian. It is time to confess that they cannot defend their system of religion as "Christian." Their behavior in recent years is an admission that they cannot defend it—it is an admission of their own guilt. All of those who have challenged them beg them to give up their satanic methods and call them to a new restoration and a turn to those things that Christianity has always believed to be true.

When they have turned from character assassination, half truths, and lies, then they will be headed in the right direction. Little by little they can move from the sinking quicksand of their bogus prophet's work to firm ground. Since they do not like the message being brought to them about their teachings, they need to change their message!

Their repeated claims of being truly Christian is an admission that there are major cracks in their doctrinal foundation. An honest person needs not plead his honesty, nor a wise man, his wisdom. Neither does a church have to use the media to convince others of their true Christianity. If honest, they must discontinue trying to convince unsuspecting people that they are what they presently are not. Instead of singing a tune with a false melody, why not get to work and turn to what they must know is truth?

We who love them cry out in prayer to God for them to give up the hoax and together turn to the Christian fold. All of Christendom calls out, turn home! My prayer is that one of three things will happen soon.
1. That a strong leader within the church will call for widespread study and turn to truth.
2. If there is no one with the courage to speak and lead them out of bondage to the freedom in Christ, then I pray that the whole system will implode, as has Armstrongism.
3. Let it become a large American business corporation.

Conclusion

MORMONISM IS NOT A MAINSTREAM CHRISTIAN RELIGION

Honesty insists that they not continue to perpetrate a hoax on unsuspecting people by suggesting that they are mainstream Christianity. They are not! Mainstream Christianity must be warned that at the present time the LDS church is most glaringly a cult. That as Christians together we no longer ignore our friends and neighbors who are in a bondage much more damaging than that of the slaves in the day of Abraham Lincoln. Is there anyone willing to take the challenge of being liberators of those so long held in spiritual bondage? Many young people need to rise to this challenge.

If you are LDS, and have read to this point, hear the gentle voice of Jesus who calls you to freedom, a freedom that begins in time and reaches to eternity. It is so much easier to be a real Christian and follow the real Jesus than to continue in Mormon bondage. Besides, for those who follow Jesus, there is salvation, peace, and eternity in heaven. Jesus offers a "Welcome Home!" to all of you who wish to find salvation in Him. If He cannot save, we are all lost. Fortunately for us He saves to the uttermost.

SUMMARY

Remember, Jesus can save everyone.
It has never taken
Jesus + the Pope, Jesus + Joseph Smith, Jesus + any other human.
Jesus can save and He alone.
Anyone who requires more is a false prophet!

"It was for freedom that Christ set us free.... So if the Son makes you free, you will be free indeed" (Galatians 5:1; John 8:36).

FROM BONDAGE TO FREEDOM

The Bars of Bondage
1. What has been the most interesting new information regarding the LDS church that you have learned in this study?
2. Explain three ways that Mormonism has borrowed from different sources.
3. How does Mormonism compare with Islam? Contrast their leaders and scriptures.
4. Is Mormonism a mainstream Christian church? Why or why not?
5. What do Mormons, as well as all people, need to know about Jesus?

CHRISTIANITY & MORMONISM

The Keys to Freedom

1. Keep your notebook ready to add new insights into approaching LDS church members. Changing revelations and changing advertising methods will reveal what their leadership is actually thinking. Pray for Mormons to turn to Christ and abandon their life of bondage.

2. Rent or check out of an audio-visual library videotapes, DVDs, or movies on Mormonism. Discuss your reactions in a group setting.

3. Review the bad approaches to witnessing to Mormons listed in the Introduction. Pray for opportunities to speak with Mormons in protected environments, that is, with Christian friends or during church activities. Keep a record of your personal ministry in your notebook.

Select Bibliography

BOOKS

A Compendium of the Doctrine of the Gospel. 2nd ed. Compiled by Franklin D. Richards and James A. Little. Salt Lake City: Deseret News Publishing Co., 1884.

Adair, James. *The History of the American Indians.* London: Edward and Charles Dilly, 1775.

Adamson, Jack, and Dr. Reed C. Durham, Jr. *No Help for the Widow's Son.* Nauvoo, IL: Martin Publishing Co., 1980.

Ankerberg, John, and John Weldon. *Everything You Ever Wanted to Know about Mormonism.* Eugene, OR: Harvest House, 1992.

Arrington, Leonard J. *Brigham Young American Moses.* New York: Alfred A. Knopf, 1985.

Bates, Ernest Sutherland. *American Faith.* New York: W.W. Norton Co., 1940.

Benson, Ezra Taft. *The Teachings of Ezra Taft Benson.* Salt Lake City: Bookcraft, 1956.

Berrett, William E. *The Restored Church.* Salt Lake City: Deseret Book Co., 1956.

Biederwolf, W.E. *Mormonism under the Searchlight.* Grand Rapids: Eerdmans, 1956.

Bjornstad, James. *Counterfeits at Your Door.* Glendale, CA: Regal Books, 1979.

Boudinot, Elias. *A Star in the West, or A Humble Attempt to Discover the Long-Lost Tribes of Israel.* Trenton, NJ: D. Fenton, S. Hutchinson, and J. Dunham, 1816.

Brodie, Fawn M. *No Man Knows My History: The Life of Joseph Smith the Mormon Prophet.* 2nd Ed. New York: Alfred A Knopf, 1978.

Braden, Clark. *These also Believe.* New York: The Macmillan Co., 1949.

Bruce, F.F. *The Books and the Parchments: How We Got Our English Bible.* Old Tappan, NJ: Fleming H. Revell, 1984.

Bushman, Richard L. *Joseph Smith and the Beginnings of Mormonism.* Chicago: University of Illinois Press, 1984.

Cowan, Marvin W. *Mormon Claims Answered.* Salt Lake City: Self-published, 1975.

Corrill, John. *A Brief History of the Church of Christ of Latter Day Saints.* Saint Louis: Self-published, 1839.

Cowdery, Wayne L., Howard A. Davis, and Donald R. Scales. *Who Really Wrote the Book of Mormon?* Santa Ana, CA: Vision House, 1977.

Crane, Charles. *The Bible and Mormon Scriptures Compared.* Joplin, MO: College Press, 1992.

Crane, Charles and Steven. *Ashamed of Joseph: Mormon Foundations Crumble.* Joplin, MO: College Press, 1993.

Crawford, Charles. *An Essay upon the Propagation of the Gospel.* 2nd ed. Philadelphia: J. Gales, 1801.

Davies, Horton. *Christian Deviations.* New York: Philosophical Library, Inc., 1954.

Davis, Inez Smit. *The Story of the Church.* Independence, MO: Herald Publishing House, 1964.

Evans, R.C. *Forty Years in the Mormon [RLDS] Church: Why I Left It.* Toronto, Canada: Self-published, 1920.

Evening and Morning Star. Independence, MO and Kirtland, OH: W.W. Phelps and Co., 1832-1834.

Flanders, Robert B. *Nauvoo: Kingdom on the Mississippi.* Urbana, IL: University of Illinois Press, 1965.

Fraser, Gordon H. *Is Mormonism Christian?* Chicago: Moody, 1977.

_____. *What Does the Book of Mormon Teach?* Chicago: Moody, 1964.

_____. *Joseph and the Golden Plates.* Eugene, OR: Industrial Litho, Inc., 1978.

Fry, Evan. *The Restoration Faith.* Independence, MO: Herald Publishing House, 1962.

Garcia, Gregorio. *Origen de los Indios del Nuevo Mundo, e Indias Occidentales.* Valencia, Spain: Pedro Patricio Mey, 1607.

Geisler, Norman L., and Ron Rhodes. *When Cultists Ask: A Popular Handbook on Cultic Misinterpretations.* Grand Rapids: Baker, 1997.

Hallwas, John E., and Roger D. Launius. *Cultures in Conflict: A Documentary History of the Mormon War in Illinois.* Logan, UT: Utah State University Press, 1995.

Harrison, G.T. *That Mormon Book: Mormonism's Keystone Exposed or The Hoax Book.* N.p.: Self-published, 1981.

Hickman, Bill. *Brigham's Destroying Angel: Being the Life, Confession and Startling Disclosures of the Notorious Bill Hickman.* Salt Lake City: Shepard Book Company, 1904.

Hiles, Norma Derry. *Gentle Monarch: The Presidency of Israel A. Smith.* Independence, MO: Herald Publishing House, 1991.

History of the Reorganized Church of Jesus Christ of Latter Day Saints. 7 Vols. Independence, MO: Herald Publishing House, 1967-1973.

Hoekema, Anthony A. *The Four Major Cults.* Grand Rapids: Eerdmans, 1988.

Holley, Vernal. *Book of Mormon Authorship: A Closer Look.* Ogden, UT: Zenos Publications, 1983.

Horton, Davies. *Christian Deviations.* New York: Philosophical Library, Inc., 1954.

Howard, Richard P. *Restoration Scriptures: A Study of Their Textual Development.* Independence, MO: Herald Publishing House, 1969.

Howe, Eber D. *History of Mormonism.* Painesville, OH: Self-published, 1840.

Select Bibliography

_____. *Mormonism Unveiled*. Painesville, OH. Self-published, 1834.

Hunt, Dave. *The Cult Explosion*. Eugene, OR: Harvest House, 1980.

Hunter, Milton R. *The Gospel Through the Ages*. Salt Lake City: Deseret Book Co., 1945.

Jenson, Andrew. *The Historical Record*. Salt Lake City: 1866-1890.

Jonas, Larry. *Mormonism Claims Examined*. Grand Rapids: Baker, 1961.

Joseph Smith's "New Translation" of the Bible. Independence, MO: Herald Publishing House, 1970.

Kennedy, D. James, and Jerry Newcombe. *What if the Bible Had Never Been Written?* Nashville: Nelson, 1998.

Kingsborough, Lord. *Antiquities of Mexico*. 7 Vols. London: Augustine Aglio, 1830.

Larson, Charles M. *By His Own Hand Upon Papyrus*. Rev. ed. Grand Rapids: Institute for Religious Research, 1992.

Launius, Roger D. *Zion's Camp*. Independence, MO: Herald Publishing House, 1984.

Lee, John D. *Confessions of John D. Lee*. Saint Louis: Bryan, Brand & Company, Original Ed., 1878.

LeSueur, Stephen C. *The 1838 Mormon War in Missouri*. Columbia, MO: University of Missouri Press, 1987.

Marquardt, H. Michael. *The Use of the Bible in the Book of Mormon*. Saint Louis: Personal Freedom Outreach, 1979.

_____. *Inventing Mormonism*. Salt Lake City: Signature Books, Inc. Clothbound 1994, paperbound 1998.

Martin, Walter. *Essential Christianity*. Ventura, CA: Regal Books, 1990.

_____. *The Kingdom of the Cults*. Limited Ed. Minneapolis: Bethany House, 1992.

_____. *The Maze of Mormonism*. Revised edition. Ventura, CA: Regal Books, 1978.

Maston, T.B. *The Bible and Race*. Nashville: Broadman, 1962.

Mayer, F.E. *The Religious Bodies of America*. Saint Louis: Concordia, 1954.

McConkie, Bruce R. *Doctrines of Salvation*. Salt Lake City: Bookcraft, 1954.

_____. *Mormon Doctrine*. Salt Lake City: Bookcraft, 1966.

McDowell, Josh. *Evidence That Demands a Verdict*. 2 Vols. San Bernardino, CA: Here's Life Publishers, 1990.

_____. *Research in Christian Evidences*. San Bernardino, CA: Here's Life Publishers, 1979.

McElveen, Floyd C. *The Mormon Illusion*. Ventura, CA: Regal Books, 1983.

_____. *The Mormon Revelations of Convenience*. Minneapolis: Bethany Fellowship, 1978.

McKay, David O. *Gospel Ideals*. Salt Lake City: The Church of Jesus Christ of Latter-day Saints, 1953.

Miller, H.S. *General Biblical Introduction*. Houghton, NY: The Word-Bearer Press, 1959.

Nelson, Dee Jay. *The Joseph Smith Papyri–A Translation and Preliminary Survey*. Salt Lake City: Modern Microfilm Company, 1978.

———. *The Joseph Smith Papyri*. Pt. 2. Salt Lake City: Modern Microfilm Company, 1978.

Parkin, Max. *Conflict at Kirtland: A Study of the Nature and Causes of External and Internal Conflict of the Mormons in Ohio Between 1830 and 1838*. Salt Lake City: Max Parkin, 1966. (Originally a thesis, Brigham Young University, 1966.)

Pratt, Orson. *The Seer*. Washington, DC: 1853-54. Photo-reprint. Salt Lake City: Eugene Wagner.

Priest, Josiah. *The Wonders of Nature and Providence Displayed*. Albany: E. and E. Hosford, 1825.

Principles of the Gospel. Salt Lake City: The Church of Jesus Christ of Latter-day Saints, 1976.

Quinn, D. Michael. *Early Mormonism and the Magic World View*. Salt Lake City: Signature Books, 1987.

———. *The Mormon Hierarchy*. Salt Lake City: Signature Books in Association with Smith Research Assn., 1994.

Reed, David A., and John R. Farkas. *Mormons Answered Verse by Verse*. Grand Rapids: Baker, 1992.

Religious Truths Defined. Pp. 175 & 337. Cited by Jerald Tanner and Sandra Tanner. *Mormonism–Shadow or Reality?* P. 64. Salt Lake City: Modern Microfilm Co., 1964.

Rhodes, Ron. *The Culting of America: The Shocking Implications for Every Concerned Christian*. Eugene, OR: Harvest House, 1994.

Richards, LeGrand. *A Marvelous Work and Wonder*. Salt Lake City: Deseret Book Co., 1976.

Richards, Stephen L. *Contributions of Joseph Smith*. Salt Lake City: The Church of Jesus Christ of Latter-day Saints.

RLDS Committee on Basic Beliefs. *Exploring the Faith*. Independence, MO: Herald Publishing House, 1970.

Roberts, B.H. *A Comprehensive History of the Church of Jesus Christ of Latter-day Saints*. Salt Lake City: Deseret News Press, 1930.

———. Ed. *History of the Church of Jesus Christ of Latter-day Saints*. 7 Vols. 2nd ed. Rev. Salt Lake City: Deseret News Press, 1963.

Ropp, Harry L. *The Mormon Papers*. Downers Grove, IL: InterVarsity, 1977.

Shields, Steven L. *Divergent Paths of the Restoration*. Los Angeles: Restoration Research, 1990.

Shook, Charles A. *The True Origin of the Book of Mormon*. Cincinnati: Standard Publishing, 1914.

———. *The True Origin of Mormon Polygamy*. Mendota, IL: The Western Advent Publication Assn., 1910.

Skousen, Cleon W. *The First 2000 Years*. Salt Lake City: Bookcraft, 1971.

Smith, Ethan. *View of the Hebrews; or the Tribes of Israel in America*. Second edition. Poultney, VT: Self-published, 1825.

Smith, Frederick M. *The Higher Powers of Man*. Independence, MO: Herald Publishing House, 1968.

Smith, Joseph, Jr. *A Book of Commandments*. Independence, MO: W.W. Phelps and Co., 1833.

Select Bibliography

_____. *Book of Doctrine and Covenants*. Independence, MO: Herald Publishing House, 1974.

_____. *The Book of Mormon*. Independence, MO: Herald Publishing House, 1953.

_____. *Inspired Version of the Holy Scriptures*. Independence, MO: Herald Publishing House, 1944.

_____. *The History of the Church of Jesus Christ of Latter-day Saints*. 7 Vols. Salt Lake City: Deseret News Press, 1951.

_____. *Times and Seasons*. Vol. 5. Pp. 613-614. Cited by Jerald and Sandra Tanner. *Mormonism–Shadow or Reality?* P. 137. Salt Lake City: Modern Microfilm, 1964.

Smith, Joseph Fielding. *Essentials in Church History*. Salt Lake City: Deseret News Press, 1942.

_____. Comp. *Gospel Doctrine: Selections from the Sermons and Writings of Joseph F. Smith*. Salt Lake City: Deseret Book Co., 1975.

_____. *Teachings of Prophet Joseph Smith*. Salt Lake City: Deseret Book Co., 1976.

_____. *The Way to Perfection*. Salt Lake City: Genealogical Society of Utah, 1931.

_____. *Doctrines of Salvation*. Compiled by Bruce R. McConkie. 3 Vols. Salt Lake City: Bookcraft, 1960.

Smith, Lucy Mack. *Biographical Sketches of Joseph Smith the Prophet*. Liverpool, England: S.W. Richards, 1853.

_____. *History of Joseph Smith by His Mother*. Salt Lake City: Bookcraft, 1979.

Stewart, Georgia Metcalf. *How the Church Grew*. Independence, MO: Herald Publishing House, 1959.

Stewart, John J. *Brigham Young and His Wives*. Salt Lake City: Mercury, 1961.

Stout, Hosea. *On the Mormon Frontier, the Diary of Hosea Stout*. Edited by Juanita Brooks. Salt Lake City: University of Utah Press, 1964. Vol. 1, 1844-1848. Vol. 2, 1848-1861.

Swartzell, William. *Mormonism Exposed*. Pekin, OH: Self-published, 1840.

Talmage, James E. *A Study of the Articles of Faith*. 36th ed. Salt Lake City: The Church of Jesus Christ of Latter-day Saints, 1957.

Tanner, Jerald and Sandra. *Magic and Masonry*. Salt Lake City: Utah Lighthouse Ministry, 1983.

_____. *Joseph Smith's 1826 Trial*. Salt Lake City: Modern Microfilm, 1971.

_____. *Joseph Smith's Successor–An Important New Document Comes to Light*. Salt Lake City: Jerald Tanner, 1981.

_____. *Mormonism–Shadow or Reality?* Salt Lake City: Modern Microfilm Co., 1972.

_____. *Mormonism: A Study of Mormon History and Doctrine*. Clearfield, UT: Utah Evangel Press, 1962.

_____. *The Case against Mormonism*. Salt Lake City: Utah Lighthouse Ministry, 1967.

_____. *The Changing World of Mormonism*. Chicago: Moody, 1980.

_____. *The First Vision Examined*. Salt Lake City: Modern Microfilm Company, 1969.

The New Schaff-Herzog Encyclopedia of Religious Knowledge. 13 Vols. Grand Rapids: Baker, 1957.

Trask, Paul T. *Part Way to Utah: The Forgotten Mormons*. Independence, MO: Refiner's Fire Ministries, 1997.

Trevor, John C. *The Untold Story of Qumran*. Westwood, NJ: Revell, 1952.

Turner, Wallace. *The Mormon Establishment*. Boston: Houghton Mifflin, 1966.

Walters, Wesley P. *New Light on Mormon Origins from the Palmyra, NY Revival*. Salt Lake City: Modern Microfilm Company, 1967.

_____. *Joseph Smith among the Egyptians*. Salt Lake City: Modern Microfilm Company, 1973.

_____. *Joseph Smith's Bainbridge, NY, Court Trial*. Salt Lake City: Modern Microfilm Company, 1977.

Watt, G.D. Ed. *Journal of Discourses*. 26 Vols. Liverpool: F.D. & S.W. Richards, 1854; reprint ed., Salt Lake City, 1966.

Whitmer, David. *An Address to All Believers in Christ*. Reprint, Searcy, AR: Bales Bookstore, 1960.

Widtsoe, John A. *Evidences and Reconciliations*. Salt Lake City: Bookcraft, 1969.

_____. *Joseph Smith–Seeker after Truth*. Salt Lake City: Bookcraft, 1951.

Wilson, Robert Dick. *A Scientific Investigation of the Old Testament*. Chicago: Moody, n.d.

Wood, Wilford C. *Joseph Smith Begins His Work: The Book of Mormon*. First Edition 1830. 2 Vols. The Book of Commandments, i.e., *The Doctrine and Covenants*. First Edition. Salt Lake City: Deseret News Press, 1958.

Worsley, Israel. *A View of the American Indians*. London: R. Hunter, 1828.

Young, Brigham. *Journal of Discourses*. 27 Vols. Liverpool: F.D. and S.W. Richards, 1966.

JOURNALS, LETTERS, PAMPHLETS, NEWSPAPERS, PERIODICALS

Amboy Journal. April 30, 1879, and June 11, 1879.

"Apostle's Humor Draws Laughter." *The Salt Lake Tribune*, April 8, 1973.

Barnes, Shelby M. "The Higher Powers: Fred M. Smith and the Peyote Ceremonies." *Dialogue: A Journal of Mormon Thought*. Winter, 1995.

Biblical Archaeology Review. September-October, 1980, p. 26.

Bodine, Jerry and Marian. *Whom Can You Trust?* Santa Ana, CA: Christ for the Cults, 1978.

Brigham Young University Studies. Provo, UT: 1959-Present.

Budvarson, Arthur. *The Book of Mormon: True or False?* Concord, CA: Pacific Publishing Co., 1959.

Campbell, Alexander. *The Millennial Harbinger*. Bethany, VA: February, 1831.

Cushing, Bruce L. *An Open Letter to My Brother: Mormonism vs. the Bible*. Bakersfield, CA: Self-published, n.d.

Deseret News. Salt Lake City: 1850-Present.

Dialogue: A Journal of Mormon Thought. Arlington, VA: 1966-Present.

Evening and The Morning Star. Independence, MO: 1832-1834.

Select Bibliography

Everyday Life in Bible Times. Washington, DC: National Geographic Society, 1967.

Fraser's Magazine. London: February, 1873.

Hansen, Klaus J. "The Theory and Practice of the Political Kingdom of God in Mormon History, 1829-1890." Master's Thesis: Brigham Young University, typed copy: 1959.

Helland, Dean Maurice. "Book of Mormon Problems." *Saints Alive Journal,* Spring/Summer, 1988.

"History of Joseph Smith." *Millennial Star.* April 6, 1861:23:246-247.

Journal of Pres. Rudger Clawson, pp. 374-375. Cited by Ogden Kraut, *Jesus Was Married,* p. 97. Dugway, UT: Self-published, 1970.

Juvenile Instructor. Salt Lake City: 1866-1970.

Kansas City Daily Journal. Kansas City: June 5, 1881.

Lancaster, James E. "By the Gift and Power of God." *Saints Herald.* November 15, 1962.

Latter-day Saints' Messenger and Advocate. 3 Vols. Kirtland, OH: 1834-1837.

Launius, Roger D. "The RLDS Church and the Decade of Decision." *Sunstone Magazine.* September, 1996.

Law, William. *Nauvoo Expositor.* June 7, 1844.

McConkie, Bruce R. *What the Mormons Think of Christ* (tract). Salt Lake City: Deseret News Press, n.d.

McKay, Robert. "Joseph Smith's False Prophecies." *The Salt Lake Tribune,* n.d.

Merson, Ben. "Husbands with More than One Wife." *Ladies Home Journal.* June 1967, pp. 78-79.

Neal, R.B. *Did Oliver Cowdery Renounce Mormonism and Join the Methodist Protestant Church at Tiffin, Ohio?* Grayson, KY: Gospel Dollar League, 1915, photocopied.

News Review. Nampa, ID: 1978.

Peck, Reed. *The Reed Peck Manuscript.* Quincy, IL: Self-published, 1839.

Roberts, B.H. *The Modern Doctrine of Deity.* Salt Lake City: Deseret News Press, 1903.

Salt Lake Tribune. Salt Lake City: September 24, 1972.

Salt Lake Tribune. Salt Lake City: 1871-Present.

Senate Document 189 (Missouri) "Concerning the Mormon Danite Band." (Photomechanical reprint 26th Congress, of 2nd Session, February 15, 1841).

Sheen, Isaac. *The True Latter-day Saints' Herald.* Cincinnati. Published by the New Organization of the Church of Jesus Christ of Latter-day Saints, January, 1860.

Smithsonian Institution, Department of Anthropology. "Statement Regarding the Book of Mormon." Washington, DC: Smithsonian Institution, 1988.

Spaulding, F.S., and Samuel A.B. Mercer. *Why Egyptologists Reject the Book of Abraham.* Salt Lake City: Utah Lighthouse Ministry, n.d.

Tanner, Jerald and Sandra. "Joseph Smith's Use of the Apocrypha." *Salt Lake City Messenger.* (89), December, 1995.

_____. "Legacy: A Distorted View of Mormon History." *Salt Lake City Messenger,* May, 1995.

Times and Seasons. 6 Vols. Nauvoo, IL: 1839-1846.

CHRISTIANITY & MORMONISM

U. S. News and World Report. September 28, 1992.

Utah Holiday Magazine. Salt Lake City: 1976.

White, Bob. Comp. *Where Does It Say That?* Scottsdale, AZ: Cult and Occult Unification Program, [date?].

Young Brigham. *Deseret News.* February 10, 1867. Cited by Ogden Kraut, *Jesus Was Married,* p. 62. Dugway, UT: Self-published, 1970.

STANDARD WORKS OF THE MORMON CHURCH

Smith, Joseph, Jr. *Book of Doctrine and Covenants, Pearl of Great Price.* Salt Lake City: The Church of Jesus Christ of Latter-day Saints, 1971.

_____. *The Book of Mormon.* Salt Lake City: The Church of Jesus Christ of Latter-day Saints, 1950.

_____. *History of the Church.* Salt Lake City: Deseret Book Co., 1963.

_____. *Inspired Version of the Holy Scriptures.* Independence, MO: Herald Publishing House, 1970.

Smith, Joseph Fielding. *Doctrines of Salvation.* Salt Lake City: Bookcraft, 1954.

Young, Brigham. *Journal of Discourses.* London: F.D. and S.W. Richards, 1851.

FOR ADDITIONAL INFORMATION

Christian Research Institute—PO Box 7000, Rancho Santa Margarita, CA 92688-7000.

Ernie Jorgenson—Restoration Books—PO Box 1161, Lewiston, ID 83501.

Gospel Truths Ministries—1340 Monroe Avenue, NW, Grand Rapids, MI 49505-4604.

Life-Line Ministries—PO Box 1536, Independence, MO 64055.

Personal Freedom Outreach—PO Box 26062, Saint Louis, MO 63136.

Refiner's Fire Ministries—PO Box 3343, Independence, MO 64055.

Religion Analysis Service, Inc.—4724 42nd Avenue, N., PO Box 22098, Robbinsdale, MN 55422-0098.

Utah Lighthouse Ministry—PO Box 1884, Salt Lake City, UT 84110.

Utah Missions Inc.—PO Box 348, Marlow, OK 73055.

Watchman Fellowship—PO Box 13340, Arlington, TX 76094-0340.

About the Author

Charles A. Crane was born and raised in Linn County, Oregon. He was ordained into the preaching ministry following graduation from college in 1962. For twenty-eight years he served as a pulpit minister and has served as President of Boise Bible College since 1990.

His education includes a Bachelor of Sacred Literature degree, Master of Arts, Master of Divinity, Doctor of Ministry, and CPEC. He has taught college and seminary in the areas of Theology, Church Administration, Psychology, Textual Criticism, and Practical Ministries. He has strong interests in church planting and world missions and has been a guest lecturer to church leaders in Germany, France, Zimbabwe, and India.

He is the author of numerous articles and books, including *The Bible and Mormon Scriptures Compared; A Practical Guide to Soul Winning, Do You Know What the Mormon Church Teaches?; Mormon Missionaries in Flight; Ashamed of Joseph: Mormon Foundations Crumble; Is Mormonism Christian?* (a rewrite of Harry Ropp's *Mormon Papers*); and *Christian Money Management.*

He has served three terms on the North American Christian Convention Board of Directors; has been a director on two different college boards for a total of twelve years; and was a trustee six years and chairman for two years of the Navajo Christian Churches Mission. He has served as both a director and as President of Intermountain Christian Convention.

His interests include writing, reading, textual criticism, photography, piloting a private airplane, riding motorcycles, and worldwide travel. The emphasis of his life has always been the church of Christ.

COVENANT PUBLISHING

Christianity and Islam
Bridging Two Worlds
Glover Shipp

Many people do not realize that Islam is second numerically to Christianity among world religions. But that may not be the case for long. Since its beginning in AD 622, it has become the fastest growing religion in the world and may overtake Christianity. The startling reality of this phenomenal growth is that Islam has closed the gap in a relatively short time! The question that is facing Christianity today is—*how will the church respond to Islam?*

Christianity and Islam: Bridging Two Worlds answers many of the questions raised about Islam since the attacks of September 11, 2001. Glover Shipp briefly reviews Islamic history and reveals Islamic strategy as a world religion.

ISBN: 1-892435-17-9   **128 pages, 6x9 softbound**   **Retail Price: $9.99**

**Christianity and Islam, Bridging Two Worlds
is available at your local Christian bookstore
or you can order today by calling
877-673-1015** *(toll free)*!

Helping people keep faith with God and one another!

Covenant Publishing, Inc. • PO Box 390 • Webb City, MO 64870-0390
417-673-1015 • 877-673-1015 • 417-673-1065 fax